THE
UPWARD
CALL

DAVID JEREMIAH

Turning
Point

with Dr. David Jeremiah

www.davidjeremiah.org

Special thanks to William Kruidenier and Robert J. Morgan
Managing Editor: Myrna Davis
Editorial and Design Services: Mark Gilroy Creative, LLC with ThinkPen Design, Inc.

Printed in China.

As for God, His way is perfect; the word of the LORD is proven; He is a shield to all who trust in Him. For who is God, except the LORD? And who is a rock, except our God? It is God who arms me with strength, and makes my way perfect. He makes my feet like the feet of deer, and sets me on my high places.

PSALM 18:30-33

He who dwells in the secret place of the Most High shall abide under the shadow of the Almighty. I will say of the LORD, "He is my refuge and my fortress; my God, in Him I will trust."

PSALM 91:1-2

INTRODUCTION

Much is discussed—especially in educational settings—about a person's calling in life. This goes beyond a vocational choice and extends to the purpose one has for living and the role each of us has in our world to make it a better place to live. All of that is good. Even those who claim no religious affiliation or faith understand the importance of giving back. But as Christians we have a higher calling—to be in the world helping others, taking care of those less fortunate, and extending God's love whenever and wherever possible.

Brother Andrew, the author of the bestselling 1967 book, *God's Smuggler*, made this comment in his book:

> I have come to see clearly that life is more than self. It is more than doing what I want, striving for what will benefit me, dreaming of all I can be. Life is all about my relationship with God. There is no higher calling, no loftier dream and no greater goal than to live, breathe, and be poured out for Jesus Christ.

So the question is, How do we pour ourselves out for God? There must be something for us to give to others, but what is the source? In order to pour out God's love, we must immerse ourselves in Him through the study of His Word, through prayer, through worship, through our finances, through our families, our very being. He cannot be set on a shelf and taken down occasionally. He must be in all of our pursuits, all of our desires—He must be our focus. This 366-day devotional is one way to begin your pursuit. Read the daily Scripture—contemplate the truth found there—and consider the devotional thought that follows. Take time after this devotional to pray, to ask God to help you grow in your walk, to focus your thoughts not on your desires or needs, but on *The Upward Call* of God—what He would have you do that day. As we allow Him to guide our thoughts, our emotions, and our desires, our perspective changes, we begin looking up toward higher ground, *The Upward Call* of God on our lives.

O God, You are my God; early will I seek You; my soul thirsts for You; my flesh longs for You in a dry and thirsty land where there is no water. So I have looked for You in the sanctuary, to see Your power and Your glory. Because Your lovingkindness is better than life, my lips shall praise You.

Psalm 63:1-3

JANUARY

WHATEVER YOU DO

*And whatever you do, do it heartily, as
to the Lord and not to men.*

COLOSSIANS 3:23

One of the thorniest issues to arise in the first-century Christian church came from that hotbed of controversies, Corinth. Because Corinth was a seat of pagan worship and idolatry, much of the meat that found its way into the local markets was meat that was left over from pagan sacrificial and worship rituals. And the question arose: Should Christians eat meat that had been sacrificed to idols?

Long story short (1 Corinthians 10:14-32), Paul said not to participate in pagan feasts; but once the meat was removed from the pagan temple and sold in the market, its religious taint was lost and it was acceptable to eat. But more importantly, he said that each Christian's conscience was the final arbiter and no one should criticize another for his or her decision. Some may choose to eat, others may choose not to. Then Paul said the most important thing: "Therefore, whether you eat or drink, *or whatever you do*, do all to the glory of God" (verse 31, italics added). *Everything* in life is to be done with a view toward pleasing God.

Whatever you have planned to do today, consider how it might be done heartily for the Lord in a way that glorifies Him.

DAVID JEREMIAH

As Your Days...

As your days, so shall your strength be.

Deuteronomy 33:25

Only one man is listed twice among the presidents—Grover Cleveland. He served two non-consecutive terms, so he's listed as the twenty-second and the twenty-fourth president. Cleveland was a Presbyterian preacher's kid who was trained in Christian truth. He faced a lot of troubles in office, but was considered honest. His dying words seem to have summed up his life: "I have tried so hard to do right."

Cleveland had a motto he lived by, and it hung directly over his bed where he would see it every night on retiring and every morning when awakening. He once said, "If I have any coat of arms and emblem, it is that." It was a verse of Scripture—Deuteronomy 33:25: "As your days, so shall your strength be."

That's a verse for you too. As we face a new year, none of us knows the challenges ahead. But as a believer, you have the strength of God in you just waiting to be made manifest in your life. He gives strength for each new day. "The God of Israel *is* He who gives strength and power to *His* people. Blessed be God!" (Psalm 68:35) In Him, you will find strength for today and hope for tomorrow.

HE WATCHES

The eyes of the LORD are in every place,
keeping watch on the evil and the good.

PROVERBS 15:3

As we welcome a new year, Proverbs 15 is a very helpful chapter to turn to. Every verse is applicable to our daily life. It begins with the ever-relevant advice: "A soft answer turns away wrath." Verse 2 counsels us to speak wisely about the state of our lives and the world. Verse 3 reminds us that all our actions and reactions are observed by the Lord. His eyes are always open, watching both the good and the evil.

Those who don't know the Lord never pause to think that God is observing them like bees in a glass hive, aware of all they say, think, do, and plan. Those of us who *do* know and love Him are grateful we have someone watching over us.

In 1926, George and Ira Gershwin wrote a popular song entitled, "Someone to Watch Over Me." How wonderful to know we have someone watching over us every moment of the year. As Psalm 145:20 says, "The Lord watches over all who love Him" (NIV). Great is His faithfulness to us!

The Bond of Perfection

But above all these things put on love,
which is the bond of perfection.

Colossians 3:14

Where can you find the strongest glue in the world? Not in a store or factory. Dive into the ocean instead and take a look at barnacles and mussels, which fasten themselves to boats, piers, and rocks. Many shellfish secrete a protein that allows them to firmly cling to any surface, even in salt water. Researchers at the Massachusetts Institute of Technology are currently studying shellfish in an attempt to develop a stronger kind of waterproof glue that can be used in ship repair and even with surgical incisions.[1]

For an even stronger kind of glue, dive into the Bible and study the subject of love. The apostle Paul said that nothing can separate us from God's love and that God has shed abroad His love in our hearts (Romans 8:39; 5:5). According to Colossians 2:2, our hearts are "knit together in love."

Although the church is made up of people from all walks of life, our love of Christ must unite us. That means we must exercise patience, meet needs, and put the interests of others first. Love is the opposite of being self-centered—it is selfless.

---

1 http://www.natureworldnews.com/articles/9138/20140922/shellfish-inspired-sticky-glue-to-repair-ships.htm

Exception to the Rule

The first of all the commandments is: "Hear, O Israel,
the LORD our God, the LORD is one. And you shall love
the LORD your God with all your heart, with all your
soul, with all your mind, and with all your strength."

Mark 12:29-30

Carl J. Printz, Norway's Consul to Canada during World War II, lived a long life and left a deep legacy. When he was ninety-nine years old, Printz was interviewed on television. The journalist asked, "Give us the rule you have followed during your long and useful life, the rule which has most influenced your life and molded your character." Printz replied, "I would mention one definite rule—one must be temperate in all things." But he paused and added, "Perhaps I should say temperate in all things except one—fulfilling the commandment to love God with all your heart, soul, and mind and your neighbor as yourself. These are the only things we can rightly do with excess."

He's right. The Bible tells us to offer ourselves as living sacrifices to the Lord and to serve Him with passionate zeal. We can't love God too much, but we can love Him better. Rather than being conformed to the world, let's be transformed by the renewing of our minds. Let's be temperate in all things this year—except in loving God with all that's within us.

Flaring Up

The LORD will guide you continually.

Isaiah 58:11

Recently a series of solar flares disrupted air traffic over the North Pole. The solar eruptions, described as "huge expulsions of magnetic field and plasma," shot from an area near the center of the sun's disc. Scientists feared they were strong enough to touch off geomagnetic storms on earth. Airlines rerouted flights between America and Asia to avoid disturbances to the planes' GPS systems.

Most of us have traded in our folded maps for GPS devices, but we know they aren't perfect. Sometimes they lead us down the wrong road, and occasionally they stop working altogether. But God's guidance system is nonstop and never failing. He continually guides His children.

The Bible says that when we offer ourselves as living sacrifices—refusing to be conformed to this world, and are transformed by the renewing of our minds—we will prove what is "that good and acceptable and perfect will of God" (Romans 12:1-2). We have the assurance that when we trust in the Lord with all our hearts and lean not to our own understanding (acknowledging Him in all our ways)—He will direct our paths (Proverbs 3:5-6, paraphrase). That is a fail-safe guidance system.

STRENGTH TRAINING

But David strengthened himself in the Lord his God.

1 SAMUEL 30:6

If you feel weary or weak, think of these Bible verses on the subject of strength. Choose one to commit to memory and ask God to use it to impart strength to your fainting heart.

Your sandals shall be iron and bronze; as your days, so shall your strength be (Deuteronomy 33:25). *Seek the Lord and His strength; seek His face evermore!* (1 Chronicles 16:11). *Do not sorrow, for the joy of the Lord is your strength* (Nehemiah 8:10). *The Lord is the strength of my life… Wait on the Lord; be of good courage, and He shall strengthen your heart* (Psalm 27:1, 14). *The Lord will give strength to His people; the Lord will bless His people with peace* (Psalm 29:11). *My flesh and my heart fail; but God is the strength of my heart and my portion forever* (Psalm 73:26). *Strengthened with might through His Spirit in the inner man* (Ephesians 3:16). *I can do all things through Christ who strengthens me* (Philippians 4:13).

When our strength is exhausted, His is undiminished. The supply of His strength will equal the length of your days, and you can lean on His words and fortify yourself in His strength today.

THE GIFT OF TIME

See then that you walk circumspectly, not as fools but as wise, redeeming the time, because the days are evil.

EPHESIANS 5:15-16

A lmost everything in life is "stoppable." Even gravity can be suspended temporarily. But one part of life cannot be stopped by us. And that is TIME. Right now, as you read these words, time is marching on. But it doesn't march without a purpose. Time marches toward the consummation of God's redemptive plan for planet Earth and its inhabitants.

The apostle Paul didn't advise the Ephesians to redeem the time just so they would be busy. It was because he knew that the kingdom of darkness is always at work to stop the advancement of God's kingdom. His words are a reminder that Satan never stops working *against* God and that we should never stop working *for* God. But there is another reason: stewardship. Like everything we have—life, breath, material goods, salvation, abilities—time is a gift from God. Our responsibility as stewards (managers) of God is to use time in the way the Owner of time wants it used.

Consider today: The next 24 hours belong to God. They have been given to you as a gift. Be sure to use this day in a conscious manner, consistent with God's desires.

BURDENED

For the love of Christ compels us, because we judge thus:
that if One died for all, then all died; and He died for all,
that those who live should live no longer for themselves,
but for Him who died for them and rose again.

2 CORINTHIANS 5:14-15

Journalists often use the word "burden" in their headlines. They talk about tax burdens and the burden of health care, the burden of student debt, and how to ease the burden of our overcrowded prison system. The word "burden" comes from an old term for *load* or *weight*.

The Bible tells us to cast our burdens on the Lord (Psalm 55:22). But there's one burden God wants to cast on us—the burden to evangelize the world. Dr. Lee Roberson once said, "Some Christians have never had a real burden for souls. When they were saved, they had a temporary desire to see others converted. There was a brief concern for their families; then this concern was gone." In his book *Touching Heaven,* Roberson suggests rekindling a burden for souls by getting a new glimpse of our Savior dying for us, reading our Bibles to see what God says about hell, praying for sinners by name, and learning how to share the Gospel.[2]

Evangelizing begins when the love of Christ compels us to share the Gospel. It begins with a burden for the lost.

2 Lee Roberson, *Touching Heaven* (Murfreesboro, TN: Sword of the Lord Publishers, 1994), 116-117.

A MERRY HEART

*A merry heart makes a cheerful countenance, but
by sorrow of the heart the spirit is broken.*

PROVERBS 15:13

After Richard Norris was badly disfigured by a gunshot wound in 1997, he remained hidden at his parents' home for years. They covered the mirrors to keep him from glimpsing his face. But a team of doctors changed that by performing a "face transplant." Using medical advancements, the physicians gave Richard a new countenance. In 2014, his transformational story was featured in a major magazine.

While Richard's story is unusually dramatic, there's a sense in which we all need a new countenance. Study the faces of people you meet every day. Steal a quick glance at your own face as you pass a mirror or reflective window. How stressed and grim we look! Our emotions inexorably flash through the forty-three muscles in our face, and we communicate our feelings through our eyes, our brows, and the set of our mouths. One smile can light up a room; one frown can darken a day.

The Bible tells us a merry heart makes a cheerful countenance. Rejoice in the Lord today, and let the joy of Jesus shine through.

HOPE IN THE LORD

For the Lord Himself will descend from heaven with a shout, with the voice of an archangel, and with the trumpet of God. And the dead in Christ will rise first.

1 THESSALONIANS 4:16

Anyone standing by the graveside of a departed loved one or friend considers the questions that arise: What do I believe about this event called death? Even knowledgeable Christians have to defend themselves against waves of sadness and longing by remembering the promises of Jesus Christ concerning faith and eternal life. Those promises—promises based on the Resurrection—give the Christian renewed hope that is sometimes clouded by grief.

Job asked the same question: "If a man dies, shall he live *again*?" (Job 14:14) And Jesus answered, straight to the point: "He who believes in Me, though he may die, he shall live" (John 11:25b). But the new, first-century believers living in far-flung places didn't have Jesus' words at hand, so they were often concerned about death. Paul wrote to the church in Thessalonica to assure them that when Jesus appears, "the dead in Christ will rise first" (1 Thessalonians 4:16).

Christ was the firstfruits from the grave; we are the harvest to follow (1 Corinthians 15:20). The grave of those who die in Christ is a place of hope.

DAVID JEREMIAH

HOW JESUS ENRICHES EVERYTHING

*Command those who are rich in this present age not to
be haughty, nor to trust in uncertain riches but in the
living God, who gives us richly all things to enjoy.*

1 TIMOTHY 6:17

Christopher Hitchens was a leading voice among the new militant atheists, and his dislike of the Lord was evident in the title of one of his books: *God Is Not Great: How Religion Poisons Everything.* He and other secularists accuse Christianity of robbing life of its joys. Christianity, they say, spoils the fun and ruins everything for everyone.

Oh, how wrong they are! Those of us who are Christ-followers can't imagine a life without Jesus. Every day with Him is sweeter than the day before. Jesus came to give us life and to give it more abundantly (John 10:10). His laws are not given to prevent pleasure but to bless and protect us. His Word is for our good (Deuteronomy 10:13), for our learning (Romans 15:4), and for our benefit (2 Timothy 3:16-17). God's plans for us aren't intended to harm but to prosper us (Jeremiah 29:11). We have a living God who gives us richly all things to enjoy.

Let's write a book with our daily lives with the pages open for all to see, and let's title it: *God Is Very Great: How Jesus Enriches Everything.*

The Time of Life

Is anything too hard for the LORD? At the appointed time I will return to you, according to the time of life, and Sarah shall have a son.

Genesis 18:14

At the beginning of the twentieth century, women began wearing wristwatches, but not men. World War I changed that, for it's hard to use a pocket watch in a battle zone. Now a hundred years later, our wristwatches have become small computers giving us total access to all our electronic needs.

Still, for the Christian, our best sense of timing isn't found on our wrists but on our knees. In Genesis 18, the Lord appeared to Abraham promising a son to be heir of God's covenant. This wasn't something God intended to do immediately, but "at the appointed time." Who set the time? The Lord! He had His own schedule; the timetable was His; and things happened according to His agenda. To Abraham and Sarah, they were so old that Sarah laughed at it. But the Lord's clock never missed a beat. He had His appointed times.

Perhaps you're looking at your wristwatch wondering why God isn't moving more quickly. But He knows what He's doing. Stop looking at your wrist, fall on your knees, and trust Him for His perfect sense of timing.

FROM WEAKNESS TO STRENGTH

I can do all things through Christ who strengthens me.

PHILIPPIANS 4:13

In the several years following the diving accident that left her a quadriplegic, Joni Eareckson Tada struggled with every imaginable emotion. She was helpless, but came to discover that God was not. The more she accepted her weakness and limitations, the greater her realization of God's strength arose within her. She has written, "Deny your weakness, and you will never realize God's strength in you."

When Paul wrote the often quoted words found in Philippians 4:13, he was in prison. "I can do all things through Christ" is not a magic formula. It is not a promise that we can do anything *we* want. Rather, it is a promise that we can do anything *God* wants. Paul was confident God was orchestrating his life and was with him even in prison. He knew that what God expected of him—faith, endurance, perseverance, boldness—he would be able to accomplish, not through his strength, but through the strength of the One who lived in him (Galatians 2:20).

If God is asking something of you today for which you feel inadequate, it's okay to agree that you are! Confessing your weakness is the first step toward allowing Christ to manifest His strength in you.

FISHERS OF MEN

*And as [Jesus] walked by the Sea of Galilee, He saw Simon
and Andrew his brother casting a net into the sea; for
they were fishermen. Then Jesus said to them, "Follow
Me, and I will make you become fishers of men."*

MARK 1:16-17

"Brother Dave Gardner," a stand-up comedian active in the
1960s, had a favorite saying: "God must have really loved the
common people because He made so many of them!" Conversely,
it was mostly common people who were attracted to Jesus during
His ministry. He even called twelve common men to be His
first disciples.

God loves the poor and powerful alike, of course. But sometimes
wealth and power can insulate man from seeing his need for
God's love. That's why Jesus said He came not to call the healthy
and wealthy, but the sin-sick souls who recognized their need for
salvation (Mark 2:17). Jesus demonstrated and taught that the
kingdom of God is not based on rank or class but on spiritual
willingness to embrace God's presence. Jesus ministered to
everyone, poor and powerful alike, but it was crowds of common
folk who followed Him, not crowds of the wealthy.

Don't let poverty or wealth, averageness or exceptionality, keep
you from Jesus (Proverbs 30:7-9). His call goes to each one alike,
as all have the same need.

SERVANT LEADERSHIP

*Whoever desires to become great among you
shall be your servant. And whoever of you
desires to be first shall be slave of all.*

MARK 10:43-44

Researchers at Arizona State University released a study showing that while arrogance and self-importance impress outsiders, it's the bosses with humility who impress their employees. When a CEO displays a humble spirit, he or she gains the long-term respect of coworkers. The Arizona researchers called this kind of attitude: "Servant Leadership."

Management expert Ken Blanchard points out that Jesus Christ not only taught servant leadership; He modeled it perfectly. One of the indications we're following His example, says Blanchard, is how we respond to feedback. When self-serving leaders get feedback, they tend to become defensive or resentful. They're interested in protecting their status, their turf, and their system. But servant leaders welcome feedback, for it's how they learn, change, respond to the thoughts and needs of others, and show respect to the one speaking to them.

Jesus came not to be served, but to serve. As we humble ourselves and serve others, God will increase our influence and extend our effectiveness in arenas both large and small.

PRAISING GOD FOR MIRACLES

My help comes from the LORD, who made heaven and earth.

PSALM 121:2

Among the stories connected to the memory of Francis of Assisi is this one: One day Francis gathered his friends at a remote monastery in central Italy. When he asked them about their journeys, each brother had an exciting tale to report. One had been riding his mule across a narrow bridge that spanned a deep gorge. When the mule bolted, the man was nearly thrown into the ravine. He praised God he hadn't been killed.

Another brother had nearly drowned fording a river but, he said, "God in His grace provided a tree that had fallen across the water. I was able to grasp a branch and pull myself to safety." Other brothers expressed similar stories of God's protection. Then someone asked Francis about his trip. "I experienced the greatest miracle of all," said the famous friar. "I had a smooth, pleasant, and uneventful journey."

We should always remember to praise God for His miracles in whatever form they come. He blesses, heals, rescues, delivers, helps, and uplifts more times every day than we can count. We should always be saying, "Thank You, Lord!"

Lifting Up Christ

And I, if I am lifted up from the earth,
will draw all peoples to Myself.

John 12:32

Preachers stand on platforms; flags are raised to the top of poles; signs are put high up on billboards. Raising something high makes it visible to more people and gives it a sense of importance. That's why God told Moses to make a serpent out of bronze, set it on a pole, and raise it up so the Israelites could see it. God had punished their sin by allowing serpents into their camp, and Moses' bronze serpent became a source of deliverance for them when they gazed on it and believed (Numbers 21:4-9).

Knowing the Jews would grasp the metaphor immediately, Jesus said that He would be "lifted up" and become a source of salvation to all who looked to Him (John 3:14-15; 12:32). By "lifted up," He was referring to the Roman cross that lay ahead of Him. His words were prophetic—His death on a cross has drawn millions to Him for two thousand years. We continue to lift up Christ today in the Lord's Supper, "[proclaiming] the Lord's death till He comes" (1 Corinthians 11:26). We also lift Him up as we praise Him for His blessings in our lives.

Our lives should continually point the world to Jesus Christ—lifting Him up for all to see and be saved.

STAND FIRM

But Peter and the other apostles answered and said:
"We ought to obey God rather than men."

ACTS 5:29

Think how often God's will is challenged in life. Examples range from national issues like government-sanctioned abortion to private matters like the temptation to shade the truth on a tax form or other legal document. It's so easy to believe that we are not accountable to God to do the right thing *in every single situation* in life.

It is especially true when we are trying to do what pleases God and we are met with opposition or criticism—and we are standing alone in our desire to please God. That was young David's situation when Israel was confronted by the Philistine giant, Goliath (1 Samuel 17). Everyone from King Saul to David's own brothers was an obstacle in his path. Yet he refused to back down. David knew that God's name was at stake and needed to be defended. So he put his faith in God and went into the battle, armed with the only things he knew how to use: faith and a sling—and was victorious.

God does not promise physical victory in every confrontation. But He does expect faithfulness and commitment to Him. If you are being opposed in your desire to please God, clothe yourself in God's armor and stand firm (Ephesians 6:10-18).

January 20

Our Advocate

*And they stoned Stephen as he was calling on God
and saying, "Lord Jesus, receive my spirit."*

In the fullest version (1563 edition) of his work (*Foxe's Book of Martyrs*), John Foxe chronicled, in more than 2,300 pages, the lives of Christians who were persecuted, and often martyred, in England and Scotland during the sixteenth-century Protestant Reformation.

Though it is true that many faithful ones lost their lives, something else is true: God defended each one who died in true faith. Which raises a question: If God defended them, why did they die? Which begs an answer to this question: What does it mean to be defended by God? The story of Stephen in Acts 7 gives insight. When Stephen stood firm for Christ in the face of Jewish persecution in Jerusalem, he was stoned. But just before the stones began to fly, he had a vision of Jesus in heaven standing at the right hand of God, waiting to receive Stephen's spirit. Normally, Jesus is pictured *seated* at the right hand of God (Ephesians 1:20; Hebrews 8:1). But Jesus stood in honor of Stephen's courage and commitment.

There is something more important than life, and that is *eternal* life. God defends the eternal life of all who, in true faith, stand for Him.

UNENDING LOVE

Therefore, there is now no condemnation
for those who are in Christ Jesus.

ROMANS 8:1, NIV

After serving two terms as president, James Madison and his wife, Dolley, retired to Montpelier, their Virginia home. In Madison's final days, he was weak and bedridden. Madison's personal servant, Paul Jennings, wrote later in his memoir that Dolley Madison sat by her husband's bedside up to 18 hours a day. She never left his side for more than 15 or 20 minutes at a time.

We could easily say that very little could separate James Madison from the love of his wife, Dolley. Her love for him was constant. But we can say with greater confidence that nothing can separate the Christian from the love of God in Christ. Is it right to picture God by our side 24 hours a day, even while we are sleeping? Through the power of the indwelling Holy Spirit, that is a most appropriate image. The apostle Paul suggests a number of things we might think could separate us from God's love—the condemnation of sin, death, spiritual powers, things unimagined—and says none of them are that strong. Nothing can separate us from God in Christ.

If you are a Christian, remind yourself today that you are safe in God's presence. His love attends your every need in life or in death.

DAVID JEREMIAH

JANUARY 22

THE DEFEAT OF DEATH

*For You will not leave my soul in Sheol, nor will
You allow Your Holy One to see corruption.*

PSALM 16:10

It is commonly known that in many surveys of people's greatest
fears, fear of public speaking ranks higher than the fear of
death. Comedian Jerry Seinfeld observed that most people are
more afraid of delivering a eulogy at a funeral than of being in
the casket. Something seems wrong with these surveys. Given the
choice, right now, would most people rather die—actually die—
than speak in public? That seems unlikely.

Death has always been humanity's greatest unknown and thus
man's greatest fear. We tend to fear what we don't understand
and can't control. Religions have made attempts through the
centuries to unravel the mystery of death. But no explanation of
death satisfies reason and intellect, and gives hope to the heart,
like the Christian explanation. Very simply, Jesus Christ defeated
death by returning to life. Had the Resurrection not happened,
we Christians would look foolish with our Gospel of eternal life
(1 Corinthians 15:14, 18).

But the Resurrection did happen! Death has been defeated!
And we Christians, in Christ, have been given the victory (1
Corinthians 15:57).

HUNGRY?

*Blessed are those who hunger and thirst for
righteousness, for they shall be filled.*

MATTHEW 5:6

In the fall of 2014, a homeowner in Rockland, Massachusetts, was awakened at 1:30 a.m. by sounds in his kitchen. After calling the police, he went to investigate himself. An intruder was cooking corn on the cob. The two men got into a scuffle, but police officers arrived in time to arrest the thief before anyone was hurt. What happened to the corn wasn't reported.

Everyone knows what it's like to be hungry. We have stomach pains, feel weak and famished, and crave our favorite foods. But how is our spiritual appetite? Do we ever feel spiritual hunger pains? Jesus told us we should be hungry and thirsty every day—that we should crave righteousness. But this might not come naturally; it's an acquired taste.

Like a child learning to like a new food, let's begin tasting what God desires for us. Turn away from sin; give up spiritual junk food. Start reading your Bible more, living it out, and practicing the Spirit-filled life. Soon you'll notice if you miss a day of conscious fellowship with the Lord. That's when you'll discover that a good spiritual appetite is a blessing.

FORGOTTEN, BUT NOT FORGOTTEN

Yet the chief butler did not remember Joseph, but forgot him.

GENESIS 40:23

After spending years in slavery and prison, Joseph finally found a possible way of escape—through the help of Pharaoh's butler, whose dream he had wisely interpreted. But the butler forgot him, and Joseph's hopes again faded. Still, he waited on the Lord. He had no choice; but no other choice could have been better for him. Taking the long view, God was planning a coming day when Joseph would be released, exalted, and mightily used to change human history.

Though forgotten by the butler, Joseph was not forgotten by the Lord.

John Piper wrote, "To wait! That means to pause and soberly consider our own inadequacy and the Lord's all-sufficiency and to seek counsel and help from the Lord… The folly of not waiting for God is that we forfeit the blessing of having God work for us. The evil of not waiting for God is that we oppose God's will to exalt Himself in mercy. God aims to exalt Himself by working for those who wait for Him."[3]

> *Wait on the LORD; be of good courage, and He*
> *shall strengthen your heart (Psalm 27:14).*

---

3 John Piper, *Desiring God* (Colorado Springs: Multnomah WaterBrook Publishing Group, 2003), 170.

A PICTURE OF SIN

Take note, you have sinned against the LORD;
and be sure your sin will find you out.

NUMBERS 32:23

A man in Palm Beach County, Florida, was arrested for theft last year, and he unwittingly provided the evidence. He might have gotten away with it except he posted "selfies" of himself with the loot on his Instagram page. Officials searched his house and found a quarter-million dollars' worth of stolen plunder. As they filled out the arrest warrant, they asked the man his occupation. He replied, "Thief."

It's strange when we're proud of the things we should be ashamed of—and ashamed of the things we should boast about. The Bible tells us to boast in the Lord, but to avoid the appearance of evil. Even as fully forgiven, born-again Christians, we can become proud of some evil habit in our lives. And, sad to say, we can be ashamed of serving Jesus. That's a terrible condition.

Although we enjoy God's grace here on earth, we need to remember He is just in all His dealings with us and we should never take His grace for granted. Listen instead to 2 Corinthians 7:1: "Therefore, having these promises, beloved, let us cleanse ourselves from all filthiness of the flesh and spirit, perfecting holiness in the fear of God."

SEATED WITH CHRIST

*Do you not know that the saints will judge the
world? And if the world will be judged by you, are
you unworthy to judge the smallest matters?*

1 CORINTHIANS 6:2-3

In 1 Corinthians 6, Paul chided the Corinthians for failing to resolve difficulties without suing one another. We should be able to settle matters with each other, he said, because one day we'll judge the world. It's hard to foresee how that will happen, but similar verses reinforce the point. The Bible teaches we will reign with Christ and have part in His kingship. When He judges the world, we'll be there to agree with His judgment.

Jesus told His disciples in Matthew 19:28, "You who have followed Me will also sit on twelve thrones, judging the twelve tribes of Israel." Revelation 3:21 adds, "To him who overcomes I will grant to sit with Me on My throne." The Bible says, "If we endure, we shall also reign with *Him*" (2 Timothy 2:12). In Revelation 20, John envisioned God's faithful children reigning with Christ a thousand years.

If we'll one day judge the world, shouldn't we be able to work out our disagreements now? Think of a troubled relationship in your life and ask God for wisdom to improve it.

THE POISON GARDEN

...looking carefully lest anyone fall short of the grace of God; lest any root of bitterness springing up cause trouble, and by this many become defiled.

HEBREWS 12:15

In Eureka, California, best-selling author Amy Stewart tends an unusual garden behind her house. Every plant could kill you. Some of her plants, if ingested, would paralyze you. Some would stop your heart. Amy is a specialist in poisonous plants, about which she often writes and lectures. They are grown behind a secure fence.

Few of us would want such a garden, but how many of us have allowed a root of bitterness to spring up within us? How many have a little toxic garden in our hearts?

If anyone had reason to remain bitter, it was Joseph in the book of Genesis. Yet he forgave his brothers, was reconciled to them, and provided for them. His forgiveness melted their hearts, and old wounds were somehow healed. Forgiveness isn't just a behavioral adjustment or psychological device. It is the sum and substance of every page and paragraph of the Bible. It's what the Bible is all about. It's the theme of the ages, the crux of the cross and gist of grace.

Beware lest any root of bitterness spring up within you.

The Gift of Work

And out of the ground the LORD God made every tree grow that is pleasant to the sight and good for food.

Genesis 2:9a

There is a stark difference between Genesis 2 and Genesis 3—but there is also an underlying and uniting theme. The difference is in how man was to procure what he needed to live on and provide for himself and his family. In Genesis 2, before sin entered the world, mankind was given a lush, abundant environment in which to live. Everything man needed was there for the taking. But in Genesis 3, after man's sin, man would be forced to work by "the sweat of [his] face" to coax out of the ground what he needed.

But here's what unites the two different situations: God's provision was present in both. In Eden, God provided abundantly from an earth devoid of sin. Outside of Eden, the earth was still God's provision, but it was changed. A cursed earth (Genesis 3:17) would yield its resources only by the hardest of labor. Yet the ability to secure what was needed was the gift of God in both eras.

The work you do today may be difficult and tiring, but we should still thank God for it because it is His gift to us—the ability to provide for our needs. Thank Him today for that gift and pray for the ability to work "as to the Lord" (Colossians 3:23).

WHAT IS POSSIBLE?

*Jesus said to him, "If you can believe, all things
are possible to him who believes."*

MARK 9:23

There is a part of the body of Christ that has adopted a slogan from the secular self-help movement: "If you can conceive it and believe it, you can achieve it!" If you can conceive of yourself as an astronaut or a star player in the NBA, and believe it with all your heart, are you likely to achieve such a goal? The answer for most adults is "No."

What's good about the "name it and claim it" school is that it encourages us not to limit ourselves or God. What's wrong with this approach is that it misapplies the words of Jesus. For example, a corollary of Jesus' words in Mark 9:23 is that "all things *are* possible for [God]"—words Jesus spoke on the night of His arrest in the Garden of Gethsemane (Mark 14:36). Jesus believed it was possible for Him not to go to the cross, and He also believed it was possible for God to keep Him from that suffering. Yet He went to the cross anyway.

Our beliefs and possibilities have to be in line with the will of God. That's how Jesus lived His life and how He taught His disciples to live (John 5:30). When our lives are lived in obedience to God's will, nothing is impossible. Dream big—but dream biblically!

WISE SPEECH

The heart of the righteous studies how to answer,
but the mouth of the wicked pours forth evil.

PROVERBS 15:28

According to *A Dictionary of American Proverbs,* there are lots of variations to the rule, "Think before you speak." One version says, "Think before you leap." Another says, "Think more and talk less." Another says, "Think twice and say nothing." And yet another says, "You can think what you like, but don't say it." [4]

However it's put, this is biblical advice. It's easy to open our mouths and let the words fly. We're living in a day when people talk without using the filters of wisdom. But wise people study how to answer. One of the best ways of doing this is to pray before speaking. This is what Nehemiah did. "Then the king said to me, 'What do you request?' So I prayed to the God of heaven. And I said to the king…" (Nehemiah 2:4-5).

Every child of God can develop a reputation for giving good advice. We can be people to whom others come for counsel. By God's grace, we can be respected for our quiet wisdom. But only if we learn to think—and to pray—before we speak.

---

4 *A Dictionary of American Proverbs* (New York: Oxford University Press, 1992).

SPIRITUAL MENTOR

*Now Joshua the son of Nun was full of the spirit of
wisdom, for Moses had laid his hands on him.*

DEUTERONOMY 34:9

Greg Rubar, a waiter at an Italian restaurant in Houston, served a particular couple many times over eight years. One day they left him an unusual tip—fifty $100 bills. Greg tried to return the money, but the two customers told him to take it and buy himself a car. It turned out they knew Greg had recently lost his car in a flood, and they wanted to help him in gratitude for his years of serving them.

If customers and acquaintances can be generous in expressing gratitude, shouldn't we seize every opportunity to thank those who have meant the most to us? That certainly includes our spiritual mentors. Someone prayed for you before you were saved. Someone—perhaps several—were instrumental in leading you to Christ. Someone taught you the Bible. Someone showed you how to pray. Someone guided you into personal ministry and taught you to serve.

Joshua was full of wisdom because Moses had laid his hands on him. Who has laid their hands on you? Have you ever thanked them for their influence? You don't have to buy them a car. Just a word of thanksgiving will do.

FEBRUARY

WHATEVER COMES

…being persecuted, we endure.

1 CORINTHIANS 4:12

According to *The Voice of the Martyrs,* a Christian named "Edward John" was teaching classes at a sewing center in Karachi, Pakistan, where he opened his classes with Bible reading and prayer. A Muslim girl, showing interest in Christianity, asked for a Bible. Edward gave her one and never saw her again. Instead, Edward was beaten by a mob, his sewing center was closed, and his landlord evicted him. Edward and his family have moved to a new location, where, being persecuted, they endure. "Although I was in trouble," he said, "I haven't stopped my evangelism work."

We must follow the Lord's example not only in the good things that come but also in suffering and persecution. Depending on our location, we might face unpopularity, ridicule, insults, rejection, or intimidation. Even in America, those reactions are no longer unexpected. In other parts of the world, the persecution is physical, financial, and life-threatening.

We have a faith worth defending and a Savior worth proclaiming. Whatever comes, let's endure with the message of Jesus on our lips and His love in our hearts.

FEBRUARY 2

WHO AM I?

What is man that You are mindful of him…? For You
have made him a little lower than the angels, and
You have crowned him with glory and honor.

PSALM 8:4-5

There are only two ways we humans can posture ourselves. Either we're bent over like a question mark or we're straight as an exclamation point. It depends on our view of God. Our lives only have meaning within the context of a Creator. His life, love, holiness, and ultimate ends—these are the things that give us hope and purpose. Reject God, and the answer to "Who am I?" doesn't even require a single word. A simple question mark will do. Without Him, we feel we're nothing but momentary sparks that flicker in meaninglessness and die into nothingness. There are no answers, only question marks.

When our view of God is true and biblical, we're as upright as an exclamation point. We're made in God's image for His purposes, recipients of His peace and perpetual life through Jesus Christ who loved us and died for us. We stand firm with hope and purpose.

We're only able to understand who we are when we understand the Creator. Our secularized culture yields despair, but our faith produces joy as we exclaim with Psalm 8: "O LORD, our Lord, how excellent is Your name in all the earth!"

HEART TO HEART

*He answered and said to them, "I tell you that if these
should keep silent, the stones would immediately cry out."*

LUKE 19:40

Are you a hyperpolyglot? That's the term for people who can
speak six or more languages fluently. Alexander Arguelles,
an American scholar, speaks 36 languages. Timothy Doner was
featured in the *New York Times* as a teenager who can speak 20
languages. In yesteryear, John Milton spoke 11 languages and
Noah Webster mastered 23. Even so, there are more than 6,500
languages in the world, so even hyperpolyglots have a long way to
go before being able to communicate with everyone.

One of the aspects of being made in God's image is our ability
to communicate. God created our mouths to make sounds while
exchanging air in our lungs. Those sounds become syllables,
giving us the capacity to speak with each other and with our
Creator. That enables us to praise Him, to pray to Him, and to
preach Him. God created us with the ability to respond to Him,
and that is what separates us from the rest of the world.

Whether you have a thousand tongues or only one, use your
lips today to sing, speak, and share Jesus from dawn to dusk.

CHRIST IN US

For He shall grow up before Him as a tender plant, and as a root out of dry ground. He has no form or comeliness; and when we see Him, there is no beauty that we should desire Him.

ISAIAH 53:2

If you had lived in first-century Israel and crossed paths with Jesus in a market (before He became well known), you would not have given Him a second glance. Outwardly, there was little or nothing about Jesus' external appearance that would have commended Him (Isaiah 53:2).

That wasn't true of all of Israel's kings. First Samuel 16:18 says that David, son of Jesse of Bethlehem, was a "fine-looking man" (NIV). The Hebrew word for "fine-looking" is the same word translated "beauty" when describing what Jesus the Messiah lacked in Isaiah 53:2. David was fine-looking, but Jesus, apparently, was not. That's a comfort, because it indicates that external attributes are not the point. You can be beautiful, handsome, or plain in the world's sight; and God can use you all the same. Why? Because it is Christ *in us* that matters (Galatians 2:20).

Our self-worth comes from how we reflect Christ, not how we are reflected in the mirror. Our appearance should enhance the image of Christ as an appropriate frame enhances a priceless painting.

Precious in His Sight

My frame was not hidden from You, when I was made in secret, and skillfully wrought in the lowest parts of the earth.

Psalm 139:15

Monozygotic (identical) twins result when one fertilized egg divides to form two separate but "identical" embryos. Fraternal (dizygotic) twins are as different as any two siblings. But even in the case of identical twins, they are not totally identical— different fingerprints being an example. Several hundred genetic differences can occur in identical twins that may eventually manifest themselves in slight, but noticeable, ways.

In short, every human being is unique—including you! You are the only version of you God has ever made. The biblical writers understood and expressed this using pre-scientific language. David knew that he was "fearfully and wonderfully made" in his mother's womb (Psalm 139:13-14). Job knew that God had "shaped [him] and made [him]," and "molded [him] like clay" (Job 10:8-9, NIV). The knowledge that the God of the universe has known and loved us from the moment of conception puts to flight any of Satan's strategies to suggest that we are unloved or of no value.

Never doubt that you are unique and precious in God's sight. Just as He watches over the sparrow (Luke 12:6), He watches over you.

DELIGHT IN THE LORD

*Make me walk in the path of Your
commandments, for I delight in it.*

PSALM 119:35

We don't often hear it said, "God happy you!" But it would be entirely appropriate. "God bless you!" could accurately be translated, "May God grant you happiness, joy, favor, and spiritual prosperity!" The so-called Beatitudes of Jesus (Matthew 5:2-11) are normally rendered, "Blessed are those who . . ." but could just as easily be translated, "Happy are those who . . . ."

"Blessed is" or "Blessed are" was a common Old Testament expression, one of the most well-known being from Psalm 1: "Blessed is the man who" avoids the way of the ungodly. Instead, "his delight *is* in the law of the LORD, and in His law he meditates day and night" (verse 2). Finding delight, prosperity, favor, and happiness by walking according to God's statutes is an underlying theme of both the Old (Joshua 1:7-8; Psalm 119) and New Testaments (2 Timothy 3:16; 2 Peter 1:4).

Rather than seeking happiness in the temporary things of this world, let your daily delight be in the Word of God: "The grass withers, the flower fades, but the word of our God stands forever" (Isaiah 40:8). The things that offer a momentary source of delight cannot compare with true, eternal joy.

The Great Encourager

And the glory which You gave Me I have given them,
that they may be one just as We are one . . . and
that the world may know that You have sent Me,
and have loved them as You have loved Me.

John 17:22-23

Every parent has had the privilege of being a source of encouragement to a discouraged child. When children's lives are going well, they seem to fuel themselves with renewed energy. But when life hits a roadblock, they need someone to draw them close. And parents usually get the call.

That is true not just for our sons and daughters, but it was true for the Son of God as well. There were times when Jesus was appreciated and sought after—when feeding the multitudes or making a triumphant entry into Jerusalem (Matthew 14; 21). But there were other times when He heard jeers instead of cheers. In those situations Jesus turned to His Father, the one Person He knew would understand and confirm for Him that there was purpose in His troubles. When Jesus' arrest was imminent, He poured out His heart to the Father (John 17). Right before it happened, He was still praying (Matthew 26).

If you are experiencing more discouragement than encouragement today, do what Jesus did: Turn to the Father who loves you.

SPIRIT POWER

But you shall receive power when the Holy Spirit has come
upon you; and you shall be witnesses to Me in Jerusalem,
and in all Judea and Samaria, and to the end of the earth.

ACTS 1:8

Generally, the theory of causation seeks to explain the
connection between one event (the cause) and another (the
effect). There are causes and effects throughout life—even in the
Christian life.

A clear cause and effect is seen in Acts 2. The effect was that
the apostles of Christ suddenly began carrying out Christ's Great
Commission to preach the Gospel and teach and baptize new
believers. And the cause? The descent of the Holy Spirit to fill
the apostles. Prior to ascending into heaven, Christ connected the
spiritual cause with the practical effect: "You shall receive power
when the Holy Spirit has come . . . ; and you shall be witnesses to
Me" (Acts 1:8). Prior to Pentecost, the disciples had been fearful
and intimidated. After Pentecost, they were powerful witnesses.
The cause of this transforming effect was the Holy Spirit.

Is it any wonder that Paul admonished the church in Ephesus
to be filled with the Holy Spirit (Ephesians 5:18)? Create a clean
vessel (1 John 1:9) for the Spirit to fill on a daily basis.

SUCCESS—GOD'S WAY

*I have glorified You on the earth. I have finished
the work which You have given Me to do.*

JOHN 17:4

"Success," said General George S. Patton, "is how high you bounce when you hit bottom." That's not a bad definition, but here's a better one: Success is faithfully tackling and accomplishing the work God gives us day by day. In biblical terms, success has nothing to do with wealth, position, power, respect, or awards. God promises to grant us success in life, but He views success as finishing the work He has assigned us. Colossians 4:17 says, "Say to Archippus, 'Take heed to the ministry which you have received in the Lord, that you may fulfill it.'"

The Bible tells us to persevere in obedience: "Be careful to obey all the law my servant Moses gave you … that you may be successful wherever you go. Keep this Book … meditate on it day and night, so that you may be careful to do everything written in it. Then you will be prosperous and successful" (Joshua 1:7-8, NIV).

Don't worry about failure; just be faithful in your Christian walk and work. That's SUCCESS in capital letters.

Pause to Refresh

The law of the LORD is perfect, refreshing the soul.

Psalm 19:7, NIV

According to motivational speaker David Gee, NBA star Rajon Rondo takes five showers on game days, the last one just a few minutes before tip-off. The reason? He says he does his best thinking in the water.

That might be a little excessive; but surveys tell us that most of us do our best thinking while we're showering, driving, or exercising.[5] For Christians, those simple pauses in the day are great opportunities to practice the art of meditation. When the Bible is inscribed in our minds, it's waterproof, so we can take it into the shower or bath. We can wash our souls and be doubly refreshed for the day. It's portable; as we drive to work or school or jog or exercise, we can use the time to meditate on God's Word and let beloved Scriptures sink into our thoughts.

In 1929, Coca-Cola coined one of its most famous slogans: "The Pause That Refreshes." For the Christian, the most refreshing pauses during the day are moments when we recall a verse of Scripture and let our minds dwell on it richly.

5 http://3secondselling.com/2013/04/the-pause-that-refreshes/

FEBRUARY 11

THE RIGHT LOT

*Therefore whoever hears these sayings of Mine, and does them,
I will liken him to a wise man who built his house on the rock.*

MATTHEW 7:24

Newspapers recorded the story of a Missouri couple who built their 5,300-square-foot home in a gated community in Florida. The three-story house had five bedrooms, three floors, beautiful verandas, and it was bordered with palm trees. The only problem: The contractor built the house on the wrong lot. The builder is tracing the mistake to an error in a land survey, but is assuring all concerned that a fair settlement will be made to this couple.

In building your life, make sure to construct it on the right lot. Build your life on the Lord Jesus Christ and on the foundation of obedience to His Word. The Bible is a firm foundation for our faith, and Jesus is a cornerstone that will never collapse. When we hear His sayings and do them, we are likewise people being built up into a holy temple for His glory (see Ephesians 2:21).

While we don't want to think of the Bible as simply a list of dos and don'ts, we do respect it as the foundation and authority for life itself. By revering, reading, and obeying it, we can keep ourselves from … lots of problems.

DAVID JEREMIAH

TIED TO THE ROCK

The LORD God is my strength; He will make my feet like deer's feet, and He will make me walk on my high hills.

HABAKKUK 3:19

Ever done any rock climbing or seen pictures of climbers clinging to the sheer sides of enormous cliffs? It can be a terrifying sight, but a recent book on the sport offers some advice: "The fear of heights and high places is a natural human fear. That fear keeps you alive. Sometimes a fear of heights comes from ignorance of your safety system. If you're afraid, check your knots, your belay anchor (which ties you to the rock), and don't look down. You can build up a tolerance for heights by climbing higher each time you go."[6]

That's great advice for all of us. It's natural to suffer pangs of fear as we go through life, and that fear can be healthy and keep us alert. But sometimes we live in fear because we're ignorant of our safety system in Christ. We need to check our knots and anchors, make sure we're tied to the Rock, and learn to look up rather than down as we climb higher from day to day.

6 Stewart M. Green and Ian Spencer-Green, *Rock Climbing* (Augusta, GA: Morris Book Publishing, 2010), 7.

CONCEDING WEAKNESS

If any of you lacks wisdom, let him ask of God, who gives to all liberally and without reproach, and it will be given to him.

JAMES 1:15

You've heard the old joke that "denial" is not a famous river in Egypt. Actually, denial is no joke. It is a serious impediment to spiritual maturity.

Everyone is tempted occasionally to engage in denial by saying something that is not true to others, to ourselves, or to God. Denial is the opposite of confession, which means "to agree with"—to say what God says about our lives. If we are weak or sinful in an area of life, we shouldn't deny it. We should say what is true about it: "God, I am weak in this area of my life." God knows it's true, so we may as well agree with Him. But that's only half the story. We should also say what else is true: "I can do all things through Christ; with every temptation comes a way of escape; I am no longer a slave to sin but now a slave to righteousness; when I am weak, Christ is strong" (Philippians 4:13; 1 Corinthians 10:13; Romans 6:13-16; 2 Corinthians 12:10).

We should not live in denial about either our weakness or God's strength. By confessing both, we avail ourselves of God's help.

LOVE

*Greater love has no one than this, than to
lay down one's life for his friends.*

JOHN 15:13

It was the English poet Elizabeth Barrett Browning who began one of her most famous poems with this line: "How do I love thee? Let me count the ways." She went on to enumerate the various ways her love could be measured and described. And her last line comes close to a biblical thought: "I love thee with the breath, smiles, tears, of all my life; and, if God choose, I shall but love thee better after death."

Saying that her love would only be perfected in heaven comes close to the idea Jesus shared with His disciples: "Greater love has no one than this, than to lay down one's life for his friends." Love may be perfected in heaven, but the pinnacle of love on earth is to deny oneself and prefer the needs of others over one's own—even to the point of laying down one's life, as Jesus would demonstrate only a few hours after stating these words. It would be wrong to think Jesus was talking only about literal death. There are many ways to die to oneself in the pursuit of loving and serving others while living.

Paul said the greatest virtue of all is love (1 Corinthians 13:13), and Jesus said the best way to demonstrate it is by dying to self while living for others.

THE FOURTH WATCH

Now about the fourth watch of the night He came to them,
walking on the sea, and would have passed them by.

MARK 6:48

Once after a busy day, Jesus hurried His disciples onto a boat and sent them across the lake while He retreated to a hillside spot for prayer and solitude. A storm descended, and for hours the disciples strained at their oars in the raging darkness. Jesus didn't show up to help them until shortly before sunrise. Why did He wait so long?

We don't know all the reasons, but we recognize the same is true for us. Sometimes the Lord doesn't seem to show up as quickly as we'd like. Yet our times are in His hands, and He is always perfectly on time. Perhaps the apparent delays are His way of developing our faith, patience, perseverance, prayer habits, endurance, and courage. Sometimes it's for testimony's sake or to allow circumstances to align correctly.

If you're impatient today for the Lord to answer your prayers and relieve your burden, remember the disciples on Galilee's lake and our Lord's words to them: "Be of good cheer! It is I; do not be afraid" (Mark 6:50). Trust His timing and wait patiently on Him.

HEAD OF THE HOME

*So he built an altar there and called on the name
of the LORD, and he pitched his tent there;
and there Isaac's servants dug a well.*

GENESIS 26:25

D r. Nelson Bell was a missionary physician who became the mentor and father-in-law of evangelist Billy Graham. In his book, *Convictions to Live By,* Dr. Bell spoke of the primacy of a godly family, writing: "In the Old Testament we read that the patriarchs 'pitched their tents, digged a well and built an altar.' How many people today pitch their tents and dig their wells but make no provision for the spirit! The altar is never built. There are thousands of houses across America fabulous in their appointments for gracious living, but they remain houses only, not homes."

In order to have success in our family life, we must build an altar and put God at the head of our homes. Husbands, wives, dads, and moms should keep their Bibles open, their knees bent, and the joy of the Lord dialed up on the family thermostat. The Christian home should be church-going, Bible-reading, and Christ-honoring. We need to pitch our tents and dig our wells, but let's not forget to build our altars.

GOD'S IDEA

*It is not good that man should be alone; I will
make him a helper comparable to him.*

GENESIS 2:18

The family is God's idea. In fact, it's His primary idea. Civil government and the church also came from the mind of God; but long before He created those institutions, God thought of the family. In the very beginning, He looked at Adam and said, "It is not good for him to be alone." He brought a woman to him and family life began.

Since the family is God's idea, it operates best when it follows His patterns and operates under His lordship. Until Christ is the center of our homes, all our attempts to improve our families will end in frustration. Unless the Lord builds the home, we labor in vain in building it.

Even in the easiest of times and best of circumstances, it's hard to build a Christian home; but any attempt apart from the lordship of Christ is doomed to failure. God loves you and wants to be the Lord of all your moments, days, attitudes, and habits. When He is Lord, it changes the atmospherics of the family. Problems may not disappear overnight; but when Christ dwells under your roof, He brings hope to the home and healing to the heart.

PUT AWAY ENVY

*For I was envious of the boastful, when I
saw the prosperity of the wicked.*

PSALM 73:3

"Paparazzi" comes from "Paparazzo," a news photographer character in the 1960 film, *La Dolce Vita*. Thanks to the ever-present paparazzi today, the whole world is treated to the luxuries and lifestyles of contemporary celebrities. The world sees their clothes, their cars, their cash, and their careers as the badges of success and happiness.

There were no paparazzi in the Old Testament period, but the lifestyles of the wealthy and famous were still well-known. And the psalmist Asaph admitted to struggling with envy (Psalm 73). The wealthy wicked (as he saw them) seemed to ignore God and be no worse off for it. They had everything they wanted and more than they needed. On the contrary, Asaph declared his own attempts to live a life of purity and devotion to be vanity: "Surely I have cleansed my heart *in* vain" (verse 13). But one day, while worshiping God, he had an epiphany: The wicked were on slippery ground while God held tightly to his hand.

Do you ever envy those who seem to have it all without giving a single thought toward God? Meditate on Asaph's confessions and conclusions as you renew your faith in God.

PONDERING

*But his delight is in the law of the LORD, and
in His law he meditates day and night.*

PSALM 1:2

Harvard scientists released a study last year demonstrating how meditation helps "fight the crippling high stress levels we experience during our busy lives…[and] it can change the physiology of a person's brain."[7] The study wasn't referring to biblical meditation, just human-based techniques. Imagine how much better the scores would have been had the participants meditated on Scripture!

In order to be a true New Testament church, we must study the Scriptures and apply them to our lives; and that involves the practice of meditation. The writers of Psalms gave testimony to this: *I meditate within my heart… I will also meditate on all Your work…. I will meditate on Your precepts… My eyes are awake through the night watches, that I may meditate on Your word…. I will meditate on the glorious splendor of Your majesty* (Psalm 77:6, 12; 119:15, 148; 145:5).

We meditate when, after having studied God's Word, we ponder what we've studied, mulling it over as we shower, drive, exercise, walk, work around the house, and rest in bed. Let your delight be in the Word of God, and meditate on it day and night.

7 http://mic.com/articles/103790/science-has-amazing-news-for-people-who-meditate

DAVID JEREMIAH

A CONTRITE HEART

*The sacrifices of God are a broken spirit, a broken and
a contrite heart—these, O God, You will not despise.*

PSALM 51:17

It is not uncommon for a student who is hoping to be successful in a specific subject area to retain the services of a tutor. While the role of a tutor is important, it is a temporary assignment. The tutor's mission is to move a student to a new level of understanding on a specific course of study. When Paul says that the Mosaic Law was "our tutor *to bring us* to Christ" (Galatians 3:24), he illustrates the law's temporary status. We can even see glimpses of the changing status of the law in the Old Testament.

In spite of the central place of animal sacrifices, by the time of King David we find him writing that God does not desire sacrifices (Psalm 40:6-8). The focus was moving from external sacrifice to internal sacrifice: "the sacrifices of God *are* a broken spirit, a broken and a contrite heart" (Psalm 51:17). We find Jesus helping the Pharisees make that shift in Matthew 23:23—moving from the letter to the spirit of the law. Now that Christ has come, when we sin, God desires that we act as living sacrifices with broken and repentant hearts (Romans 12:1), confessing (agreeing with God about) our sins, that we may find His forgiveness (1 John 1:9).

If you have sins to confess, let them spill out of a broken heart before God. The sacrifice of Christ means our only sacrifice is humble confession.

NO OTHER NAME

Nor is there salvation in any other, for there is no other name under heaven given among men by which we must be saved.

ACTS 4:12

A radical group once threatened to kill prominent African-American pastor Dr. E. V. Hill if he preached one more sermon about Jesus. This wasn't in another country; it was in Los Angeles. Police officers told Hill he shouldn't fill the pulpit the following Sunday, but Dr. Hill replied, "It's your job to keep me living, and it's my job to keep on preaching." The church's deacons came and sat on the front row, and Dr. Hill preached on the name of Jesus. "I want to call His name out loud!" he proclaimed. "So if it's my last time and a bullet strikes me down, I want to go out saying, 'Jesus!'"

No other name has the power of Jesus. No other name can raise the dead, strengthen the living, save the lost, defeat the demons, delight the angels, and bear us through perilous times. Only Christ could offer Himself as a righteous sacrifice for sin and shed His blood as an everlasting atonement. If we reject Christ, we are rejecting the only possible means by which we can receive forgiveness and salvation.

There is no other name.

BIBLICAL BOASTING

My soul shall make its boast in the LORD; the humble
shall hear of it and be glad. O, magnify the LORD
with me, and let us exalt His name together.

PSALM 34:2-3

You've seen the bumper sticker: "He who dies with the most toys wins." Yes, it's a cynical statement about our materialistic culture; but there's another layer of insight there concerning competition. Down to one's dying day, life is all about comparisons and competitions.

The apostle Paul wrote that it is not wise to engage in such activity. The subject came up in Corinth when false teachers and apostles boasted about their accomplishments (2 Corinthians 10). But Paul refused to be drawn into such fruitless debates. When people who were all on the same plane—dead in trespasses and sin, redeemed only by the grace of God—began to boast about their greatness, Paul chose to focus on two things: carrying out his apostolic mission and focusing on the greatness of Christ. Paul loved to boast—but only about Christ and never about himself (2 Corinthians 10:17-18).

If you are ever tempted to feel large or small based on comparisons with others, shift your focus to Christ and boast in Him.

BEING CLEANSED

*If we confess our sins, He is faithful and just to forgive us
our sins and to cleanse us from all unrighteousness.*

1 JOHN 1:9

Making a mess of our lives comes naturally to us, but some make a bigger mess than others. One woman in Michigan was convicted of embezzling more than $10,000 from her employer. During her sentencing, she admitted, "I have shamed myself and my family, but by the grace of God they have forgiven me. It will take a long time for me to forgive myself. I know that people will never look at me again the same way, and I am very sorry."[8]

It's sad to see people who have made life-altering mistakes, and sometimes it's hard to forgive ourselves when we're the one who sinned. Left to ourselves, we're a constant source of shame and sorrow to ourselves and others. Since the "wages of sin is death," we're all condemned to hell apart from the forgiveness of the Lord Jesus Christ.

The essence of the Gospel is this: We have a forgiving God who will restore us if we confess our sins to Him. The blood of Jesus Christ cleanses us from all sin. We can forgive ourselves only because He washes away our sins and makes us holy in His sight. He can clean up whatever mess we make. He forgives to the uttermost.

8 http://www.uppermichiganssource.com/news/story.aspx?id=1106611#.VEFPiL42XA4

PERSIST IN BEING POSITIVE

Do all things without complaining....

PHILIPPIANS 2:14

According to a news item, a man in California had a pet parrot with a lovely British accent, but somehow the bird escaped and went missing four years. Finally the owner and bird were reunited, but there's an odd twist in the tale. The parrot now speaks Spanish. No one knows where the bird went during his sabbatical, but he came back with a whole new vocabulary, jabbering away with words like: *gracias, amigo,* and *por favor.*

Life has its odd twists and ruffled feathers; but as we grow in Christ, our vocabulary changes. As we mature in Christ, we do less complaining and more thanking. We learn to look at things through the lens of God's providence and to thank Him for His overruling grace. The apostle Paul said, "Rejoice always, pray without ceasing, in everything give thanks; for this is the will of God in Christ Jesus for you" (1 Thessalonians 5:16-18).

Our lips are the barometer of the heart, and His praise should be continually in our mouths. Today, try to restrain the complaining spirit; in everything give thanks.

TROUBLE OR TRUST?

When you hear of wars and rumors of wars, do not be troubled; for such things must happen, but the end is not yet.

MARK 13:7

The newspapers today are filled with troubling stories— frightening pandemics and deadly viruses; radical extremists swallowing vast chunks of the Middle East; biblical standards collapsing in a culture that no longer fears the Lord. But remember, these things are predicted in advance. Notice that Jesus didn't say "*If* you hear…," but "*When* you hear…." Trouble will come, yet our Lord told us not to be troubled by trouble.

The Psalms teach us the same lesson. Ponder these verses: "In the time of trouble He shall hide me in His pavilion…. This poor man cried out, and the Lord heard him, and saved him out of all his troubles…. God is our refuge and strength, a very present help in trouble…. Trouble and anguish have overtaken me, yet Your commandments are my delights… Though I walk in the midst of trouble, You will revive me." (Psalm 27:5; 34:6; 46:1; 119:143; 138:7).

It's not *if* but *when* trouble comes. Yet God's answer to trouble is trust; our answer to fear is faith.

Come One, Come All

*But in every nation whoever fears Him and
works righteousness is accepted by Him.*

Acts 10:35

In 1883, American poet Emma Lazarus wrote a sonnet to raise money for the pedestal of the Statue of Liberty; it was later mounted inside the Statue. The most well-known lines of the sonnet say, "Give me your tired, your poor, your huddled masses yearning to breathe free, the wretched refuse of your teeming shore. Send these, the homeless, tempest-tost to me, I lift my lamp beside the golden door!" Those words became prophetic as millions of immigrants from many countries entered the U.S. through the immigrant station on nearby Ellis Island between 1892 and 1934.

Just as America opened its doors to the world, so God through the Gospel has opened the doors of His kingdom to humanity's "huddled masses yearning to breathe free." Even though God worked through Israel He always had a heart for the nations (Genesis 12:3; Isaiah 11:10; 42:1, 6). Reluctant at first, the Jews finally saw that the Gospel of Christ was for the Gentiles as well: Jew, Gentile, slave, free, male, female—all are "one in Christ Jesus" (Galatians 3:28).

If you are yearning to be free, embrace the Savior of all mankind. He invites all to come unto Him (Matthew 11:28-30).

A COMMUNITY OF ENCOURAGERS

Rejoice with those who rejoice, and weep with those who weep.

ROMANS 12:15

The Hebrew culture had a unique way of referring to "everything": identify two opposite poles and let them represent everything in between (Psalm 139:8-12). There are traces of that figure of speech in Romans 12:15 where Paul writes about our need to identify with and encourage each other. The two opposite extremes are when someone weeps and when he rejoices. The implication is, "those two and all the times in between."

If we are honest, we might say it is easier to "weep with those who weep" than to "rejoice with those who rejoice." Another person's pain or hardship evokes empathy and compassion in us. We ourselves have suffered and we know what the other person is going through. Rejoicing in another's success is more challenging. Perhaps we have experienced no equal successes or joys and find ourselves envious, even jealous, of another's good fortune. Paul doesn't place one need above the other; they are equally our responsibility.

You will meet someone today who is at either end of the emotional spectrum or somewhere in between. Ask God for grace to identify with them—especially to applaud them in their success.

RESTORING THE FRAGMENTS

*Create in me a clean heart, O God, and
renew a steadfast spirit within me.*

PSALM 51:10

The Dead Sea Scrolls were discovered from 1946 to 1956 in 11 caves near the Dead Sea. Over 900 manuscripts were discovered representing hundreds of texts and more than 15,000 fragments of linen, papyrus, and parchment (animal skin). So—10 years, 11 caves, hundreds of manuscripts and texts, and *thousands* of fragments ranging in size from 27 feet long to fingernail size. It fell to scholars to try to piece the fragments back together to create the original priceless documents.

Fragments—that's how we view our life at times. If we have had a failure, a sin of omission or commission that shames or embarrasses us, we feel crushed and broken. We wonder if God can put the pieces of our life back together again. The good news is that He can! The psalmist David knew of God's restoration work first hand (Psalm 32, 51), as did the apostles Peter (John 21:15-19) and Paul (Acts 22:6-16).

If sin or failure has fragmented your heart and soul, confess to God and let Him restore the joy of your salvation (Psalm 51:12). God is the ultimate scribe—He will restore the pieces of your life.

THE HEART OF OBEDIENCE

If you love Me, keep My commandments.

JOHN 14:15

One of the most challenging periods for parents is when a toddler experiences the "terrible twos." With a two-year-old child, learning to be obedient is tested frequently. Obedience by definition is "compliance with an order, request, or law or submission to another's authority." Since true obedience requires "first-time" compliance, young children have to be taught to obey—often responding to praise and encouragement or, when necessary, discipline. All parents look forward to the day when a child obeys out of love rather than for praise or fear of discipline.

For a believer, our obedience to the Lord also emanates from a mixture of fear and love. In Deuteronomy 13:4 we are told to "fear Him, and keep His commandments and obey His voice." This was not a suggestion but rather an admonition to be true to God and His purposes.

How is your heart? Is it willful? Stubborn? Do you obey the "first time"? Throughout the Word of God we see that His plans for us are for good, and yet sometimes we fail to obey—perhaps thinking more of His love for us than the possible discipline we might experience later. February 29 only appears on our calendar once every four years—don't let your obedience be as sporadic as this date. The true test of obedience is consistency.

MARCH

BATTLE READY?

For the word of God is living and powerful and
sharper than any two-edged sword.

HEBREWS 4:12

Modern readers have nearly forgotten *The Pilgrim's Progress*, yet John Bunyan's famous allegory still provides enriching reading as it covers every aspect of the Christian life. Here's a scene to whet your appetite. Near the beginning of his journey toward the Celestial City, Christian stopped at the Palace Beautiful, constructed by God as a place to refresh pilgrims. In the armory there, Christian was fitted with armor: "Sword, shield, helmet, breastplate, all-prayer, and shoes that would not wear out."

It's a good thing Christian armored up, for he had no sooner resumed his journey than he met the enemy—Apollyon—who savagely attacked him. The battle lasted hours, and the enemy rained scores of flaming darts at him. But Christian prevailed thanks to his armor and sword.

When it comes to facing the enemy, the question isn't *if* but *when*. The probability of battle is one hundred percent. If you're under attack today, it means the enemy feels he needs to stop you. Resolve to resist the devil with all your might. Grip the shield of faith in one hand and the sword of the Spirit in the other. Armor up for the battle.

Wait on the Lord

*My flesh and my heart fail; but God is the strength
of my heart and my portion forever.*

Psalm 73:26

Robins and sparrows *fly*. But when you look up and see an eagle or a vulture floating high above, you're looking at a bird *soaring*. Yes, the eagle has to do some flying in the beginning, but eventually it connects with the thermal updrafts and taps into their power. The difference between flying and soaring is relying on a source of power beyond oneself.

The majesty of the eagle was noticed by the Old Testament writers as a symbol of strength and ability (Deuteronomy 28:49; Psalm 103:5). Isaiah thought the eagle was the perfect metaphor for the person who gained strength from God. The person who waits on (depends on, trusts in) the Lord will find the strength to "mount up with wings like eagles" (Isaiah 40:31). By definition, soaring means to be far above the problems of life; it means seeing what's happening on earth from God's perspective. With soaring comes understanding; with understanding comes patience and contentment.

If you are flying by your own strength today, wait on the Lord. Rise up with His power and gain His perspective on your circumstances.

A BREATH OF FRESH AIR

Be filled with the Spirit.

EPHESIANS 5:18

Environmental engineers call China one of the most smog-polluted nations on earth, with only 3 of its 74 largest cities meeting air quality standards. In Beijing, for example, the smog is so heavy that residents sometimes can't see the end of the block. Now the government is teaming up with innovators to bottle air from the distant Laojun Mountains and transport it to urban areas. Residents can now stop at breathing stations, don an air mask, and breathe the atmosphere of another land. China's president, Xi Jinping, has endorsed the idea, saying, "Air quality is now a deciding factor in people's perception of happiness."

In the Bible, the same Greek word is translated *wind, breathe, spirit,* and *Spirit*—as in Holy Spirit. In a sense, the Holy Spirit is God's oxygen in the lungs of our soul. The atmosphere of our culture is toxic; but when we're filled with the Spirit, it's like getting an oxygen transfusion. It clears our thoughts, refreshes our hearts, and keeps us healthy.

The Spirit of God is the breath of God. In order to live spiritually, we need His breath—the Holy Spirit.

The Way Up Is Down

The humble shall increase their joy in the Lord.

Isaiah 29:19

The Journal of Positive Psychology released a survey last year showing that people looking for someone to date gravitated toward those displaying signs of humility. Arrogance and egos were turn-offs for both men and women looking for romantic relationships. According to the *Journal*, a woman looking for a man wants someone quick to see the other's point of view, who expresses remorse at mistakes, and who forgives easily.

It's funny how modern research keeps affirming the truths of the Bible. The Bible advocates a humble heart, saying, "Better *to be* of a humble spirit with the lowly, than to divide the spoil with the proud. … The humble in spirit will retain honor" (Proverbs 16:19 and 29:23). The apostle Paul wrote, "Do not set your mind on high things, but associate with the humble" (Romans 12:16).

Resolve to treat the next person you meet with humility. Listen to their conversation, open the door for them, compliment them, avoid self-centered comments, and seek to serve them in some way. You'll find that the best way to go up is to reach down to others.

GOD'S PROMISES

*For all the promises of God in Him are Yes, and in
Him Amen, to the glory of God through us.*

2 CORINTHIANS 1:20

When people talk about politicians, especially during heated races prior to elections, a frequently heard complaint is that politicians make promises they can't keep. Politicians can promise change, but only Congress can legislate change. Not keeping a promise one *can* keep is bad; making a promise one *can't* keep may be even worse. But that's true for all of us, not just politicians. Better not to vow than to vow and not pay, Solomon wrote (Ecclesiastes 5:5).

God is different on both accounts. He is *capable* of making any promise and keeping it—a reflection of His omnipotence (power). But He is *incapable* of making a promise and not keeping it—a reflection of His never-changing character. God's words are always true and always trustworthy (Psalm 19:7-9). When God says something or makes a promise—about forgiveness, eternal life, grace and mercy, His love, His provision for our needs—those words are trustworthy.

That is why the proverb says to trust in the Lord with *all* your heart. In times of trouble, trust in the promises of God—He will keep every promise He has ever made.

DAVID JEREMIAH

IN WEAKNESS

*He gives power to the weak, and to those who
have no might He increases strength.*

ISAIAH 40:29

When we talk about weakness, we're admitting inadequacy. Perhaps you don't have all the strength needed to perform some task. Maybe you give out before the day is over or the job is done. Perhaps you're disabled and unable to function as independently as you'd like. Perhaps your finances are tight and you're not able to give as much as you want. Perhaps you feel inadequate in the role you're trying to fill at church. Do you feel unusually weak in the face of some temptation right now?

The Lord knows all about it. Jesus suffered weakness in His flesh so He can sympathize. He understands your feelings of inadequacy better than anyone.

He can also give needed strength for whatever He calls you to do today. The apostle Paul said, "I can do all things through Christ who strengthens me." The phrase "all things" refers to whatever God has assigned to us. We can live in victory and obedience, even when we're weak. In our weakness, Jesus understands and He undertakes for our needs. He is always present in our weakness, and you can trust Him today.

LOVING GOD, LOVING OTHERS

*He who says he is in the light, and hates his
brother, is in darkness until now.*

1 JOHN 2:9

Horticulturists in the United Kingdom have developed
a plant they are calling the "tomtato." Above ground it
produces tomatoes, but below ground it produces potatoes. This
is unnatural, of course. The apostle James said, for example, that a
fig tree can't bear olives or vice versa (James 3:12). Jesus made the
same point when He said, "You will know them by their fruits"
(Matthew 7:16).

The apostle John applied these botanical lessons to the spiritual
life in a plain way: You can't say you love God and hate your
brother at the same time (1 John 2:9-11). If you love God, the fruit
in your life will be that you will love others—especially others
in the body of Christ who also love God. In fact, Jesus told His
disciples that their love for one another was how the world would
be able to identify them as His followers (John 13:34-35). And it
applies to more areas than just love. Anyone who claims to know
God through Christ but doesn't obey all His commands "is a liar,
and the truth is not in him" (1 John 2:4; Matthew 28:19-20).

The way we demonstrate that we love God is by loving others.
Failing to love others calls into question our love for God.

THE SOVEREIGNTY OF GOD

He does according to His will in the army of heaven and among the inhabitants of the earth. No one can restrain His hand.

DANIEL 4:35

The Sovereignty of God is the title of a book by scholar Arthur W. Pink, who laments that many Christians overlook the concept of God's sovereignty. Pink argues that while this theme was once expounded in the pulpit, now it's like a phrase borrowed from a dead language. "Alas!" he wrote, "that the doctrine which is the key to history, the interpreter of Providence, the warp and woof of Scripture, and the foundation of Christian theology should be so sadly neglected."

The word *sovereign* means, "reigning over all." When we speak of the sovereignty of God, we're referring to His absolute control over everything from the tides of history to the details of our days. The Most High rules over heaven and earth, over the large and the small. Psalm 115:3 says, "Our God *is* in heaven; He does whatever He pleases."

God is in control, and everything plays out according to His ultimate plan. When we grasp the significance of the sovereignty of God, our cares are lessened, our hearts are calmed, our spirits are lifted, and our days are brighter.

BE ANXIOUS FOR NOTHING

*Be anxious for nothing, but in everything by prayer
and supplication, with thanksgiving, let your
requests be made known to God; and the peace of
God...will guard your hearts and minds.*

PHILIPPIANS 4:6-7

What's the most popular verse in the Bible? Last fall, the retailer Amazon released a list of the most popular passages from its most popular books, and the most commonly highlighted portion of the Bible was Philippians 4:6-7. Readers of e-Bibles underlined that passage more often than any other in Scripture.

When we look around at our anxious world and our fretful lives, we can understand why people are drawn to the promises of Philippians 4. But notice the context of the passage. The Lord tells us here to rejoice in Him (verse 4); to be gentle in our dealings with others (verse 5a); to remember how near He is to us (verse 5b); to pray earnestly about our concerns (verse 6a); to count our blessings with thankfulness (verse 6b); and to focus our minds on what is true, noble, just, pure, lovely, and praiseworthy (verse 8).

What a wonderful description of the life of faith! When we trust the Lord like this, we don't have to fret about the small details of life. We can rely on God with issues both big and small.

OUR INDISPENSABLE WEAPON

*Put on the whole armor of God, that you may be
able to stand against the wiles of the devil.*

EPHESIANS 6:11

If you were a dog working alongside Navy SEALs, how much would your body armor cost? Would you believe $30,000? Many elite military units employ canine partners, and every dog sent into combat is outfitted with a tactical bulletproof vest that includes a waterproof high-definition camera, a harness for rappelling with its handler from helicopters, integrated microphones and speakers, and the most current woven technology for stopping bullets or knives. These dogs can move faster than the SEALs, and they can detect smells and sounds crucial to the mission. They're worth every penny of the gear they carry.

Our Master in heaven has purchased the armor we need. "Truth, righteousness, peace, faith, and salvation are more than words," says Ephesians 6:14-18 in *The Message*. "Learn how to apply them. You'll need them throughout your life. God's Word is an *indispensable* weapon. In the same way, prayer is essential in this ongoing warfare."

Our adversity is deadly, but the armor of God is proficient and able to keep us safe and victorious. Determine today to live a righteous life, to trust God in the crossfire, to appropriate the Scriptures, and to be faithful to prayer.

SAVED TO SERVE

For you, brethren, have been called to liberty;
only do not use liberty as an opportunity for the
flesh, but through love serve one another.

GALATIANS 5:13

Children think that the absence of rules means the absence of restraint—and not just physical children; spiritual children often think that too. Paul dedicated part of his letter to the Galatians, teaching that "liberty"—freedom from the law—is not a license for the unbridled appetites of the flesh. Rather, the energy formerly spent obeying the law is now to be redirected to serving others.

Jesus told His disciples that He did not come into the world to be served but to serve and to give His life for others (Mark 10:45). Indeed, He said that greatness is determined by the humility of service. Two of Isaiah's most powerful images are that of the nation of Israel as a servant to the Gentiles (Isaiah 49:3), then of the Messiah as the Suffering Servant for both Jews and Gentiles alike (Isaiah 53:11). If Christ came to honor God by serving the will of God, we who go by His name must do the same.

Look for an opportunity today to serve someone in your life. Serve them as Christ would serve—sacrificially and unconditionally.

THE UNHOLY TRINITY

*And I saw three unclean spirits like frogs coming out
of the mouth of the dragon, out of the mouth of the
beast, and out of the mouth of the false prophet.*

REVELATION 16:13

Counterfeit money is as old as money itself—coins were first used in Greece around 600 B.C. Counterfeits were made of less valuable metals but looked the same. It is estimated today that for every one million true United States dollars in circulation there are one hundred counterfeit dollars.

At every opportunity Satan will seek to counterfeit God's work (2 Corinthians 11:13-15). Everything he says is a lie, as worthless as counterfeit currency (John 8:44). In the coming Tribulation, Satan will deploy his most dramatic counterfeit strategy of all: an unholy trinity. Just as the Holy Trinity consists of God the Father, Son, and Holy Spirit, Satan's unholy trinity will consist of himself (counterfeiting God the Father), the Antichrist (paralleling the Son), and the False Prophet (imitating the Spirit) (Revelation 16:13). They will seek to deceive the whole world into worshiping the Antichrist instead of Jesus Christ.

The spirit of the Antichrist is at work today (1 John 4:3). Do not be deceived by what you see or hear (1 Peter 5:8).

PEOPLE

*Make no friendship with an angry man,
and with a furious man do not go.*

PROVERBS 22:24

The seasons of the year change naturally without any assistance from us. But there is another kind of change that is wholly dependent on our choices and actions: changes in relationships. Sometimes we can tell when a change is needed—for positive or negative reasons.

For instance, Proverbs 22:24 warns against becoming friends with an angry person. Why? Because "an angry man stirs up strife, and a furious man abounds in transgression" (Proverbs 29:22). So the chances of becoming involved in strife and sin are multiplied when we form a friendship with an angry person. On the positive side, Paul writes that we should "associate with the humble. Do not be wise in your own opinion" (Romans 12:16). In short, just as iron sharpens iron (Proverbs 27:17), so people have a telling influence on each other—for good or for ill. Paul also warned about the dangers of believers becoming partners with nonbelievers, whether in business, marriage, or other intimate relationships (2 Corinthians 6:14-18).

Ask God to show you any changes you need to make in your relationships. And make sure your closest relationship continues to be with Jesus Himself.

PRACTICING PATIENCE

Knowing that the testing of your faith produces patience.

JAMES 1:3

When we pray, "Lord, give me patience," what is the cause? A traffic jam? A spouse's irritating habit? A child's messy room? We know God will answer that prayer because we know He wants us to be patient; patience is a fruit of the Spirit (Galatians 5:22—"longsuffering"). But the reasons we pray for patience are several degrees removed from how the New Testament portrays the need for patience.

Over and over in the epistles, patience is linked to persecution and troubles (2 Corinthians 6:4; Colossians 1:11). That is not to say that our need for patience in the everyday "trials" of life is inconsequential. But compared to persecution and trouble relating to one's faith—that calls for a deeper level of patience. In short, the deeper the trial, the deeper the lesson of patience learned. That doesn't mean we have to invent trials in order to learn patience; the trials will come on their own. But it does mean we must welcome them as teachers and tutors in the spiritual life.

Regardless of why you need patience today, embrace the cause and ask the Spirit to manifest patience in your response so "you may be perfect and complete, lacking nothing" (James 1:4).

BE THE MAN FOR GOD

For I am not ashamed of the gospel of Christ, for it is the power of God to salvation for everyone who believes.

ROMANS 1:16

Evangelist George Whitefield was asked to preach at the fairgrounds in Marylebone Fields in London, where a Quaker gentleman had built a platform and pulpit for the occasion. Whitefield arrived after dark to find a vast crowd, but some of them had come to see the bare-fisted boxing matches taking place nearby. When George started preaching, the crowds flocked to him, and rough, bare-chested boxers marched in his direction to break up the meeting. To make matters worse, the Quaker's pulpit tottered every time George moved or even gestured. Just when Whitefield was about to lose his nerve, his wife, Elizabeth, tugged on his clothing and called up to him, "George, play the man for God!" As a riot ensued, Whitefield kept preaching, his text from Romans 1:16.[9]

From the days of the Acts of the Apostles, opponents have tried to silence our witness. But when we are struck down for sharing the Gospel, we must get back up and speak with more boldness, just as the apostles did. We must be men and women for God.

9 John Pollock, *George Whitefield and The Great Awakening* (Garden City, NY: Doubleday, 1972), 198-199, 248.

DAVID JEREMIAH

PEACE BE WITH YOU

*Then, the same day at evening, being the first day of the
week, when the doors were shut where the disciples were
assembled, for fear of the Jews, Jesus came and stood in
the midst, and said to them, "Peace be with you."*

JOHN 20:19

When a mother and child become separated at the mall, the
parent is filled with anxiety over the lost child. Then the
mom sees a security guard approaching, holding the hand of
the child, and anxiety is turned to joy and peace. The transition
happens in a moment—what was missing has been found.

On the third day after Jesus' crucifixion, His disciples and
followers were filled with anxiety. They huddled together behind
locked doors for fear that the people who put Jesus to death would
be coming next for them (John 20:19). The anxiety of some was
heightened even further when they went to visit the tomb where
Jesus lay, only to discover that His body was missing. Not only was
He dead, His body had been stolen! But then Jesus made Himself
known to Mary Magdalene at the Garden tomb. Peace replaced
anxiety as she returned to tell the others that Jesus was alive.

We serve a living Savior, not a dead one. When your fear or
anxiety level is high, let the presence of the resurrected Jesus give
you peace.

PATRICK'S TROUBLES

Always carrying about in the body the dying of the Lord Jesus,
that the life of Jesus also may be manifested in our body.

2 CORINTHIANS 4:10

Today is the day that the patron saint of Ireland, Saint Patrick, is honored. A native of Britain, he was captured in the late fourth century A.D. by Irish pirates at age sixteen and enslaved for six years in Ireland. During that time he committed himself to Christianity. He escaped and returned to his family in Britain where, a few years later, he had a vision of the Irish calling him to return and minister to them.

Rather than resenting his years as a slave to the Irish, Patrick used the time as a shepherd to contemplate what it meant to know Christ, what it meant to know God's forgiveness. He left Britain as an unconverted teenager but returned as a believer in Christ. Without those six years of suffering, who knows how different Patrick's life might have been. And who knows how many Irish might never have heard the Gospel through Patrick's ministry in Ireland in the fifth century?

Times of trouble in life, be they brief or extended, require a change in perspective. Instead of asking, "Why is this happening to me?" we must ask, "What is God doing in my life? What does He want me to learn in this situation?"

My Friends

*No longer do I call you servants, for a servant does not know
what his master is doing; but I have called you friends, for all
things that I heard from My Father I have made known to you.*

JOHN 15:15

No wonder a dog is called man's best friend. Dogs always
forgive, they never judge, they patiently listen, they are
always willing to go places with us, they aren't demanding, jealous,
or possessive, they like to be around us . . . and more. Those aren't
perfect definitions of a good friend, but they're close. And they
explain why dogs are such popular pets.

That said, dogs can't do what we often need the most when
we're in trouble. They can't pray with us, give us words of
encouragement, or provide wisdom or correction when we're on
the wrong path. Sometimes even our best human friends can't do
all that we need when we are hurting. But there is one friend who
can, and His name is Jesus. He exemplifies the friend described in
Proverbs 18:24—a friend who sticks closer than a brother. Jesus
told His disciples that He considered them His friends, not His
servants, because of what He had revealed to them. Friendship
implies the deepest level of intimacy and trust.

If you need a friend who is completely trustworthy and loyal,
His name is Jesus.

GOD'S WISDOM

*For there is not a word on my tongue, but
behold, O LORD, You know it altogether.*

PSALM 139:4

The original goal of Google Books, which began in 2004, was to digitize (scan the pages of) "all" the world's books—and by extension, all the world's knowledge. Many copyright issues delayed the project within its first 10 years, but as of April 2013, Google Books' database contained more than 30 million scanned books.

Only part of the world's knowledge is contained in books, so no database of scanned books could contain all knowledge. But there is a "database" that does: the mind of God. "Omniscient" is the word used to describe God's infinite, all-encompassing knowledge. He knows not only what has happened but what has not yet happened. David understood that God knew what he would say before he spoke the words, and where he would walk before he took a step (Psalm 139:4, 16). Jesus said God knows the number of hairs on our head and knows when a sparrow falls from the sky (Matthew 10:29-30).

God's omniscience warns us to avoid sin and comforts us when we wonder about the future. God knows what we know and everything we don't.

UNENDING PRAISE

Praise the LORD! Oh, give thanks to the LORD, for He is good! For His mercy endures forever. Who can utter the mighty acts of the LORD? Who can declare all His praise?

PSALM 106:1-2

When the Bible directs us to give thanks to the Lord, it reminds us of the importance of extoling His goodness to us. As sinners saved by grace, we have much to praise Him for! The benefits of living a praise-filled life are too numerous to mention, but know this: Changing your focus from "me to Thee" will radically change your perspective in life.

Psalm 106:2 says, "Who can declare all His praise?" Think about it—who, indeed, can declare all His praise? Our praises should be unending! Don't limit your worship of the Lord to an hour on Sunday. Keep a song in your heart throughout your day. Begin first thing each morning. Scottish preacher Duncan Campbell resolved to bless the Lord at all times, starting with his morning devotions. According to his biographer, Campbell rose each morning as the farmers harnessed their horses to the plows. He was convicted by their work ethic and determined to be as diligent with his spiritual harvest as they were with their crops.

When we start the day praising the Lord, it keeps a song in our hearts throughout our waking hours. As we offer our praise and worship to the Lord, He dries our tears and banishes our fears. Remember that the Lord is good—be thankful to Him and bless His name (Psalm 100).

HOW LONG?

*Attend to my cry, for I am brought very low; deliver me
from my persecutors, for they are stronger than I.*

PSALM 142:6

Anyone who has been on long road trips with children knows these questions: "Are we there yet?" "How much longer?" "Why is it taking so long?" Little children can't comprehend things like time and distance, delays and detours, stops and starts, as well as adults. So even when parents give the answers—"About 50 more minutes" or "About 50 more miles"—children ask the same questions again.

There is a lesson there for us. Jesus said that unless we become like little children, we will never enter the kingdom of heaven (Matthew 18:3). Part of that childlikeness is honesty. Just as children ask their parents the same question repeatedly without shame, so David questioned God the same way. We love David and his psalms because he was willing to say what we are often afraid to say to God: "How long?" "Why?" "Where are You?" But we shouldn't be. God is not afraid of our questions or our needs. He is our Father and we are His beloved children in whose questions He delights (Luke 11:11-13).

If there is something you need to know from God, cry out to Him in boldness (Hebrews 4:16) and humility (James 4:6) as often as it takes (Luke 11:5-8).

GOD'S JUSTICE

Surely God will never do wickedly, nor
will the Almighty pervert justice.

JOB 34:12

One of the most unfair parables Jesus told—unfair to the natural mind—concerned a landowner who hired men throughout the day to work in his vineyard. They all stopped work at the same time and were paid the same wage. The last men hired were paid the same as the first men hired—and the first men hired grumbled about the unfairness of everyone being paid the same amount even though not everyone worked the same amount (Matthew 20:1-16). The landowner replied, "What's unfair about me doing with my money what I will?"

Jesus' parable was directed toward the religious leaders who thought it unfair that latecomers to the kingdom of heaven should receive the full measure of grace and kingdom standing as those who had devoted their life to God. Jesus' point is that God's actions are a blend of justice, grace, and mercy, all balanced by His perfect purposes. God is never unfair, but He is always just, gracious, and merciful. Faith comes when we trust Him to blend those elements perfectly in every situation.

God is the landowner and we are the workers. It is His right to do as He will with what is His.

UNCHANGEABLE

For I am the LORD, I do not change....

MALACHI 3:6

We're like twigs caught in an ever-rolling stream of change. Every moment is different than the previous one. Our bodies change, our children change, our work changes, our health and wealth change; our culture and world are constantly in flux. But at the core of the universe is an unchanging God—immutable, enduring, abiding, changeless, the same yesterday, today, and forever. In Him we have "an anchor of the soul, both sure and steadfast" (Hebrews 6:19).

The Scottish pastor Alexander Maclaren wrote about Malachi 3:6, "This is the confidence with which we should cheer ourselves when we look upon the past and when we anticipate the future… We have… an unchanging love… a faithfulness that never departs from its word… a purpose of blessing that will not be turned aside…Trust yourself, weak and sinful as you are, to that unchanging love."

We can have confidence in our Lord because of His unchanging ways. We will always experience trials in life, but He will never be moved.

RAISED TO LIFE

*And if Christ is not risen, then our preaching
is empty and your faith is also empty.*

1 CORINTHIANS 15:14

When we look at the two sides of a coin, the two halves of a pair of scissors, or the two wings on a bird, it seems they are of equal value—that neither side nor half is more important than the other. We might look at the death and resurrection of Christ in a similar way—but we would be slightly wrong.

In 1 Corinthians 15 the apostle Paul does not say that without the *death* of Christ our preaching and faith are empty (verse 14). Nor does He say that without the *death* of Christ our faith is futile and we are still in our sins (verse 17). Instead, he says that without the *resurrection* of Christ all those things are true. It is a fine shade of difference, to be sure—but important. The death of Christ satisfied God's wrath against sin and paid the penalty for which only death would suffice. But in order to prove that the penalty of sin had been paid once and for all, death—the consequence of sin—had to be defeated. If Christ had not defeated death by rising from the dead, we would still be in our sins.

Give thanks to God today for the death of Christ—and especially for the resurrection of Christ and eternal life ensured by the empty tomb.

STAND UP AND SPEAK UP

Nor do they light a lamp and put it under a basket, but on a lampstand, and it gives light to all who are in the house.

MATTHEW 5:15

When the apostle Peter was confronted by a servant of the high priest, he lost his tongue. Rather than speaking up for Christ, he denied knowing the Savior. But after the Resurrection and Pentecost, Peter couldn't keep quiet. "We cannot but speak the things which we have seen and heard," he told his critics (Acts 4:20). As *The Living Bible* puts it, "We cannot stop telling about the wonderful things we saw Jesus do and heard him say."

When we share the Gospel, we must stand up and speak up for everyone to hear. Don't be deterred by criticism, and don't let timidity keep you from telling others what God has done for you. Listen to the advice of Jesus: "Return to your own house, and tell what great things God has done for you" (Luke 8:39).

When we think of the wonderful things we've seen Jesus do and heard Him say, and when we consider the great things He has done for us, how can we be silent or hide our light under a basket? Let's look up, stand up, and speak up for Him!

PRAYING FOR UNITY

*These all continued with one accord in prayer
and supplication, with the women and Mary the
mother of Jesus, and with His brothers.*

ACTS 1:14

There was a time when there was only one Christian church. It was the church in Jerusalem and, immediately after Christ's ascension, it appears to have had 120 members (Acts 1:15). By contrast, today there are more than 40,000 Christian denominations in the world.

The most striking difference between the first church and today's worldwide church is that they were all of "one accord in prayer" (Acts 1:14). Jesus had told them to wait in Jerusalem for the gift of the Holy Spirit, so that was likely the focus of their prayer (Acts 1:4). But after the Spirit came at Pentecost, their unity in prayer continued as they chose a replacement for Judas Iscariot and chose men to assist the apostles in serving the church (Acts 1:24-25; 6:1-6). Jesus had made unity among His followers a matter for His own prayer (John 17:20-21).

It is to be expected that human beings, even Christians, will differ in their ideas. But the goal of unity through prayer is always the highest priority. If there is "one body and one Spirit" (and there is—Ephesians 4:4), unity should be the result.

SIGNS OF EASTER

A wicked and adulterous generation seeks after a sign, and no sign shall be given to it except the sign of the prophet Jonah.

MATTHEW 16:4

America begins showing signs of Easter earlier and earlier every year. Plastic eggs for sale by the millions, chocolate eggs and bunny rabbits in every store, pastel colored Easter baskets and bundles of plastic green "grass" to fill them—the world's signs of Easter can't be missed. But today's signs of Easter are a far cry from the signs that proved the reality of the very first Easter morning.

Jesus told His detractors who had asked Him for a miraculous sign that they would see only one sign—the sign of Jonah, who spent three days in the belly of a great fish before being rescued from death. On the third day after Jesus' own death, He came out of the grave to give the world a sign it cannot deny. For a man to predict His own death and resurrection was something only God could do. The Gospel writers give us many proofs of His resurrection: sightings by witnesses, nail-scarred hands, a stone rolled away, and more. Truly, Jesus was—is—alive!

As you prepare to celebrate Easter, give thanks to God that your faith is not in vain—that Christ was raised for you (1 Corinthians 15:14).

RESURRECTED SAVIOR

*Jesus answered and said to them, "Destroy this
temple, and in three days I will raise it up."*

JOHN 2:19

How would knowing the outcome of a difficult situation change your outlook while going through it? Jesus knew He was going to die in Jerusalem, but He also knew He was going to be raised from the dead. He believed the Messianic psalms applied to Him: "For You will not leave my soul in Sheol, nor will You allow Your Holy One to see corruption" (Psalm 16:10).

Did that lessen the anguish of the moments prior to His death? No, He was human and He grieved the pain and suffering He was about to endure (Luke 22:44). But His faith in His Father's plan and protection was greater than His anticipation of suffering. He was wholly submitted to the Father's will (Luke 22:42). Jesus knew nothing could separate Him from God's love, and we have been given the same promise (Romans 8:35-39). And we have also been given the same promise of resurrection Jesus was given (1 Corinthians 15:12-19; 1 Thessalonians 4:16). And we are to comfort one another with these promises (1 Thessalonians 4:18).

Easter is the time when we remember the Savior's resurrection, which makes our own resurrection sure. Comfort yourself with these words today.

STEADFAST FAITH

*Therefore, my beloved brethren, be steadfast, immovable,
always abounding in the work of the Lord, knowing
that your labor is not in vain in the Lord.*

1 CORINTHIANS 15:58

Three years of growing faith and hope among His followers were dashed on the shoals of despair when Jesus was apprehended and killed. Typical of the despair felt by those in Jerusalem were two despondent followers of Christ who left Jerusalem to walk to the village of Emmaus. On the way, they encountered a stranger who seemed to know nothing of the past days' events in Jerusalem. Yet he rebuked them for their despondency, for not recognizing the meaning of the death of the Nazarene. And then He revealed to them that He was the Christ, raised from the dead. "So [the two] rose up that very hour and returned to Jerusalem . . . and they told about the things *that had happened* on the road" (Luke 24:33, 35).

When the two disciples saw that Jesus had been given new life, they received new life as well. Such is the power of the Resurrection; such is the meaning of Easter!

If you grow despondent in the face of life's circumstances, remember the Resurrection—proof that God's power is sufficient to resurrect your faith.

TRUSTWORTHY AUTHORITY

Then He appointed twelve, that they might be with Him and that He might send them out to preach.

MARK 3:14

When considering matters of life, death, and eternity, nothing could be more important than authority. That is, who do we believe, and why? The world is full of people claiming to speak for God, but credentials are of the utmost importance. There are false apostles today just as there were in the first century (2 Corinthians 11:13-15).

The common denominator of apostolic authority in the first century was having seen and heard Jesus Christ in person: "How shall we escape if we neglect so great a salvation, which at the first began to be spoken by the Lord, and was confirmed to us by those who heard *Him*" (Hebrews 2:3). Spiritual and divine authority began with Christ and continued through those He appointed and sent out. Their authority was confirmed by "signs and wonders and mighty deeds" (2 Corinthians 12:12)—confirmation that was lacking among false apostles who sought to establish themselves through deceit and counterfeit means.

The reason the New Testament epistles are trustworthy is because they were written by those who were called to speak for Christ.

YOUR SOCIAL NETWORK

*Let your light so shine before men, that they may see
your good works and glorify your Father in heaven.*

MATTHEW 5:16

With the click of a button, we can reach hundreds or even thousands of people. Social media has created a way to instantly share our thoughts. Most people use social media for this purpose alone, but we have the opportunity to use it for more.

The power of the Holy Spirit equips us to be Christ's witnesses, and social media can be a method of sharing Christ. When a friend shares their struggles, we can pray and send a message of encouragement. Social media can also bring opportunities to serve as we hear of friends going through sickness or difficulties.

People are drawn to the fruit of the Spirit: love, joy, peace, longsuffering, kindness, goodness, faithfulness, gentleness, and self-control (Galatians 5:22-23). As we ask the Holy Spirit to guide us, we can become active witnesses instead of passive observers. Social media does not have to be a black hole of wasted hours. We can be intentional in our use of social media and allow the Holy Spirit to work through our posts and comments.

DAVID JEREMIAH

APRIL

REFLECTING HIS HOLINESS

So I said: "Woe is me, for I am undone! Because I am a man of unclean lips, and I dwell in the midst of a people of unclean lips; for my eyes have seen the King, the Lord of hosts."

ISAIAH 6:5

Tennis players like to play opponents who play at a higher level than themselves. Parents encourage their children to make friends with upstanding peers. Teachers encourage promising students to take advanced placement classes. Why? Because we can always do better; there is always a higher level of potential achievement. Fortunately, in most areas of life there are examples of outstanding achievement to emulate.

When it comes to holiness, however, grasping the concept is harder because none of us knows a perfectly holy person. That is, it is not normal today for people to have personal, face-to-face encounters with God, the Angel of the Lord, or Jesus Christ—those who personify pure holiness. But we can read from Scripture what happened to people who did: Their lives were radically changed; they became more holy.

When Moses met with God face-to-face, it was obvious to everyone (Exodus 34:29-30). That's why worship, Bible study, and communion with God are so important. The more we see His holiness, the more like Him we can become.

OUR REPLACEMENT

*Have mercy upon me, O God, according to Your
lovingkindness; according to the multitude of Your
tender mercies, blot out my transgressions.*

PSALM 51:1

The concept of being replaced usually has a negative connotation. We work hard to become important and irreplaceable. While this mindset has its benefits at work, it will not work when it comes to our relationship with God where we are always on the receiving end. God does not need us.

We can ignore the truth and try to earn God's favor, or we can accept this truth and come to God in humility. In Luke 18, Jesus describes a Pharisee who is consumed with his own merit. His prayers reveal his blindness to his own shortcomings and to God's perfection and holiness. Meanwhile, a tax collector clearly sees his need for God's grace and forgiveness (verses 9-14).

God's mercy is revealed in the life, death, and resurrection of Christ. He stands in our place, and His perfection and purity make us acceptable to God. One way to remind ourselves of this is to pause, asking God to shine His light into any areas of our lives that we may need to confess or recommit to Him. This will keep our hearts tender and honest and we will find deep joy in His compassion toward us.

THE KING ETERNAL

*Now to the King eternal, immortal, invisible, to God who
alone is wise, be honor and glory forever and ever. Amen.*

1 TIMOTHY 1:17

There are two eternities in 1 Timothy 1:17. There is a King who
reigns eternally; and there is praise that greets Him forever
and ever. Because God is eternal, His praise is everlasting.

One of the reasons God promises us eternal life is so we can
render everlasting praise. The Bible says, "Even from everlasting
to everlasting, You are God" (Psalm 90:2). The cry of the holy
ones in heaven is: "Blessing and honor and glory and power be to
Him who sits on the throne, and to the Lamb, forever and ever!"
(Revelation 5:13)

If Christians only think in terms of time, our lives are miserable.
The Bible says that without the reality of the Resurrection and
its ensuring eternal life, we are the most pitiful of people (1
Corinthians 15:19). But Christ *has* risen from the dead! The Day
of the Lord is coming. Eternity is our inheritance. As we better
contemplate the nature of our eternal King, we'll better cope with
the tensions of time. Since we're going to praise Him forever, why
not begin now? Why not start living with eternity in view!

WHAT GOD KNOWS

Declaring the end from the beginning, and from ancient times things that are not yet done, saying, "My counsel shall stand, and I will do all My pleasure."

ISAIAH 46:10

An obscure literary figure of speech, called *merism*, occurs often in Scripture. A *merism* is the use of two contrasting words to refer to something in its entirety. For example, if we say, "He searched high and low," we are really saying, "He searched everywhere." Or if we say, like the psalmist, "You know my sitting down and my rising up" (Psalm 139:2), we would be saying that God knows everything about us. That's what God meant when He said, through Isaiah, that He declared "the end from the beginning." That is, God knows everything "from A to Z" about everything! He knows A, He knows Z, and everything in between.

God employed *merism* to describe Himself. Christ called Himself "the Alpha and the Omega, *the* Beginning and *the* End," and then explained the figure of speech: "Who is and who was and who is to come, the Almighty" (Revelation 1:8). Christ is eternal and His knowledge is complete.

There is nothing God doesn't know about your life. You may know the past and present, but God also knows the future. Choose today to walk securely—not in what you know, but in what you believe.

No Credibility Gap

*...being fully convinced that what He had
promised He was also able to perform.*

ROMANS 4:21

Several years ago when a particular United States governor was caught breaking an oft-repeated campaign promise, he explained that his prior words were simply "political statements" that had to be adjusted with changing circumstances. He was adopting the philosophy of Machiavelli, the prince of politicians, who said, "The promise given was a necessity of the past; the word broken is the necessity of the present." Promise breaking seems to be standard operating procedure for many of today's politicians. Still, we somehow expect our leaders to keep their promises; and when they break them, it creates a credibility gap with those they govern.

God is different. His promises are sure. No matter how many promises He has made, each one is more certain than the sunrise, more enduring than the highest mountain, more abiding than the deepest sea.

When Abraham believed the promises of God, it was credited to him as righteousness. Whenever in a time of doubt or darkness we find a promise in Scripture and cling to it in faith, God is pleased. He is faithful. He will always do as He has said.

Abide With Me

My days are like a shadow that lengthens, and I wither away like grass. But You, O Lord, shall endure forever.

Psalm 102:11-12

When you see a butterfly with its beautiful wings fluttering around your yard or park, you might wonder about its longevity. It has a one-month lifespan. Alligators live about 50 years. There are whales swimming in the oceans today that still carry ivory points of spears flung at them 200 years ago. A giant tortoise can celebrate 250 birthdays. The Antarctic Sponge has a lifespan of 1,500 years. And there is a species of jellyfish said to be virtually immortal. When it grows old, it has the ability to cycle back to an immature stage and start all over again.

Regardless of our ingenuity or initiative, however, time cannot be stored, stopped, or slowed. There is an end to everything in this life. The time we have is a gift from God, and we must be mindful that whatever this moment holds, this too shall pass. In each season of life, God has a purpose and an enduring plan. The psalmist reminds us of God's enduring presence: "But You, O Lord, shall endure forever." In an ever-changing world, we have the confidence that God is our anchor. He is our stability in unstable times. He is the Rock that abides forever. He offers eternal life for those who abide with Him.

APRIL 7

THE FATIGUE FACTOR

*I know that You can do everything, and that no
purpose of Yours can be withheld from You.*

JOB 42:2

The word "fatigue" frequently shows up in the headlines, preceded by a host of adjectives. Congress suffers budget fatigue. Sports teams lose because of travel fatigue. Trains derail because of driver fatigue. Soldiers face battle fatigue. Ministries go unfunded because of donor fatigue. There was even a report recently about young people suffering Facebook fatigue. All these reports—and more—are accurate. We are a society of tired people in a tired world.

But God isn't tired. "Have you not known? Have you not heard? The everlasting God, the Lord, the Creator of the ends of the earth, neither faints nor is weary" (Isaiah 40:28). Since God possesses all the power in the universe, He can do anything He chooses. He can do everything as easily as He does anything. Nothing is more difficult for God than anything else; He does all things with the same amount of ease. Nothing is too hard for Him. Nothing is remotely hard for Him. He never grows tired.

The Bible repeatedly reassures us of God's strengthening grace. So take care of yourself, avoid unnecessary weariness, rest in Him, and draw from His strength.

THE POWER OF JESUS' NAME

Every tongue should confess that Jesus Christ is Lord.

PHILIPPIANS 2:11

In his 1875 book on the history of hymns, Edwin Long tells of a missionary in India named Reverend E. P. Scott who determined to reach a dangerous tribe with the Gospel. His friends sought to dissuade him, saying, "We will never see you again." He said, "But I must carry Jesus to them." Traveling through the area, Scott found himself surrounded by warriors brandishing spears pointed at his chest. The missionary, expecting to die, quietly extracted his violin from its case, closed his eyes, and decided to die singing "All Hail the Power of Jesus' Name."

The expected attack didn't come. On the third verse ("Let every kindred, every tribe, on this terrestrial ball..."), Scott opened his eyes to see the spears lowered and tears in the eyes of the warriors. Reverend Scott went on to devote years of labor to evangelizing this tribe.

The power of the Lord Jesus exceeds all the dangers and demands of earth. Nothing is too difficult for Him, and no prayer too hard to answer. Praise Him today for His power, find strength in His omnipotence, and crown Him Lord of all.

PEACE WITH GOD

*Peace I leave with you, My peace I give to you; not
as the world gives do I give to you. Let not your
heart be troubled, neither let it be afraid.*

JOHN 14:27

Have you ever found yourself preoccupied or obsessed with something? Whether it's planning for a big event or watching back-to-back episodes of your favorite show, it's easy for a single train of thought to crowd out all others. While we may have little control over circumstances and the thoughts that come knocking on our mind's door in response, there is hope: we can choose the direction of our thoughts.

"Peace I leave with you." Jesus spoke these words knowing the pain and suffering awaiting Him the next day. He knew the fear and confusion His disciples would face and that they would flee in fear. We are simple creatures who struggle to hold multiple thoughts in our minds at once, especially when our worries and fears try to take over. Despite our weakness, God's promise never changes. We can return to Him time and again. His peace never fades. We can welcome it into our hearts and minds despite the chaos and storms of life swirling around us.

His peace can become our anchor, holding us steadfast despite crashing waves and forceful winds. Have you sought His help and peace today?

Facing the Giants

Only do not rebel against the Lord, nor fear the people of the land, for they are our bread; their protection has departed from them, and the Lord is with us. Do not fear them.

Numbers 14:9

When first graders start grammar school, and ninth graders start high school, they can feel like grasshoppers in a land of giants. Everything seems bigger and scarier. While things normally turn out okay, for one group of "new students," they didn't.

When Moses sent the 12 spies from Kadesh into Canaan to spy out the land, 10 of the 12 returned shaking in their sandals because of the giants in the land. They told Moses they would never be able to conquer such people and their walled cities. Their fear spread throughout the assembled nation and they were forced to spend their lives wandering in the wilderness. But when Jesus commissioned His apostles to go throughout the world to preach the Gospel to people who might be opposed, they obeyed wholeheartedly in spite of "giants" in the land.

By the Holy Spirit, God has not given us a spirit of fear but of power and love and a sound mind (2 Timothy 1:7). Don't worry about the assignments God gives you. We've read this page-turner and know that we win in the end!

AN OVERCOMING FAITH

In the world you will have tribulation; but be of
good cheer, I have overcome the world.

JOHN 16:33

Recently Britain's Prince Charles added his voice to those alarmed about the dramatic increase of violence against Christians. He warned that Islamic militants are deliberately targeting Christians in parts of the Middle East and seeking to wipe out the followers of Christ in Arab lands. It's true, but that's not the half of it. The crisis is global. Christians are the most persecuted group in the world today—with millions facing pressure, danger, and death because of their faith. One expert called Christian persecution a worldwide human rights disaster of epic proportions.

When we see the violence against believers escalating, and the Western world becoming increasingly secularized and given over to sin, we can grow discouraged.

According to Jesus, discouragement isn't the correct response. We should maintain our cheerfulness, knowing He is in control. "In the world you will have tribulation," He said, "but be of good cheer, I have overcome the world."

IF THEY WERE WISE

He makes His sun rise on the evil and on the good,
and sends rain on the just and on the unjust.

MATTHEW 5:45

Jesus told us to treat people as kindly as we can, for that emulates our heavenly Father. He shares His sun with everyone whether they are good or evil; and He waters the fields of both the righteous farmer and the ungodly landowner.

Were they wise, people everywhere would look to the sky, see the beauty of the sunrise, feel the refreshing drops of replenishing rains, watch the migration of the birds, and praise God for the genius of His Creation.

Were they wise, secularists and atheists and skeptics would notice the brilliance of the stellar heavens and their self-evident intelligent design, and they would praise the God of the stars. Were they wise, all the hedonistic, self-absorbed people on earth would pause to thank God for their pulsing hearts and breathing lungs and incredible brains.

The evidence of God's goodness is everywhere to be seen. Some people are blind to it, but they're the ones most needing our kindness. Let's praise God for His power, and let's share His compassion today even with those who don't believe in it.

THE DIVINE CARETAKER

Consider the lilies…

MATTHEW 6:28

In her book, *God of All Comfort,* devotional writer Hannah Whitall Smith said, "The Lord assures us that we need not be anxious about anything, but may commit all our cares to Him; for He careth for us. We are all familiar with the passages where He tells us to 'behold the fowls of the air,' and to 'consider the lilies of the field' and assures us that we are of much more value than they, and that, if He cares for them, He will much more care for us. One would think there was comfort enough here for every care or sorrow all the wide world over. To have God assume our cares and our burdens and carry them for us; the Almighty God, the Creator of Heaven and earth, who can control everything, and foresee everything, and consequently can manage everything in the best possible way, to have Him declare that He will undertake for us; what could possibly be of greater comfort?"

But, said Smith, we often don't enjoy God's comfort because we doubt the power of His promises.

Take God at His Word today. Today, know He cares for you.

HE IS PREEMINENT

*By Him all things were created ... that in all
things He may have the preeminence.*

COLOSSIANS 1:16-18

Recently the website *Wikipedia* released a report based on its research and analysis listing the ten most influential people in human history. Who tops the list? It's Jesus Christ, of course; followed by Napoleon Bonaparte, William Shakespeare, Muhammad, Abraham Lincoln, George Washington, Adolf Hitler, Aristotle, Alexander the Great, and Thomas Jefferson.

It's undoubtedly true that Jesus of Nazareth is the most influential person who ever lived. But here's what's wrong with the list. The Lord Jesus Christ is in a class all by Himself; there are no competitors, no rivals; He is unique. He is Lord of all. He is King of kings, Lord of lords, the image of the invisible God. He is Alpha and Omega, the First and the Last, the Preeminent One.

That's wonderful to contemplate. We'd be in sad shape if we had to worship Napoleon or some other name on that list. We don't pray to Shakespeare. We may admire Washington and Lincoln, but they can't give abundant life. There is only one Jesus, and He alone guides our steps, receives our worship, and gives us everlasting hope. He alone is preeminent.

SEPARATION ANXIETY

Men of Galilee, why do you stand gazing up into heaven?
This same Jesus, who was taken up from you into heaven,
will so come in like manner as you saw Him go into heaven.

ACTS 1:10-11

When young children experience separation anxiety, they become frantic when they lose sight of their loved one. Similarly, when Jesus was crucified, the disciples were devastated. In their minds, He was gone. It was not until Jesus began appearing to them that their faith grew, like children realizing their loved one will return.

By the time Jesus ascended, the disciples were secure in their relationship with Him; their outspoken witness and joy revealed their confidence in Christ's promise to return. Today, as we stand in a long line of disciples waiting for Jesus' return, we too can be confident of His return. In the midst of our circumstances, the promise remains. Jesus is coming back. His love for us was revealed through His every action: coming to earth, forgiving sins, bringing healing and being crucified on our behalf. Having loved us enough to endure all of this, He will surely return as promised. Meditating on this truth will fill us with joy and equip us to witness to others.

DAVID JEREMIAH

Always Interceding

*Therefore He is also able to save to the uttermost
those who come to God through Him, since He
always lives to make intercession for them.*

Menwith Hill, in a Yorkshire moor in the north of England, is the world's largest eavesdropping station in the world. There, American and British intelligence officers monitor worldwide electronic "chatter" coursing through the air, hoping to pick up clues to terrorist and other harmful activity before it happens. While terrorists talk on their cell phones, satellite dishes intercept their conversations.

Warfare is always going two ways—offense and defense. The same is true in spiritual warfare. While Satan is luring and tempting those he can (1 Peter 5:8), Jesus is in heaven interceding with the Father on our behalf. Luke 22 gives an example: Jesus knew that Satan wanted to trip up Peter and the disciples and "sift [them] as wheat." But Jesus said to Peter, "I have prayed for you [plural], that your faith should not fail" (Luke 22:31-32). While Satan was attacking, Jesus was interceding.

The next time you are tempted to sin, think about Jesus praying for you in heaven—praying "that your faith should not fail." And praise Him that He is your partner in prayer.

ASKING AND ANSWERING

For this reason, since the day we heard about you,
we have not stopped praying for you and asking God
to fill you with the knowledge of His will through
all spiritual wisdom and understanding.

COLOSSIANS 1:9, NIV 1984

When President James Garfield was shot by an assassin, doctors could not determine the location of the bullet since no X-ray technology existed. While Garfield clung to life, Alexander Graham Bell worked feverishly—literally, day and night, hardly stopping to sleep—to develop a device he could use to locate the bullet so doctors could remove it. The president died before Bell's technology was perfected. But the inventor of the telephone displayed what is necessary in the face of challenges: continual seeking for answers.

When we lack a specific knowledge of God's will, we must do the same. Paul wrote to the Colossians that he was praying *continually* for them, *asking* God to fill them with a knowledge of *His will*. Persistence and asking—two things Jesus taught His disciples about prayer (Luke 11:5-11; 18:1-5).

If you are seeking God's will, pray without ceasing and let God answer as He will. Before there are answers, there must be asking. We ask, He answers.

ANANIAS

But Peter said, "Ananias, why has Satan filled
your heart to lie to the Holy Spirit and keep back
part of the price of the land for yourself?"

ACTS 5:3

There were three men in the book of Acts named Ananias. The first was the man to whom Peter spoke in Acts 5. Ananias and his wife sold a piece of land and claimed they were giving all the proceeds to the church. They were lying, and their lie was exposed to protect the church from deceit.

The second Ananias was a fervent disciple of Christ in Damascus who had the joy of leading Saul of Tarsus to faith in Christ and facilitating his baptism (Acts 9:1-19). Paul later described him as a man of "good testimony" (Acts 22:12).

The third Ananias was the high priest who commanded that Paul be struck on the mouth in Acts 23:2. The apostle responded angrily, "God will strike you, *you* whitewashed wall!"

We encounter these same three men today. Some in the church have a corrupting influence. Some in the world oppose the spread of the Gospel. But here and there we encounter true saints who maintain a good testimony and seek to win others to the Lord Jesus.

What kind of Ananias are you?

WHY AFFLICTION IS GOOD

It is good for me that I have been afflicted,
that I may learn Your statutes.

PSALM 119:71

Joseph's rise to power in Egypt was amazing in a land that looked down on nomadic Semite shepherds like himself (Genesis 43:32; 46:34). We know the theological reasons—God promoted Joseph to power in Egypt to prepare a place for Jacob's family. But humanly speaking, why were the Egyptians so taken with Joseph?

A clue may be in Psalm 119:98-100 where the psalmist says God's Word made him "wiser than [his] enemies"; he had "more understanding than all [his] teachers." And how did the psalmist gain such a commitment to God's statutes? Through affliction (Psalm 119:71). Before Joseph was promoted to power in Egypt, he suffered in an Egyptian prison after being falsely accused (Genesis 39:20). Suffering and affliction accomplish one of two things. They either drive us *to* God and His Word or *away from* God. In Joseph's case, his affliction drove him back to the truths he knew about God, resulting in his knowing God better and better—something the Egyptians ultimately recognized as wisdom.

If you are suffering today, don't let it drive you away from God. Reach out to Him and embrace His promises.

Narrow Minded?

*I charge you therefore before God and the Lord
Jesus Christ, who will judge the living and the
dead at His appearing and His kingdom.*

2 Timothy 4:1

Some say biblical Christianity is too narrow. If it is true (and it is), then it is indeed narrow compared with modern sensibilities. It helps to remind ourselves of what the Bible teaches about Jesus Christ, to make sure we remain committed to a biblical faith.

For instance, the Bible says that Jesus Christ will sit as judge of all humanity one day in the future (Romans 2:16; 2 Timothy 4:1). *Do you believe this?* Jesus Himself said that He is the way, the truth, and the life—that no one comes to the Father except through Him (John 14:6). *Do you believe this?* The Bible says that one day every knee will bow and every tongue confess that Jesus Christ is Lord (Philippians 2:10-11). *Do you believe this?* Jesus said that everyone who does not believe in Him stands condemned already (John 3:18). *Do you believe this?* But the Bible also says there is no condemnation for those who are in Christ Jesus (Romans 8:1). *Do you believe this?*

The law of gravity is narrow, but it is also true. The best response to truth is to believe and rejoice in its blessing.

UNIVERSAL PRAISE

Blessing and honor and glory and power
be to Him who sits on the throne.

REVELATION 5:13

When we praise the Lord, we're joining the saints of Scripture and the hymnists of history in lifting up our worship to Him who sits on the throne. We're joining the hosts in heaven now gathered by the crystal river. We're sharing in the natural praise that arises from creation as the birds sing, the winds howl, and the thunders rumble across the sky. The whole universe is designed to praise the Lord.

A nineteenth-century English divine prayed: "We join, O God, in the blessed strain Thy holy children sang of old, when, filled full of gladness and Divine glory, they all met to sing Thy praise, to praise Thee as a God of glory, and to magnify Thy mighty name. We too would call upon all things to praise Thee, and join the song poured forth unto Thee by the sweet birds and the flowers, and by all Thy works in nature."

From first to last, Revelation brims and overflows with worship. It isn't a book of perplexity but of praise. If worship will be universal during the Millennium and eternal state, let's get a head start on it today!

HIS WAY

And you shall remember the Lord your God, for
it is He who gives you power to get wealth.

DEUTERONOMY 8:18

One day while vacationing in the south of France, singer Paul Anka heard a song titled "Comme d'habitude." He flew to Paris to negotiate the rights to translate and record it in English. Back in New York, Anka sat down late at night and began writing his version on an old electric typewriter. He had only one soloist in mind—Frank Sinatra. Anka composed the lyrics as he thought Sinatra would have written them if he were dying: "The end is near … I've lived a life that's full … I've done it my way." It became one of Sinatra's greatest hits: "My Way!"

As our culture has advanced in entertainment, technology, science, and education, a humanist philosophy has overtaken our hearts. People want to do things their way, take all the credit, and live as though God has little to do with everyday life. Like the people of Babel, we want to make a name for ourselves with no thought of God.

But it's God who gives us the ability to do things, even to gain wealth; and we must remember that what we do is only successful when we do it—His Way.

AVOID THIS SPIRIT

And every spirit that does not confess that Jesus
Christ has come in the flesh is not of God. And this
is the spirit of the Antichrist, which you have heard
was coming, and is now already in the world.

1 JOHN 4:3

We hear "Spirit of . . ." often: Spirit of Christmas, Spirit of 1776, Spirit of America, the Olympic Spirit, and others. While it's hard to define, "spirit of" means attitudes and behaviors consistent with the season or event being described.

The apostle John wrote that a diabolical spirit—"the *spirit* of the Antichrist" (1 John 4:3)—was already at work, empowering those who denied that Jesus Christ had come in the flesh as a human man—the Son of God *and* the Son of Man. The Greek word *anti* can mean "against" or "in place of." So the spirit of the Antichrist would be any attitude, behavior, or teaching that is blatantly against or subtly counterfeiting the true Christ. There is no reason to suspect that the spirit of the Antichrist was limited to the first century. Look around today at the number of ways Christ is opposed or misrepresented in our culture.

It is the Christian's responsibility to know Christ and His teaching well enough to immediately recognize "the spirit of the Antichrist."

STAY ON COURSE

If we ask anything according to His will, He hears us.

1 JOHN 5:14

When missionary J. Hudson Taylor was conducting services aboard a ship one Sunday, he noticed the captain looked troubled. A contrary wind was bearing the ship toward a dangerous reef. As the course grew more perilous, the captain said, "Well, we have done everything that can be done."

"No," said Taylor, "there is one thing we have not yet done. Four of us onboard are Christians. Let us each retire to his own cabin, and in agreed prayer ask the Lord to give us immediately a breeze." After a brief time in prayer, Taylor returned to the deck and told the first officer, a godless man, to let down the mainsail. With an oath the man did so, and a slight breeze caught it. "It's only a cat's paw," said the sailor, meaning a mere puff of wind. But it became a sustained breeze that pushed the ship back into its desired course.

Our prayers are strengthened when we know God is listening and that He is faithful. While we always say, "Your will be done," we must never lack confidence that He hears, answers, and keeps us on the right course.

THE BODY OF CHRIST

Now you are the body of Christ, and members individually.

1 CORINTHIANS 12:27

Dr. Warren Wiersbe summed up the Christian experience like this. "Salvation includes a threefold work: the work God does *for* us—salvation; the work God does *in* us—sanctification; the work God does *through* us—service."

The Bible often uses the word "through" to describe how God uses us. For example, 2 Corinthians 5:20 says, "We are ambassadors for Christ, as though God were pleading *through* us" (emphasis added). Think of it this way: In the Gospels, Christ walked on earth in a physical body. His body was literally the body of Christ. But when He returned to heaven, the church was formed, and one of the names given the church was the body of Christ. Our Lord's original body was (and still is) real and physical; but His second body is comprised of Christians everywhere. He works through us to accomplish His work on earth.

Our ministry today is in Christ, who lives and works through us. You don't have to depend on your own personality or powers of persuasion. Christ will work through you today. You are His ambassador and His body.

THE HEAVENS DECLARE

*You are worthy, O Lord, to receive glory and
honor and power; for You created all things, and
by Your will they exist and were created.*

REVELATION 4:11

Physicist Tony Rothman wrote an article for *Discovery Magazine* discussing the problem secular scientists face with the complexity of the universe and the remarkable scientific laws and fine-tuning of the cosmos. "When confronted with the order and beauty of the universe and the strange coincidences of nature," he wrote, "it's very tempting to take the leap of faith from science into religion. I am sure many physicists want to. I only wish they would admit it."

Acknowledging the creative power of God isn't really a leap of faith; it's obvious for those who are honest and objective. Psalm 19 says (in The Message): "God's glory is on tour in the skies.... Madame Day holds classes every morning, Professor Night lectures each evening. Their words aren't heard…but their…unspoken truth is spoken everywhere."

The universe is filled with the evidence of God's greatness. In awesome wonder we can consider the worlds He has made. When we see His stars and hear His rolling thunder, we can praise Him. We can say with the writer of Psalm 104:1, "O Lord my God, You are very great."

Wait Until Wednesday

But the LORD was with Joseph and showed him mercy, and
He gave him favor in the sight of the keeper of the prison.

Genesis 39:21

A tongue-in-cheek theological axiom concerning the will of God goes like this: If it's Monday, and you want to know what God's will is for Tuesday, just wait until Wednesday. The point of that saying is this: God's will is always active, always ongoing, always being worked out—even when circumstances are difficult. The mistake we make is thinking that God's will can never involve discomfort or pain.

We know for a fact that it was God's will for Joseph to be taken to Egypt; Joseph himself said as much to his brothers. In fact, Joseph said it was God who sent him to Egypt (Genesis 45:4-7; 50:20). But God's will was not just the end result—Joseph being made second-in-command in Egypt. God's will also included everything that resulted in that appointment—like being cast into an Egyptian prison for a time. Even in that dark period, "the LORD was with Joseph" (Genesis 39:21), an indication that Joseph was clearly in God's will.

When your circumstances make you question God's will, recommit yourself to His presence and His purposes.

ASK AND YOU SHALL RECEIVE

Ask and it will be given to you; seek and you will find; knock and the door will be opened to you.

MATTHEW 7:7, NIV

Evangelist D. L. Moody told of two Christian women who were burdened for their unsaved husbands. They agreed on a radical plan. They would each spend an hour a day praying for the salvation of their men. After seven years, the women grew discouraged and debated giving up. They could see no progress. But the women decided to persevere as long as they lived, so they rededicated themselves to the task. Three years later, one of the women was awakened in the night by her husband, who was in great distress about his soul. As soon as the sun rose, that woman hurried off toward her friend's house to tell her that God was about to answer her prayers. She was astonished to meet her friend coming from the opposite direction with the same news. Ten years of persevering prayer was crowned with the conversion of both husbands on the same day.

The month of April is a good time to remember that yes, we may pray anytime, anywhere, for anything. Don't grow discouraged in prayer. Ask, and it will be given you; seek, and you will find; knock, and the door will be opened to you.

BLESSED TO BE A BLESSING

*I will make you a great nation; I will bless you
and make your name great; and you shall be a blessing. . . .
And in you all the families of the earth shall be blessed.*

GENESIS 12:2-3

The next time you cut open a piece of fruit, pause to marvel at the abundance of seeds it contains. The seeds represent the process of renewal in nature, but they also represent an important necessity—plants require seeds to reproduce so that they do not become extinct! God blessed His creation so it could "be fruitful and multiply" (Genesis 1:28; 9:1). Even our own blessing of regeneration and salvation is to become a source of blessing to others.

The idea of "blessed to be a blessing" is seen earliest and most clearly in God's calling of Abraham. God didn't call Abraham out of Mesopotamia just to give him a richer life in Canaan. Yes, Abraham was blessed personally, but there was a greater purpose: "In you all the families of the earth shall be blessed" (Genesis 12:3). Through Abraham's faith and God's covenantal promise, generations of people have come to faith. "So then those who are of faith are blessed with believing Abraham" (Galatians 3:9).

Ask God to make you aware of someone who needs the blessing of God today. Plant a seed, share your faith, be a blessing.

THE BELT OF TRUTH

Stand therefore, having girded your waist with truth . . . .

EPHESIANS 6:14A

The use of "girded" (NKJV, NASB) and "girt" (KJV) in Ephesians 6:14 gave rise to the popular term "girdle of truth." But a word of clarification: Paul is not making reference in that verse to the "girdle" as it was defined in the early to mid-twentieth century—a female undergarment. Paul refers more correctly to a "belt" worn around the waist of most men in his day, and all soldiers: "the belt of truth" (NIV, NLT, ESV).

But why would Paul connect truth to a first-century belt? Probably because of the usefulness of the leather or linen belt in his day. It was used to tuck up a robe to ensure more efficient movement (1 Peter 1:13); it was used by soldiers for hanging a sword or quiver of arrows; it was used by soldiers to display medals of valor. Just so, the truth of God keeps the Christian unencumbered by false teaching and sin (Hebrews 12:1), serves as a place to hang our beliefs (John 17:17), and rewards us with salvation when we believe and obey it (2 Thessalonians 2:10). Most of all, truth allows us to love in deeds and not in words alone (1 John 3:18).

The belt of God's truth is not something that makes us look good. Rather, it is something that shapes our life into the image of Christ.

MAY

THE PERFECT ENDING

*But we see Jesus, who was made a little lower than the angels,
for the suffering of death crowned with glory and honor, that
He, by the grace of God, might taste death for everyone.*

HEBREWS 2:9

When we dislike the ending of a book or movie, we try to imagine a better one: what we think should have happened. The wonder and goodness of creation was broken when Adam disobeyed God. We feel the burden of this brokenness and separation from God. Thankfully, the Creator did not end the story there.

Just as a producer determines the last scene of a movie and a writer carefully crafts the final sentence of a book, God mercifully provided what we desire and desperately need: a Savior. We cannot save ourselves. Only God, who is powerful enough to create the world out of nothing and to give us life, could find the perfect solution to our brokenness and separation from Him: Jesus.

Jesus is God's final answer to the dilemma we face. He is God in the flesh, and the book of Hebrews elaborates on why Jesus is all we need. He is superior to every human leader, prophet, and priest. He offers us Himself along with forgiveness, life, and meaning.

MAY 2

YOUR TIME

Be hospitable to one another without grumbling.

1 PETER 4:9

In her memoirs, former Secretary of State Condoleezza Rice told of growing up in an African-American pastor's family in Birmingham. Despite her parents' busy schedules, they watched *The Mickey Mouse Club* with her every day. One afternoon, the insurance agent came to visit. "He was the only white man I can ever remember coming into our house," recalls Rice. But he came just as it was time to sing: "M-I-C-K-E-Y-...." Mr. Rice politely told the man he would have to wait until they all put on their mouse ears and engaged in the family ritual of singing along.

"This small gesture was simply one of many that communicated they always had time for me," wrote Condoleezza.[10]

One of the greatest presents we can give is time—to our children, to our spouse, to our church, to friends, and sometimes to strangers on the street or neighbors in need. It's the most hospitable kind of hospitality. When we give our time without grumbling, we're giving ourselves.

10 Condoleezza Rice, *Condoleezza Rice: A Memoir of My Extraordinary, Ordinary Family* (New York: Random House, 2010), 39.

Take the Gift

For by grace you have been saved through faith,
and that not of yourselves; it is the gift of God,
not of works, lest anyone should boast.

Ephesians 2:8-9

You work hard in your vegetable garden and harvest an abundance of fresh produce. So you collect a bag full of tomatoes, beans, cucumbers, and squash, and knock on your neighbor's door to share the bounty. As you hand her the gift from your garden, she asks if she can pay you something. You decline, but understand. If it's not Christmas, a birthday, or anniversary, people are uncomfortable with the idea of receiving a gift.

The human tendency to want to work for what we get, the feeling that what is not earned is undeserved, keeps many from understanding the Gospel of the grace of God. Salvation is no more free than the cost of growing vegetables. But just as you paid the price so your neighbor could have a gift, so Jesus Christ paid the price for salvation and offers it as a gift to us. We are "saved through faith, . . . not [by] works, lest anyone should boast" (Ephesians 2:8-9). Salvation "is the gift of God." When we pay for a gift, it ceases to be a gift at all.

There's only one thing to do with God's offer of the gift of salvation: Say "thank you" and embrace it.

FAITH IS A MUST

*By faith we understand that the worlds were framed
by the word of God, so that the things which are
seen were not made of things which are visible.*

HEBREWS 11:3

We have heard this saying before. If a tree falls in the forest, and no one is there to see (or hear) it, does it make a sound? That's one big problem Christians face every day. We haven't actually seen the physical appearance of God.

People who don't believe need to see before they believe. Believers don't need to see it. They rely on the Word of God. Faith treats things that are hoped for as reality. Faith is the solid, unshakable confidence in God which is built upon assurance that He is faithful to His promises.

Hebrews 11:6 (NIV) says, "And without faith it is impossible to please God, because anyone who comes to him must believe that he exists and that he rewards those who earnestly seek Him."

Who wouldn't want a reward from the Creator of the universe and Creator of all living things? The map to the reward is rather easy—we just need to have faith in God.

PLEASING GOD

*For before [Enoch] was taken he had this
testimony, that he pleased God.*

HEBREWS 11:5B

It is the classic theme of world literature—the need of a lesser being to please a greater being. Whether the greater being is a king, tyrant, ogre, or fantastical being, the subject's need is to discover what the ruler demands and do it. Tension in the story builds as it looks less and less likely that the subject will be able to please the ruler.

The Bible is part of world literature, and it shares that theme with other great stories. The Bible's story—the necessity for man to please God—is at the same time more and less dramatic. First, God requires only one thing to be pleased: "But without faith *it is* impossible to please *Him*" (Hebrews 11:6). Everything else we might do to please the Creator God does not qualify unless preceded by faith. Second, there is a dramatic crisis and solution: God becomes a human being so dedicated to God that He lives a *perfectly* faithful life and dies to pay for the faithlessness of all other men. The life of pleasing God is illustrated simply by Enoch: "He pleased God."

If it is your desire to please God, always begin with faith. Our belief in Him seems to bring Him more pleasure than anything else.

Practice Encouragement

Therefore comfort each other and edify one another, just as you also are doing.

1 Thessalonians 5:11

Paul wanted the Thessalonians to give one another the gift of encouragement. He encouraged them in 1 Thessalonians 5 to remember the suddenness of our Lord's return. Since Jesus will come like a thief in the night (verse 2), we're to be prepared, putting on the breastplate of faith and love and … the hope of salvation (verse 8). And since God has a great future for us, "whether we wake or sleep, we should live together with Him" (verse 10). We should therefore encourage each other to look up with hopefulness (verse 11). We should honor those who labor among us, living with peace and patience toward all (verses 12-14).

What a great chapter Paul wrote in 1 Thessalonians!

When we're conscious of the imminent return of Christ, we're filled with hope; and that helps us offer Scripture-based encouragement to others. When we encourage someone else with such scriptural truth, they will in turn encourage others. Our attitudes are passed on down the line.

Jesus is coming soon! *Therefore comfort each other and edify one another, just as you also are doing.*

WAITING

*Therefore, since we are receiving a kingdom which
cannot be shaken, let us have grace, by which we may
serve God acceptably with reverence and godly fear.*

HEBREWS 12:28

The country music band Alabama has a song about the pace of life that says: "I'm in a hurry to get things done. Oh, I rush and rush until life's no fun. All I really gotta do is live and die. But I'm in a hurry and don't know why."[11]

Waiting is part of living, and sometimes it's the hardest part. We're programmed to hurry, but sometimes God has a way of slowing us down. It's hard to serve God acceptably with reverence and godly fear when we're too busy to pray, to be still, and to give God time to resolve the issues that concern us. Maturity takes time, and time requires waiting.

Maybe you're waiting for Mr. Right or Miss Congeniality, or for a prodigal to return, or for an employer to call. As Christians, we learn more about walking with God through waiting than through anything else. Our faith grows when we're trusting in His promises and patiently laying our concerns before Him.

Remember amid the rush of life to slow down long enough to wait on the Lord.

---

11 Alabama: *American Pride*, *"I'm in a Hurry (And Don't Know Why),"* by Roger Murrah and Randy VanWarmer, writers, released 1992.

DAVID JEREMIAH

WHAT GOD CANNOT DO

God is not a man, that He should lie, nor a son of man,
that He should repent. Has He said, and will He not do?
Or has He spoken, and will He not make it good?

NUMBERS 23:19

Anxious? Fearful? Worried? Depressed? Perhaps we need to remember what Joshua said: "Not a word failed of any good thing which the LORD had spoken to the house of Israel. All came to pass…. Behold, this day I *am* going the way of all the earth. And you know in all your hearts and in all your souls that not one thing has failed of all the good things which the LORD your God spoke concerning you" (Joshua 21:45 & 23:14).

King Solomon made the same point at the dedication of the temple in 1 Kings 8:56, saying, "There has not failed one word of all His good promise."

Titus 1:2 says, "God, who cannot lie, promised."

Hebrews 6:18 adds, "It *is* impossible for God to lie"; and so, said the writer, that's why we "lay hold of the hope set before *us*." God has never broken, and will never break, a single promise—past, present, or future. Trust Him today with your anxiety, fear, worry, and depression. Lean on His power, love, grace, and mercy.

MAY 9

SIGNS OF LIFE

We know that we have passed from death to life, because we love the brethren.

1 JOHN 3:14

In earlier ages it was often hard to determine when someone was actually dead. Books of historical oddities are filled with accounts of people accidentally buried alive. Hans Christian Andersen was so petrified by the prospect that he kept a sign by his bed bearing the words: "I am not really dead." Painter Auguste Renoir insisted doctors do whatever was necessary to prove he was dead before burial. George Washington told attendants to keep his body above ground for three days before burial.

According to Scripture, those without Christ are spiritually dead, but those who know Him are alive. If we're alive, there should be signs of life. People should instantly see that we're living in Christ. There should be no mistake about it. We should bear evidence of Christ's life—a love that consumes us, a joy that sustains us, a hope that brightens our outlook, a purity that maintains our holiness, and a commitment that makes others want to follow our Savior.

It's a tragedy when people don't know if we're dead or alive in Christ. Let the world know you're alive.

GREAT PROMISES

Do not worry about your life, what you will eat;
nor about the body, what you will put on.

LUKE 12:22

Last year, a Gallup poll found large numbers of Americans in the grip of worry, and a simultaneous study by the University of Surrey in the United Kingdom warned that worry can have long-term chronic health consequences, including cardiovascular disease. No surprise there. But how do we reduce worry? The research recommended more sleep, periods of deep breathing, walks in the forest, chocolate, and smelling grapefruits. A study at James Cancer Hospital in Columbus, Ohio, found that the pleasant-smelling essential oils of grapefruit tended to reduce tension and boost the body's energy.[12]

Those ideas may have merit, but the true answer to anxiety is spiritual. Learn to meditate on God's goodness. Ponder His power. Drill into His promises. Focus your mind on Him, for Isaiah told us, "You will keep him in perfect peace, *whose* mind *is* stayed *on You*" (Isaiah 26:3).

To reduce your anxieties, take some time today to stop and think about God's many blessings in the midst of stress and pressure. Grapefruits are good; but great promises are better.

---

12 http://www.fastcompany.com/3040809/how-to-be-a-success-at-everything/7-surprising-things-that-can-help-you-stop-worrying.

PAIN AND GAIN

*And Pharaoh said to Joseph, "See, I have
set you over all the land of Egypt."*

GENESIS 41:41

Did you hear about the Christian who said his dream was to be a retired missionary? How about the person who wanted to be an author but not a writer? Or the little boy who said he'd like to be the Most Valuable Player on his team? These folks are looking at what only comes after years of work, practice, and suffering. Missionaries have to toil thanklessly, authors have to learn to write, and young athletes must practice repeatedly. It's a cliché because it is often true: There is no gain without a measure of pain.

Joseph didn't go to Egypt with his eyes set on becoming Pharaoh's prime minister. He spent more than a decade as a servant, a steward, a prisoner, and risking his life as an interpreter of Pharaoh's dreams before God rewarded his faithfulness with a place of honor. Even for Jesus Christ, the cross preceded the crown. Life is all about gaining maturity, and maturity must be tested and perfected through trials.

The path to blessing and honor always goes through the land of testing and obedience. Stay on that path and trust God for where it leads. Be faithful in the little and difficult things on the way.

DAVID JEREMIAH

WHAT OPPORTUNITY REVEALS

Thus [Potiphar] left all that he had in Joseph's hand, and he did not know what he had except for the bread which he ate.

GENESIS 39:6A

In the summer of 2014, a bank teller pled guilty to embezzling nearly two million dollars from the State Bank of Lincoln where she worked as a head teller. She pulled off her crime by having access to the bank's vault and by changing audit numbers. Because she had worked at the bank for nearly two decades, she was trusted.

Joseph, in a much shorter time, grew to be totally trusted by his master, Potiphar, a wealthy official in Egypt. In fact, Potiphar turned over so much responsibility to Joseph—managing everything he owned—that all he knew about his property was the food he ate every day. Joseph managed everything else. How easy in such a situation—complete, trusted access to great wealth—would it have been for Joseph to line his own pockets with Potiphar's goods? What the playwright Oscar Wilde said—"I can resist anything except temptation"—was not true of Joseph. His integrity was not changed because of his privileged position.

Circumstances don't create character; they reveal character. Arm yourself today with the integrity of Christ.

DESIRES OF YOUR HEART

*Delight yourself in the Lord; and He shall
give you the desires of your heart.*

PSALM 37:4

Dr. Joseph Sizoo was a Washington D.C. pastor whose parishioners included Robert Todd Lincoln, the eldest son of Abraham Lincoln. One day Sizoo was allowed to handle the late president's Bible. It was the Bible from which Lincoln's mother read to him and was the only possession he carried with him from childhood. "Book in my hand," recalled Sizoo, "I wondered where it would fall open. It opened to a page which was thumb marked and which he must have read many times. It was the thirty-seventh Psalm."[13]

How wonderful if our Bibles would turn automatically to Psalm 37. This passage tells us not to fret nor be envious. Rather trust in the Lord and feed on His faithfulness. Delight yourself also in the Lord, and He shall give you the desires of your heart.

Is this true? Absolutely. But remember—delighting in the Lord changes our desires. When we delight in Him, we begin desiring what He desires for us. And having planted those desires in our hearts, the Lord is then only too happy to fulfill them.

13 Bob Klingenberg, *Is God with America?* (Xulonpress Press, 2006), 325-326.

NOAH WALKED WITH GOD

But Noah found favor in the eyes of the LORD . . . . Noah was a righteous man, blameless in his time; Noah walked with God.

GENESIS 6:8-9, NASB

We wonder if we live in the most evil age in history given the atrocities that happen around us. But it appears there has been an age when wickedness was even more widespread than in our own: the age described in Genesis 6. That age was so wicked that God "was sorry that He had made man on the earth" (verse 6). It was the age that prompted the Flood, after which God started over with Noah and his family.

Noah was an Adam-type man whom God trusted to be the new head of the human race. Noah wasn't sinless, but he was righteous; he was a man who "walked with God." Genesis 6:9 suggests that he may have been the only human being of his kind on earth in that age, the only man who sought to follow God's will and who could be trusted with God's mission to preserve human and animal life on earth. Noah was faithful. In the face of probable derision and scorn from his community, he built an ark and preserved life on earth.

Noah raises this question: If God looked for one person who would be faithful to Him in a specific task, would His eyes rest upon you?

THE SHIELD OF FAITH

*Therefore take heart, men, for I believe God
that it will be just as it was told me.*

ACTS 27:25

When the tragic shooting of nine people of faith occurred in a South Carolina church in 2015, the hearts of not only their families grieved but the nation mourned as well. How could this happen? How could someone spend time with these lovely people in a Bible study and then turn on them? We will never have all the answers, but we do know that evil entered into the heart of that young man and he acted with hatred and malice. It was an attack not only on these precious individuals but on people of faith. It is a reminder to us all to keep our shield of faith in place at all times.

What a poignant reminder that we need the shield of faith to protect us. No, physical violence isn't the greatest threat to most of us, but Satan is still on the attack. Without the shield of faith, we're tempted to doubt the outcome of our situations, the answers to our prayers, and the promises God has made. If we lay down our shield, we're fully vulnerable to the lies launched in our direction. But Satan has no answer to those who say: "Take heart … I believe God that it will be just as He said." Faith is the victory that overcomes the world.

FIDELITY

*Praying at all times in the Spirit, with
all prayer and supplication.*

EPHESIANS 6:18A, ESV

One of the great records of correspondence by mail was between John and Abigail Adams during the founding of the American republic. She was in Massachusetts, he in Philadelphia or Europe, and the stream of letters never ceased. Likewise, the correspondence between Winston and Clementine Churchill was equally nonstop. Even when they were in the same house, working in different rooms, servants carried a constant stream of love notes back and forth between them.

Those stories are examples of "communicating without ceasing." Though not formally conversing at every moment, each spouse kept the other in mind continually so that communication was only a note away. Likewise, Paul admonishes Christians to pray "at all times in the Spirit" (Ephesians 6:18a, HCSB) and "pray without ceasing" (1 Thessalonians 5:17). That means take up the pen of faith and pray to our beloved God whenever there is a need. Keep Him in mind at all times so He is only a prayer away.

Let God be on your mind continually today so words of praise, intercession, or supplication may arise as needed.

PASS IT FORWARD

Not returning evil for evil or reviling for reviling,
but on the contrary blessing, knowing that you were
called to this, that you may inherit a blessing.

1 PETER 3:9

Francis Crick, James Watson, and Maurice Wilkins were awarded the 1962 Nobel Prize for Physiology or Medicine for their research into the nature of the genetic code—that information contained in human cells that is passed from generation to generation. We receive genetic information from our parents and pass it on to our children, a living chain that ties the human race together from beginning to end.

Scientists now know that human genes can be affected by environmental and lifestyle choices. It behooves us, therefore, to be good stewards of what we receive for the benefit of succeeding generations. And the same is true of spiritual blessings we inherit. That is, we have been blessed to be a blessing. Not only have we been called, as children of God, to inherit a blessing; we have been sent out into the world in order to be a blessing to others as well. The grace of God in us is for our giving as well as for our keeping—a never-ending supply of blessing for the world.

As God has been a blessing to you, be a blessing to someone today—pass it forward.

INSPIRATION OR IMPULSE?

Let nothing be done through selfish ambition or conceit, but in lowliness of mind let each esteem others better than himself.

PHILIPPIANS 2:3

Two men were riding their horses down a country road, discussing the question of motivation. One believed we're capable of pure motives, even without Christ. The other disagreed. They came to a ditch where a pig had gotten tangled up in fencing and was struggling to extricate himself. The latter gentlemen got down in the mud and managed to free the animal, though he ruined his clothing. Resuming their trip, the first man said, "There! That was a selfless act of kindness." But his friend replied, "No, it was pure selfishness. The only reason I helped that pig was to save myself from the guilt and torment of worrying about him all day."

Without Christ, it's impossible to operate from true love and godly motivations. But as we grow in Him, our motives gradually improve and we're increasingly compelled by His love, which is "poured out into our hearts through the Holy Spirit, who has been given to us" (Romans 5:5, ESV).

Only in Christ can we exhibit humility (lowliness of mind) and be motivated by biblical love rather than our own desires.

HUMBLE YOURSELF

*For whoever exalts himself will be humbled, and
he who humbles himself will be exalted.*

LUKE 14:11

In a study from 2014, researchers found that when company leaders exhibited humility and compassion, their employees performed at higher levels and were more committed to their work. According to the study, when these leaders let go of their ego-driven attitudes and embraced more empathetic ones, companies reaped greater success.[14]

The Bible takes a similar view on the subject of humility: If you humble yourself before God, He will lift you up (James 4:10). And if you want to follow Christ, you *will* be humble. Jesus told His disciples that truth during His last supper with them. He took on the role of a servant by washing their feet—a shocking thing for Him to have done. And when He was finished, He said they should do the same for each other—play the role of servant: "For I have given you an example, that you should do as I have done to you" (John 13:15). Followers of Christ must be reconciled to the truth that we are called to be humble servants of one another.

Ask God today to give you a servant's humble heart. Look for an opportunity today to humble yourself and serve another person. Better to humble ourselves and be exalted than to exalt ourselves and be humbled.

14 http://www.huffingtonpost.com/douglas-labier/why-humble-empathic-busin_b_6042196.html

BEFORE AND AFTER

*But you shall receive power when the
Holy Spirit has come upon you.*

ACTS 1:8A

In recent days, the media has covered many heartwarming scenes of toddlers, born deaf, hearing for the first time after a cochlear implant. That is a true "before and after" scenario—to go from not hearing to hearing with the flip of a switch.

It wasn't the result of flipping a switch, but the apostles of Jesus had their own "before and after" experience: pre-Pentecost versus post-Pentecost. Jesus had promised to send the Holy Spirit to give them power to fulfill the commission He had given them. And the Spirit was poured out on them in Jerusalem at Pentecost. Before that moment, the disciples had been fearful, uncertain, and isolated behind closed doors (Acts 1:12-13). After Pentecost, everything changed. Peter preached a bold sermon and thousands believed in Christ (Acts 2:41). In the following days, the apostles preached boldly in Jerusalem and worked powerful miracles in defiance of orders not to preach.

The Holy Spirit can make the same difference in our lives if we will remain submitted and obedient to Him—being filled with the Holy Spirit (Ephesians 5:18).

NEVER CHANGING

*The angel of the LORD encamps all around
those who fear Him, and delivers them.*

PSALM 34:7

One of Rembrandt's final paintings is considered by many to be his finest: *The Return of the Prodigal Son.* It illustrates the climax of the parable of Jesus recorded in Luke 15:11-32. The power of that parable is found in the father's unconditional love for the prodigal son who returns home after profligate living. He returns not knowing what to expect—whether the father would still love him or not.

Jesus told the parable to Jews and their leaders whose ancestors had, a few generations earlier, returned from exile in Babylon. Most of them, born in Babylon, had not known the God of their fathers personally. Would He still be angry over the sins that sent Israel into exile? The answer was no: "For I am the Lord, I do not change." God's love is not based on their, or our, goodness or sinfulness. It is based on God's choice to love unconditionally. He had told them through Jeremiah that His love was as constant as the universe (Jeremiah 31:35-37). When they returned home to Judah they discovered God's love had not changed.

His love does not change toward you either. Rest today in the unchanging nature of God and His unchanging love for you.

Hand Gestures

You open Your hand and satisfy the desire of every living thing.

PSALM 145:16

Hand gestures can communicate our innermost thoughts and emotions. Clenched fists reveal anger. White knuckles and trembling are usually the result of fear and nervousness. We close our hands around things we want to hold on to and open them to receive and give gifts.

God's generosity is described in the verse above. He created and sustains life. He opens His hand and satisfies the desire of every living thing. Our very existence is dependent on God. If we overlook God's generosity or find ourselves in the midst of a painful season, it's easy for a mindset of scarcity to take over. We become afraid of losing what we have, and our heart's stance becomes one of grasping as we seek to control our circumstances.

This is an exhausting place to be. Not only do circumstances remain outside our control, but we miss opportunities to participate in the joy of giving because we are focused on protecting what we have. We also miss God's gifts to us because we are focused on our lack. The first step to living with open hands is to embrace the truth of God's generosity. When we believe in God's goodness and His love for us, we find the freedom to receive and release His gifts.

FORGIVENESS

*"Come now, and let us reason together," says
the LORD, "Though your sins are like scarlet,
they shall be as white as snow."*

ISAIAH 1:18

Earlier this year a man in Woodland, California, lost his wallet and decided it had been thrown in the trash. He climbed into a large garbage dumpster, but the sanitation truck came by while he searched through the debris. Hoisting up the dumpster, the truck poured the trash, including the man, into its giant interior and continued toward the landfill. It took a terrifying hour for the man to climb up through the debris and signal the sanitation engineers. He barely escaped being compacted.

Have you ever heard anyone say, "I feel like garbage"? Sometimes we feel dirty, sinful, like a person in a dump truck. Isaiah 64:6 says, "We are all like an unclean *thing*, and all our righteousnesses *are* like filthy rags … our iniquities…have taken us away."

But Isaiah also said, "Let the wicked forsake his way, and the unrighteous man his thoughts; let him return to the LORD, and He will have mercy on him; and to our God, for He will abundantly pardon" (Isaiah 55:7). The Lord offers complete forgiveness of all our garbage through Jesus Christ. And yes, you may receive it today.

MARY, MOTHER OF JESUS

*Then Mary said, "Behold the maidservant of the
Lord! Let it be to me according to your word."*

LUKE 1:38A

To be one out of 7.2 billion persons in the world is a
humbling proposition. It sounds insignificant, lowly, and
inconsequential. It brings to mind the often-heard question,
"What difference can I make?" From a human point of view, it is
not an unreasonable question.

How about one out of 175 million people? Does that make
us feel more significant? Any less lowly? Not really—even that
number is beyond our comprehension. But 175 million was
approximately the world's population when God came to one
person with a mission to fulfill. That person was Mary, a young
teenage girl living in the town of Nazareth. Could anyone have
felt less important, less worthy? Mary even described her life
as a "lowly state" (Luke 1:48). And yet Mary's response to God
was surprisingly assured. She asked the angel Gabriel only one
question before responding to his description of the task, to be
the mother of the Jewish Messiah. She said, "I am God's servant,
ready to do what you have said" (paraphrase).

Given our "lowly state," would we respond to God's call with
such humble serenity and submissiveness? Be ready for God's call
and make ready your response.

WILLING TO LIVE

And whoever does not bear his cross and
come after Me cannot be My disciple.

LUKE 14:27

Americans were shocked in World War II when Japanese fighter pilots—called *kamikazes*—flew their planes directly into Allied battleships. But there is a distinct and biblical difference between dying willingly to *take* life and dying willingly to *give* life. The people of God have always been willing to give their lives so that others might live.

Even those who die for less than honorable reasons express a thread that has run throughout human history: Without something to die for, there is nothing to live for. Three Hebrew men were willing to die for God in Babylon (Daniel 3), and tradition says that all but one of Jesus' disciples, plus many others throughout history, willingly died for His sake and for the kingdom of God. The book of Revelation tells us there will be many martyrs for Christ during the Great Tribulation on earth. Whether we die for Christ in this life or not, Jesus calls all of us to carry our cross—our *willingness* to die as He died—with us daily.

A willingness to die for our faith is one thing. But a willingness to live for Him means dying to ourselves a thousand times daily so that His will might be done in us.

SOWING SEED

He who sows sparingly will also reap sparingly, and he
who sows bountifully will also reap bountifully.

2 CORINTHIANS 9:6

Once when Rosalind Goforth grew discouraged with her missionary work in China, she wrote the words of 2 Corinthians 9:6 on the blackboard in her home and she looked at them daily. "This promise remained constantly before me," she later said, "an ever-present incentive to sow bountifully the Gospel seed...even though it often seemed the seed was being cast on stony ground. The day came, however, when my beloved husband and I were permitted to see bountiful harvests of souls reaped for our Master in that region." Indeed, the crowds who came to hear Jonathan Goforth preach sometimes numbered 25,000, a multitude unheard of in Chinese evangelism. Multitudes came to Christ during their career, and fifty Chinese converts became ministers or evangelists.

We have a large assortment of seed to sow—our Gospel witness, Gospel literature, our testimonies, our tithes and offerings, our acts of kindness and charity. The Bible promises that those who sow faithfully will reap a harvest. We can only reap if we sow.

So what Gospel seed can you sow today?

GOD'S PERSPECTIVE

And God sent me before you to preserve a posterity for you in the earth, and to save your lives by a great deliverance.

GENESIS 45:7

Chameleons and dragonflies have eyes that can cover a full 360 degrees of vision. With their peripheral vision, humans can cover only half that range. At any given moment in life, we humans are missing "half" of what is going on around us. Ours is a limited perspective to say the least.

Our perspective is limited spiritually, too; we don't often see things from God's perspective with our limited spiritual vision. For instance, for years Joseph thought he was only in Egypt to be God's representative among the Egyptian nation—to demonstrate God's wisdom and righteousness. And he did that well (Genesis 41:38-40). What he didn't see at first was that God had him in Egypt to prepare a place of refuge for the descendants of promise—the family of Jacob. He was overcome when he realized he was meeting his brothers for the first time in many years, and that he could help preserve his family (Genesis 42:24).

We should live our lives with the knowledge that we are not seeing the whole picture. We must ask God to show us His perspective—and walk in confidence knowing His way is best.

DAVID JEREMIAH

From Pain to Praise

And God will wipe away every tear from their eyes; there shall be no more death, nor sorrow, nor crying. There shall be no more pain, for the former things have passed away.

Revelation 21:4

According to the Federal Centers for Disease Control and Prevention, 2,513,171 people died in America in 2011 from all causes. On average, 6,885 people died every day; 287 people every hour; five people every minute; one person every 12 seconds. In the time it takes you to read this devotional, 5 to 10 people will die in America. At this moment, tears are being shed somewhere over the pain of loss. And that's just in America, which represents only 8.5 percent of the world's population. Is it any wonder Paul spoke of creation groaning for freedom (Romans 8:20-22)?

All of us will shed tears of pain and loss and grief at some time in life. But a day is coming when all those tears will be wiped away and will never be seen again. The sounds of pain will be replaced by the sounds of praise to the One who has redeemed us from a fallen world and ushers us into a new heaven and new earth.

If you are shedding tears of loss today, ask God to help you transition from pain to praise for the One who knows your every tear.

David's Epitaph

*For David, after he had served his own generation
by the will of God, fell asleep, was buried
with his fathers, and saw corruption.*

Acts 13:36

Epitaphs on gravestones are not as popular as they once were. In previous generations, a person could write his or her own epitaph—a summary of one's life or legacy—before death or leave the task to a friend or family member. The subject of epitaphs raises a good question: How would you want your life to be permanently remembered in one short sentence or phrase?

When the apostle Paul was preaching in a synagogue in Pisidian Antioch, Israel's King David had been dead and buried for a thousand years. But in leading up to talking about Christ's resurrection, Paul cited King David as a man who was buried and whose body decayed in the ground. Unwittingly, Paul spoke what would have been a beautiful and simple epitaph for David: "He served his own generation by the will of God" (Acts 13:36). Bible students know that David was far from perfect. But in spite of his sins and errors in judgment, David had a heart for God (verse 22).

God doesn't hold us responsible for past or future generations. But He does ask us to serve Him in our own generation like David did. There could be no greater legacy or remembrance.

THE GIFT OF FORGIVENESS

*By faith the harlot Rahab did not perish with those who did
not believe, when she had received the spies with peace.*

HEBREWS 11:31

Sometimes Christians wonder if they have committed a sin that
God cannot forgive. Or they wonder if they have committed *the*
unforgivable sin (Matthew 12:31-32). As for the latter possibility,
Jesus was speaking to Pharisees who willfully rejected Christ's
divine credentials as the Son of God. No Christian is in danger of
committing that sin.

As for committing a terrible sin that God cannot forgive, the
Bible is clear: All have sinned (Romans 3:23), and all may receive
eternal life (John 3:16). Because we live in societies that are required
to exact punishment for crimes, it is difficult to comprehend the
idea that "if we confess our sins, He is faithful and just to forgive
us *our* sins and to cleanse us from all unrighteousness" (1 John
1:9). But He is! A pagan prostitute named Rahab found that out
personally. She threw herself on the mercy of the Israelites' God
when His people entered Canaan. And she was forgiven her past
and rewarded for her faithfulness (Joshua 2).

God withholds forgiveness from no one who needs and seeks
it. If that applies to you today, confess your sins and be forgiven.

BLACK SHEEP

*Likewise, was not Rahab the harlot also justified by works when
she received the messengers and sent them out another way?*

JAMES 2:25

Most families have a "black sheep" somewhere in the family.
How that person is viewed depends on distance. If the
person is a faint memory, he is seen as a laughing matter, a faint
shadow in the past. But if the person remains a fresh memory,
then there is no mention of him or her in polite company.

Such distinctions are made only among those who place great
pride in human respectability. But in biblical terms, there are no
white sheep! We are all black sheep in the family of humanity.
None of us deserves mention in the holy company of heaven—
except for the grace of God. That grace is demonstrated by God
sending His own Son to be born as the descendant of human
sinners. They ranged from a harlot like Rahab (Matthew 1:5) to
a deceiver like Jacob (Matthew 1:2); to occasional sinners like
Abraham, kings that struggled to rule righteously; and Joseph, a
seemingly good man. But they were sinners all, chosen by God to
play a role in His grand purpose of redemption.

Because all have sinned, all can be forgiven in Christ; and
all can serve. Don't ever let your human past keep you from a
redeemed future.

JUNE

JUNE 1

CHRIST ALONE

Behold I lay in Zion a chief cornerstone, elect, precious, and he who believes on Him will by no means be put to shame.

1 PETER 2:6B

Human beings are committed to making lists—and not just "To Do" lists. We create lists to rank all manner of things. Athletic teams are ranked, students in graduating classes are ranked, and music is ranked on the charts. *Fortune* magazine ranks the top companies and *Forbes* magazine ranks the richest people.

The book of Hebrews does some ranking of its own, but in a different way. The world ranks groups of equals to see who is number one. And while Hebrews ranks Jesus Christ as number one, it is not because He is first among equals. He is number one in all of creation because He has no equal. The first three verses of Hebrews 1 summarize why Christ is superior to angels, Moses, priests, and everyone else—because only Christ has taken away our sins and has sat down at the right hand of God as a sign of the Father's approval of what Christ accomplished. No one else has done for us what Christ has done for us.

Christ sets Christianity apart from all other religions. He is the only person who had the remedy for human sin and was qualified to carry it out on our behalf. For that and more, today He deserves our praise.

JUNE 2

Learning to Say "Thank You"

Therefore by Him let us continually offer the sacrifice of praise to God, that is, the fruit of our lips, giving thanks to His name.

HEBREWS 13:15

One of the first things parents do with their children is teach them to say "thank you." Later, children learn to write thank-you notes for Christmas and birthday gifts. The expression of gratitude is a learned trait, and "thank you" hopefully becomes a spontaneous response.

"Thank you" to God is a form of worship, springing from a sense of gratitude. Saying "thank you" to God is a learned expression of worship in response to His gifts. Worship is also a sacrifice. At the very least, we sacrifice time, talent, and treasure in worshiping God, all of which could have been spent differently. The first act of worship recorded in human history was an act of sacrifice by Cain and Abel (Genesis 4:1-4). While Cain's sacrifice was based on selfish interests, Abel's sacrifice was pleasing to God and cited as exemplary (Hebrews 11:4). Upon learning what God has done for him, one of the Christian's first responses should be "the sacrifice of praise" (Hebrews 13:15)—the sacrifice of saying, "Thank You."

Use your desire to worship God as a measure of your gratitude to Him.

NOT OF THIS WORLD

I have given them Your word; and the world has hated them because they are not of the world, just as I am not of the world.

JOHN 17:14

After His last sermon in the Gospels, which is recorded in John 13-16, Jesus paused to pray for His disciples; and His words are preserved in the next chapter, John 17. In verse 14 He prayed, "I am not of the world." Being eternally God, Jesus entered the world via a virgin birth and left the world by ascending to heaven from the Mount of Olives. He was truly "not of the world."

But the preceding phrase in verse 14 is mind-bending, for it says of us, His followers, "They are not of the world, just as I am not of the world." We don't belong to this world any more than Jesus did. Our citizenship is in heaven, our eternal home is there, and our values are determined from there—just like Him. These aren't easy days to be a Christian, but no such days have ever existed. The challenges of living a Christian life in today's culture can't be used as an excuse for not walking with God. Stay true to Him no matter what the world says. If you sometimes feel out of place on planet earth, remember that you are a citizen of heaven. What you feel is a longing for your native land.

BY FAITH

By his faith [Noah]… condemned the world and became heir of the righteousness that comes by faith.

HEBREWS 11:7B, NIV 1984

Since its founding in the 1770s, America was known as a Christian nation. Many pilgrims were Christians seeking religious freedom, many founding fathers were Christian, and many foundational documents expressed biblical principles. But beginning in the mid-twentieth century, America began to be known as a post-Christian nation as God was moved further toward the edge of public influence.

Is it harder to live as a Christian in a post-Christian nation than in a Christian one? Some would say so. But in truth, it doesn't matter where we live. The biblical requirement for faithfulness as the way to please God is the same. The need to remain faithful never changes. Noah proved it is possible to live in a corrupt culture and still please God. His "holy fear" (holy reverence) of God caused him to stand firm in faithfulness in spite of getting no support from the culture in which he lived.

You may feel unsupported in your nation, your home, your workplace—but you can remain faithful to the One who is always faithful to you (2 Timothy 2:13).

THE WORLD TOMORROW

For the earth will be filled with the knowledge of the glory of the LORD, as the waters cover the sea.

HABAKKUK 2:14

When we think about the future of our planet, we worry for our children and grandchildren. What kind of world will they face in coming decades? The Bible warns that perilous times will come; but the Bible is also filled with encouragement about the future and about the coming Golden Age of Jesus Christ—the Millennium. This is when the earth will be filled with the knowledge of the Lord as waters cover the sea. This is the period when God's people will reign with Him a thousand years (Revelation 20:1-6). Satan will be bound, earthly troubles will cease, and every need will be met. There will be no want in the millennial kingdom because we'll have all our needs fulfilled in a near-perfect world.

We don't have to wait for the Millennium to live under the rule and reign of Jesus Christ. We can experience that now. Our hearts can be filled with the knowledge of the Lord today as the principles of the kingdom govern our lives.

Is the King at home in your heart?

Perseverance

We also glory in tribulations, knowing that
tribulation produces perseverance.

Romans 5:3

Millions around the world have benefited from the teaching ministry of Kay Arthur, but her work wouldn't have happened apart from bitter disappointment early in her ministry. While serving as a missionary Mexico, she contracted a heart infection that forced her to return home. "I felt like a failure," she recalls. "Depression set in until I cried, 'Father, whatever You want.'" Back in Chattanooga, she began teaching the Bible to teenagers in her home, and out of those experiences came her life's work. "It would be several years before I'd see how He'd use those formative years of study in Mexico to prepare me to write inductive Bible studies that would eventually reach fifty-two countries," she wrote.

We seldom understand our trials at the time. We may feel like failures and wonder why God allows suffering. But as time passes, we learn to look back and see how He worked things for good and how every trial drove us closer to Him. With every test, our relationship with God grows more intimate and our perseverance more steadfast.

LISTENING EARS

They found Him in the temple, sitting in the midst of the
teachers, both listening to them and asking them questions.

LUKE 2:46

"Listening is such a simple act," wrote management consultant Margaret J. Wheatley. "It requires us to be present, and that takes practice, but we don't have to do anything else. We don't have to advise, or coach, or sound wise. We just have to be willing to sit there and listen."[15]

Jesus certainly knew how to advise, coach, and communicate His wisdom. The teaching of the ages rolled off His tongue, and His Words change our lives. Yet He also knew how to listen. He freely gave the present of listening ears. He heard the cries of widows, the perplexity of disciples, the voices of children, the confusion of rulers, and the voice of His Father.

According to Proverbs 20:5, people's hearts are like deep waters, "but a man of understanding will draw [them] out." Those who listen have a way of uncovering the needs of others. We can't solve everyone's problems, but sometimes listening is enough. Let every one of us be swift to hear, slow to speak (James 1:19).

---

15 Margaret J. Wheatley, *Finding Our Way* (San Francisco: Berrett-Koehler Publishers, 2007), 275.

WHAT SALT DOES

You are the salt of the earth; but if the salt loses
its flavor, how shall it be seasoned?

MATTHEW 5:13

Jesus said, "You are the NaCl of the earth"—NaCl being the chemical formula for salt, a compound of equal parts sodium (Na) and chlorine (Cl). Why did Jesus say "salt" instead of, "You are the dirt/plants/water/air of the earth"? Those latter elements of nature are certainly as indispensable as salt. It may be because salt can do things none of the others can. Salt can *change*, *preserve*, and *add value* to what it touches. But it is up to us to use it—or not.

Every culture in recorded history has valued salt for a variety of reasons. The Romans salted the fields of ancient Carthage after conquering the city so crops could not grow. Salt *changed* the ground from fertile to infertile. And prior to refrigeration, every culture used salt to *preserve* meat from spoiling. Salt was so *valuable* it was even used in place of money. *Change*, *preserve*, and *add value*—three traits that Jesus may have had in mind when He said His followers were to be the salt of the earth.

Ask God today to help you be a change agent and kingdom "preservationist," and to add spiritual value to all those you meet.

BORN TO RULE

But one testified in a certain place, saying:
"What is man that You are mindful of him, or
the son of man that You take care of him?"

HEBREWS 2:6

Eton College (founded in 1440) is a boarding school in England for boys aged 13-18, traditionally from England's privileged class. Nineteen British Prime Ministers have been educated at Eton (Churchill attended a similar school, Harrow) along with countless political elites. Eton is known as the chief nurse of England's statesmen. Unofficially, it is said that Eton students learn they are "born to rule."

Not all Eton graduates rule England, of course. But there is a class of people in this world who were born to rule: human beings. In Genesis 1, mankind is given dominion over all of creation (verses 26-28). And in Hebrews 2, the writer quotes David, the psalmist, who says, "And You have crowned [man] with glory and honor. You have made him to have dominion over the works of Your hands; You have put all *things* under his feet" (Psalm 8:5-6; Hebrews 2:7-8). So what happened? Sin. But the last Adam (1 Corinthians 15:45) has come to restore what the first Adam lost.

Remember who you are in Christ: born to rule, then born again and destined to regain your place of honor and glory.

THE GREAT WHITE THRONE

*And I saw the dead, small and great, standing
before God, and books were opened.*

REVELATION 20:12

Anyone who has sat in a courtroom awaiting a verdict knows
the stress of the moment. Innocent or guilty? Life or death?
Tension fills the courtroom like electrical voltage as the jury
renders its decision and the judge pronounces the sentence.

What, then, will it be like at the Great White Throne? God
will have a complete record of every moment of everyone's life,
everything done publicly and privately. This will be the ultimate
test for those who believe their good works will get them into
heaven. No one has lived a perfect or sinless life; no one's works
will be sufficient. Whether we view our lives as good or bad,
without Christ there is only condemnation.

That's why Christ came to save us. His blood shields us, for
"*there is* therefore now no condemnation to those who are in
Christ Jesus" (Romans 8:1). Becoming a Christian means we no
longer gain salvation by our works but by grace. The only way
to pass from death to life—to bypass the Great White Throne
Judgment—is through faith in Christ.

How much better to know Him as Savior than to meet Him
as Judge!

A HELPING HAND

And God has appointed these in the church: first apostles, second prophets, third teachers, after that miracles, then gifts of healings, helps, administrations, varieties of tongues.

1 CORINTHIANS 12:28

When an elderly person stumbles and falls to the ground, those nearby instinctively stop to lend aid. They reach out and take the person's hand or arm and *help* them to get back on their feet. That is exactly the meaning of the Greek word behind the New Testament reference to the gift of *helps* as mentioned by Paul (1 Corinthians 12:28). This rare Greek word means to reach out and "take up" or "grasp"—that is, to offer help when needed.

It is telling that Paul mentions the gift of helps in the same breath as the high profile gifts of apostles, prophets, teachers, and workers of miracles. There could not be a greater contrast—those with the gift of helps rarely seek recognition or attention. Their gift is to instinctively reach out and serve others without reward or recompense. Their reward is the satisfaction of serving others in a life-changing way.

Whether one has the gift of helps or not, all Christians are called to serve and help others. If you see someone who could use a helping hand today, why not offer yours?

Permanent, Protected, Approved

In Him you also trusted, after you heard the word of
truth, the gospel of your salvation; in whom also, having
believed, you were sealed with the Holy Spirit of promise.

Ephesians 1:13

Some people today still use a wax seal on personal correspondence. Red sealing wax is dripped onto the flap of an envelope and a seal is pressed into the wax, imprinting the author's initial or other personal symbol. An unbroken seal on a letter is a sign of permanence and protection of the contents.

Such a seal is visible and physical—and some kind of visible seal will be put on the foreheads of God's 144,000 called evangelists during the Tribulation (Revelation 7:1-8). But every Christian has been given a seal that is invisible—a seal that is God's mark of permanence and protection for eternity: the seal of the Holy Spirit. In addition to permanence and protection, the seal (gift, presence) of the Holy Spirit affirms God's approval. Just as the Holy Spirit descended upon Cornelius's household to approve Peter's message to them (Acts 10:44-47), so the Spirit of God says to the Christian, "You are approved and beloved of God" (see 1 Thessalonians 2:4).

If you are a true believer in Jesus Christ, you have been sealed by the Holy Spirit forever.

THE CLOCK IS TICKING

For this purpose the Son of God was manifested,
that He might destroy the works of the devil.

1 JOHN 3:8B

In athletic games that are played for a set number of minutes, like basketball and football, the closer the clock gets to the final seconds, the more intense the play becomes. In fact, coaches practice plays to use when time has almost expired. Immediacy increases intensity in athletics—and in spiritual warfare.

Has the world ever been in more dire straits than it is now? Revelation 12:12 tells us that the devil "knows that he has [but] a short time" left to disrupt God's plans on earth. It should come as no surprise that the closer we get to the end of the age and the Second Coming of Jesus Christ, the more Satan will increase his activity. Wars, discord, disease, strife, immorality, and more are evidence of Satan's work. But what Jesus started when He came the first time—destroying the works of the devil—will be concluded when He comes again.

The great hope of the Christian is that one day we, and the world, will be free from the attacks of God's enemy. Satan knows the clock is ticking and that he will one day be removed forever (Revelation 20:10).

DON'T FORGET

Now I beg you, brethren, through the Lord Jesus Christ, and through the love of the Spirit, that you strive together with me in prayers to God for me.

ROMANS 15:30

The apostle Paul was traveling from Corinth to Jerusalem with money for the Jerusalem church. Knowing the Jews in Jerusalem would be eager to persecute him, he wrote to the church in Rome asking for their prayers "that [he] may be delivered from those in Judea who do not believe" (Romans 15:31).

Prayer is often the forgotten ingredient in spiritual warfare. In Paul's classic passage on the believer's spiritual armor (Ephesians 6:10-18), prayer is often neglected. But it is Paul's final admonition: "With all prayer and petition pray at all times in the Spirit, and with this in view, be on the alert with all perseverance and petition for all the saints" (verse 18, NASB). It is as if Paul is saying, "Once you are clothed with God's armor against Satan, you must win the battle on the field of prayer!" He makes the point by asking for prayer for himself against the temptation to fear the repercussions from preaching the Gospel (verses 19-20).

Be clothed with God's spiritual armor—but don't neglect to pray for strength and steadfastness against "the wiles of the devil" (Ephesians 6:11).

IT'S ALL IN THE FRUIT

Make a tree good and its fruit will be good, or make a tree bad and its fruit will be bad, for a tree is recognized by its fruit.

MATTHEW 12:33, NIV

John Chapman, better known as "Johnny Appleseed," is remembered for planting thousands of apple trees in Pennsylvania and states farther west during the early nineteenth century. But planting apple seeds is like buying a lottery ticket; apple trees do not bear fruit identical to the seed that was planted. In Chapman's day, when a tree was found that bore a desirable apple, branches from that tree would be grafted to rootstock to continue getting the desired fruit. In other words, a tree was deemed to be good only if its fruit was good.

On more than one occasion, Jesus said the same thing: Bad trees produce bad fruit, and vice versa. That is, "a tree is recognized by its fruit" (Matthew 12:33). Paul used the fruit metaphor to discuss good and bad in the spiritual realm when he gave examples of "the fruit of the Spirit"—traits of Christlikeness reproduced by the Spirit in the life of the Christian (Galatians 5:22-23).

Our primary responsibility is to examine the fruit we ourselves are bearing. If we claim to be *of* Christ, we must also be *like* Christ.

LIFT HIM UP

You have made him a little lower than the angels;
You have crowned him with glory and honor,
and set him over the works of Your hands.

HEBREWS 2:7

In terms of classification, there seems to be a graduated order to creation. God Himself is over all, Lord of all, eternal and omnipotent. Below Him is the angelic order—fabulous beings of light and glory. Below them are humans, created "a little lower than the angels" (Psalm 8:5), and placed on earth to tend it. Below humans are animals—sheep, oxen, beasts of the field, birds, and fish (Psalm 8:6-9).

According to Psalm 8 and Hebrews 2, Jesus Christ moved down the chain to redeem the human race. Though He was God Himself, He became human—a little lower than the angels—in order to die for our sins. Following His resurrection, He ascended back to heaven to reassume the glory He had with the Father before the world began (John 17:5). "Therefore God also has highly exalted Him and given Him the name which is above every name... in heaven... and... on earth" (Philippians 2:9-10).

We'll never fathom all Jesus did for us; but the more we study it, the more we are able to comprehend and appreciate His great gift of salvation.

TRADITIONS

*Therefore, brethren, stand fast and hold the traditions
which you were taught, whether by word or our epistle.*

2 THESSALONIANS 2:15

Many adults today are assuming a greater share of responsibility for their aging parents. In Jesus' day, He criticized some who sidestepped that responsibility based on a Jewish tradition that had evolved. They made "the word of God of no effect through [their] tradition" (Mark 7:13). This tradition said money could be dedicated to God and thus not be used to help one's parents. That is an example of keeping the letter but violating the spirit of the law. It was a tradition that essentially negated God's Word.

Traditions are not wrong in and of themselves—they are simply practices or teachings passed from one generation to another. If the practices or teachings conform to God's Word, they are good and should be preserved—like the traditions Paul exhorted the Corinthians and Thessalonians to keep (1 Corinthians 11:2; 2 Thessalonians 2:15). The challenge is discerning which traditions are pleasing to God and which are not.

Think about the religious traditions in your own life today. How many are conscious choices, consistent with Scripture, and how many are not?

DAVID JEREMIAH

June 18

Panorama of Providence

Anxiety in the heart of man causes depression,
but a good word makes it glad.

Proverbs 12:25

Someone said, "Worry is a trickle of fear that meanders through the mind until it cuts a channel into which all other thoughts drain." Are you worried today? Perhaps you're anxious about your health, your family, your future, or your finances. Oh, what a plague is worry. It robs us of sleep, peace, and the ability to think biblically. If only we could see our problems from the panorama of Providence and from the vista of His sovereignty.

In The Living Bible, Philippians 4:6 says simply, "Don't worry about anything; instead, pray about everything; tell God your needs, and don't forget to thank him for his answers."

Worry is our natural human response to the pressures of life. Peace is God's supernatural gift for our hearts. If a trickle of fear is meandering through your mind and cutting a deep channel, unleash the flood of God's peace. He is in control. He is in His holy temple and on His mighty throne. He can bear the load and grant you peace.

BE ALERT

Little children, it is the last hour; and as you have heard that the Antichrist is coming, even now many antichrists have come, by which we know that it is the last hour.

1 JOHN 2:18

The word *antichrist* is not found in classical Greek prior to the coming of Christ. It may be a word coined by the apostle John since he is the only one who uses it in the New Testament (1 John 2:18, 22; 4:3; 2 John 7). To describe someone who was *against* Christ or drawing attention to himself *instead of* Christ, one would attach *anti* ("against, opposite, instead of") to *Christos* to create "antichrist."

John used the word two ways: to refer to *the* Antichrist (1 John 2:18; 4:3) and those who operate *like* the Antichrist (1 John 2:18, 22; 2 John 7). Like Satan and his demons, a satanically inspired individual who appears at the end of the age has satanically inspired emissaries who are doing his work at present. In truth, the antichrists that John warned against—anyone who is against the true person and work of Jesus Christ—are everywhere in the world. And like those to whom John wrote, we must be aware of their presence and deception (2 Corinthians 11:13-15).

Be alert and on your spiritual guard today for antichrists who deny and deceive.

DAVID JEREMIAH

God's Guidance System

Before I was afflicted I went astray, but now I keep Your word.

Psalm 119:67

What did we do before GPS? How did we get anywhere? We used to stop and ask for directions and unfold paper maps across the steering wheel while driving. Now we enter our destination into our smartphone or our car's GPS unit and do whatever it tells us to do. We have a destination, a goal, but don't know how to get there. Fortunately, our GPS does and takes us, by twists and turns, where we need to go.

God has a goal for our life and a way of getting us there. The goal is conformity to the image of Christ (Romans 8:29), and the way of getting there is the twists and turns of life—even the difficult parts (Romans 8:28). Could we get there without the wrong turns, the breakdowns, the potholes, and the heavy traffic? Possibly— but Jesus didn't. He suffered on the way to God's destination for Him; it was how He learned obedience to the Father—through the things He suffered (Hebrews 5:8). If there are dimensions to the faith-life that we can't learn without being tested, then we will be tested.

If you are committed to God's destination for your life, first you must be committed to the route on which He takes you. You must have faith that you will arrive.

My Father's House

In My Father's house are many mansions; if it were not so, I would have told you. I go to prepare a place for you. And if I go and prepare a place for you, I will come again and receive you to Myself; that where I am there you may be also.

JOHN 14:2-3

Do you remember that feeling when you were young, waiting anxiously for the school day to be over so that you could finally see your parents and siblings again? Or that longing to get home after a hard day at work, knowing that your loving husband or wife awaited you? There is something so compelling about being home with those we love.

That's the feeling we're to have about our eternal home, the one that awaits us in heaven. Before He ascended, Jesus told His disciples not to be troubled, that He was going to prepare a place for them in heaven. But Thomas questioned the Lord, saying, "Lord, we do not know where You are going, and how can we know the way?" (verse 5) Jesus replied to Thomas, "I am the way, the truth, and the life. No one comes to the Father except through Me" (verse 6).

If we want to spend eternity with our Father in heaven, we must believe that Jesus is the only way. Like the disciples, we too can be confident that one day we will see Him—all longing and anticipation will end—in our Father's house.

DAVID JEREMIAH

The Mother of John Mark

So, when [Peter] had considered this, he came to the house of Mary, the mother of John whose surname was Mark, where many were gathered together praying.

Acts 12:12

Being called by our name is a sign of inclusion, a sign that we are "known." But when Luke, the writer of Acts, mentioned a significant woman by name, he had to explain who she was because she was not well known: "Mary, the mother of John whose surname was Mark." Most people would have been familiar with Mark, the cousin of Barnabas and missionary assistant to Barnabas and Paul. But very few knew Mark's mother's name.

Mary was not a leader that we know of. But she used what she had to serve the Jerusalem church. She apparently had a large house—vestibule, courtyard, and possibly two stories of living area—and a servant. Her house could be the one referred to as a meeting place in Acts 1:12-14; it was definitely a meeting place in Acts 12:12-17. It was the place where the church gathered to pray for Peter when he was imprisoned in Jerusalem.

You may not have a large house and servants, but everybody has something to use—including the abilities and spiritual gift(s) God has given you. Ask God to show you how to use *for* Him what you have *from* Him.

LIGHT OF THE WORLD

Then God said, "Let there be light"; and there was light. And God saw the light, that it was good; and God divided the light from the darkness.

GENESIS 1:3-4

Physically speaking, there is one light of our world—the giant star we call the sun. The sun is so dominant in the life of planet earth that it was worshiped by some ancient cultures. In the third millennium B.C., the Egyptians worshiped Ra, the god of the sun, from whom all life was supposed to have originated.

Jesus' words about the light of the world were radically different. He told His disciples that *they* were the light of the world. But instead of the world worshiping His disciples as some sort of divine light, the disciples' light had a singular focus: to reveal the glory of God. And there was another unique slant on this spiritual light: It was not the disciples themselves but their good works that would cause the world to focus on God. Just as John the Baptist came "to bear witness of the Light" which is Christ, "that all through [John] might believe" (John 1:7), so we are to bear witness to the reality, love, and grace of God by our good works done in His name.

Think about that today: You, and your Christlike actions, can cause someone to see the reality of God. Pray that your light will reveal God's glory.

ETERNAL FOCUS

*For [Abraham] waited for the city which has
foundations, whose builder and maker is God.*

HEBREWS 11:10

Parents are sometimes heard telling their young adult children, "You need to stop dreaming about the future and get a job today!" Some adults can't stop thinking that their true destination in life is just around the corner. Instead of sowing seeds today, they dream only of a harvest (Proverbs 12:11).

Just the opposite is true of some Christians. Instead of keeping our eyes focused on our eternal calling, we become enamored with "today"—the things of this world that are only temporal (1 John 2:17). The writer to the Hebrews singled out Abraham and Moses as examples of those who lived their lives by faith in the future. Abraham might have been traveling to Canaan, but he knew he was destined for an eternal city. And Moses didn't mind giving up the riches of Egypt because "he looked to the reward" God had planned for him in eternity (Hebrews 11:26).

Both the present and the future are important, but only one will last forever. In fact, our present life is to be lived with our eternal life in mind (1 Corinthians 3:11-15). Whatever your plans are for today, fulfill them for eternal reasons.

DO WHAT IS RIGHT

Trust in the LORD, and do good.

PSALM 37:3

It took some courage, but a Texas Girl Scout Troop helped nab a shoplifter while they were selling cookies at a Houston supermarket. From their table near the entrance, they watched a suspicious man wheel his shopping cart out the door and toward the curb. The girls were suspicious because none of the items were in bags and the man looked as if he were trying to sneak out. They alerted authorities who found $2000 in stolen merchandise in the man's possession—not just groceries but small appliances and alcohol as well. "He was stealing a lot of stuff," said one girl. "We caught a bad guy."

Sometimes while minding our own business throughout the course of a day, we're confronted with a challenge—a wrong to right, a correction to make, a task to finish, or a soul to influence. Most people look the other way, apathetic or frightened. But remember that the word "bold" is a New Testament adjective for God's people; and the Lord expects us to be of "good courage."

Having faith will give us courage even when the challenge seems intimidating or the task seems impossible. We must always trust God and do what is right.

The Gift of Prayer

Epaphras, who is one of you, a bondservant of Christ, greets you, always laboring fervently for you in prayers, that you may stand perfect and complete in all the will of God.

Colossians 4:12

Marianne Adlard, a bedridden girl in 1860s London, read about the success of evangelist D. L. Moody and longed for his ministry to touch her own local congregation. She prayed, "O Lord, send this man to our church." In 1870, Moody was indeed invited to speak at Marianne's church; but that morning there was no response to his message. Marianne prayed earnestly that afternoon. In the evening Moody asked if anyone wanted to give their lives to Christ. A flood of people rose to their feet. Moody was so surprised, he had them sit down while he clarified his invitation. Still they stood. In a ten-day period, four hundred people professed faith in Christ.

Like Marianne, Epaphras wrestled in prayer for the church he loved, asking God to work among the people. He believed his greatest ministry to others was in prayer.

When we present the needs of others in prayer to God, we're exercising throne power—the power of coming to the throne of grace so another soul can receive mercy and grace to help in time of need. Only heaven knows the power of such a ministry.

The Judge of All the Earth

True and righteous are His judgments.

REVELATION 19:2

In Genesis 18:25, Abraham asked a question that puts things in perspective: "Shall not the Judge of all the earth do right?" As humans, we recoil from the concept of judgment. We question why God would condemn the world. We wonder about those who have never heard the message of the Gospel. We can't fully understand the presence of evil in the universe or the suffering that fills our world. Sometimes we're uncomfortable with the biblical concepts of God's wrath, vengeance, and judgment.

In the end, we will come to Abraham's conclusion in Genesis: The Judge of all the earth will do right. We'll agree with the angels in Revelation: "True and righteous *are* His judgments." God's wisdom knows how to handle sin; and His purity demands its condemnation. His grace is extended to us fully and freely, and His Cross frees us from condemnation.

Without the judgment of God, sin and suffering would be unhindered, unfettered, and unending. God's judgment is certain, but it's wise in its application and crucial for our happiness. We can praise Him for His judgments, for the Judge of all the world will do right. He is—and always will be—true and righteous.

His Path, Not Ours

*Trust in the LORD with all your heart, and lean
not on your own understanding; in all your ways
acknowledge Him, and he shall direct your paths.*

Proverbs 3:5-6

William Sangster began pastoring London's Westminster Central Hall just as World War II broke out. His courageous ministry, powerful evangelism, and undying optimism helped keep London alive for Christ even in her darkest hours. After the war, Sangster was diagnosed with progressive muscular atrophy. His condition deteriorated until he was virtually paralyzed. But his attitude never faltered. He told others that he had made four rules for himself at the outset of his illness: "(1) I will never complain; (2) I will keep the home bright; (3) I will count my blessings; (4) I will try to turn it to gain."

Things don't always go as we'd wish, and we often don't have all the information we desire. Such times aren't just *testing* times; they are *trusting* times. The Bible tells us to walk by faith and not by sight, for without faith it is impossible to please Him. Those who come to God must believe that He is, and that He rewards those who diligently seek Him (2 Corinthians 5:7; Hebrews 11:6).

Let's adopt Sangster's rules as our own. In times like these, it's critical to have faith in God and to trust every word of His every promise.

BRIGHTEN THE CORNER WHERE YOU ARE

By faith Moses… refused to be called the son of Pharaoh's daughter, choosing rather to suffer affliction with the people of God than to enjoy the passing pleasures of sin.

HEBREWS 11:24-25

During a hotel stay in France, the founder of Greater Europe Mission, Robert Evans, determined to share his faith with the staff he encountered there. He quickly discovered that many of them were familiar with the Gospel, and some had already come to faith in Christ. Evans was interested in how they came to know about Christ and found that it was one of the workers—the hotel painter—who had shared his faith. "Almost everything here gets constant painting," explained the man. "My work gets me into every department of the building; I know everybody and everybody knows me. Of course, I tell them about my Lord."

This is a great reminder that our mission field is wherever we are. For Moses, it was the desert. He did his greatest work for the Lord in the hardest locations. Sometimes our situations are difficult and challenging, but having a Moses-like faith can help us see beyond the temporal and into the eternal. Don't be frustrated if you're tending sheep in the desert or painting a wall somewhere. God has a wonderful way of using us to reach people wherever we are.

ALWAYS FAITHFUL

*For this reason I also suffer these things; nevertheless
I am not ashamed, for I know whom I have believed
and am persuaded that He is able to keep what
I have committed to Him until that Day.*

2 TIMOTHY 1:12

The Latin phrase *Semper Fi*—short for *Semper Fidelis*—is well known to United States Marines and their families. It means "always faithful" or "always loyal," and it has served as the motto of the Marine Corps since 1883. On the Marine Corps emblem, an eagle holds a ribbon in its mouth inscribed with *Semper Fidelis*. The words "always faithful" suggest there is never a time when a Marine will not be faithful to his or her duty to country.

The Marine Corps motto could well serve as a motto for the Christian life. The apostle Paul makes the point that "it is required in stewards that one be found faithful" (1 Corinthians 4:2). And Christians are nothing if not stewards—of creation, of spiritual gifts, of the Gospel, of time, talent, and treasure, and of the grace of God. There is never a day when we are not expected to be faithful to God, never a day when we can allow fear of the future to replace faith in the God who knows the future. Writing from prison in his final letter, Paul knew that better days were right around the corner in the presence of his Lord. In the deepest sense, nothing could really touch or harm him.

If you are a follower of Christ, let *Semper Fidelis* be your watchword today and every day: Always Faithful.

JULY

RESEMBLANCE

But we all, with unveiled face, beholding as in a mirror the glory of the Lord, are being transformed into the same image from glory to glory, just as by the Spirit of the Lord.

2 CORINTHIANS 3:18

Some time ago, the *New York Times* reported a study showing that couples who are happily married for long periods really do begin to look alike. Even if the man and woman bore no resemblance at their wedding, they showed marked resemblances later in life. Moreover, the more marital happiness a couple reported, the greater the increase in facial resemblance. The change is apparently due to decades of shared emotions and similar lifestyles.[16]

As time goes by, Christians should increasingly resemble Jesus. After all, we're the bride of Christ, and we share His emotions and lifestyle. Romans 8:29 says that God has predestined us to be "conformed to the image of His Son," and according to 2 Corinthians 3:18, the Holy Spirit transforms us by stages into the image of Christ.

Today someone will study your attitudes, words, and deeds. Make sure they see Jesus in you. We are His reflectors to the world.

16 http://www.nytimes.com/1987/08/11/science/long-married-couples-do-look-alike-study-finds.html

Law of Imitation

*And be kind to one another, tenderhearted, forgiving
one another, even as God in Christ forgave you.*

EPHESIANS 4:32

The Latin phrase *lex talionis* refers to the "law of retaliation," illustrated by the biblical instruction of "eye for eye, tooth for tooth" (Exodus 21:24). The biblical guideline was meant to limit punishment, not mandate it; and the New Testament suggests a better response to wrongdoing: love and grace instead of retaliation.

Nothing is more impulsively human than retaliation, and nothing is more supernaturally surprising than the extension of grace in all things—especially when one has been wronged. And in Ephesians 4:32, there is a reason for such an unnatural response: We should extend grace to others because of the grace that has been extended to us by God. It takes a measure of disregard and contempt to say, "Even though God has extended grace to me, I choose not to extend that same grace to others." God had every reason not to extend grace to humanity, but He did anyway. And He calls us to do the same. We can know it's the right thing to do when we feel a natural resistance to doing it.

Instead of the law of retaliation, practice the law of imitation. Do for others what you have seen God do for you.

NO "BUTS" ABOUT IT

*Then Jesus said, "Father, forgive them, for
they do not know what they do."*

LUKE 23:34

You may have heard these words from someone you hurt: "I forgive you, but . . . ." If there is a pause after "but," what are you thinking? During that moment of silence you are probably wondering if you are truly forgiven or not. The relief you heard in "I forgive you" probably vanished when you heard "but."

"But" usually means there is a condition involved. "You can ride with me, but (I have three stops to make first)." "I'll let you borrow my car, but (you'll need to return it with the gas tank full)." Sometimes conditions are expected (filling the gas tank), but sometimes they seem out of place: "I forgive you, but . . . ." Doesn't "forgive" mean, well, *forgive*—as in unconditional forgiveness? When we hear "but," we hear the prelude to conditions on which forgiveness will be extended. When Jesus Christ asked God to forgive those who crucified Him, His request was unconditional: "Father, forgive them." He didn't say, "Forgive them, but don't make it easy on them." He simply asked that they be forgiven.

The next time you are called on to extend the grace of forgiveness, make sure it is unconditional—that there are no "buts" about it.

WARNING SIGNS

And the LORD God of their fathers sent warnings to them by His messengers, rising up early and sending them, because He had compassion on His people.

2 CHRONICLES 36:15

If a society doesn't have "warnings," it doesn't care for its citizens. Depending on where we live, we need warning sirens to alert us to the dangers of tornadoes or tsunamis. We need notifications that warn us of severe weather. We need warning labels on products that may be harmful. News outlets have an obligation to warn viewers of local scams or regional epidemics.

A warning is an attempt to prevent another person from running into danger or encountering harm. The Bible is full of warnings. Sin produces sorrow; immorality brings heartache; moral depravity causes despair; and disregard for grace results in judgment. When we ignore God's greatest warnings and continue to live in sin, we miss His grace, His Gospel, and the glory He wants to give us. That's why the apostle Paul told the Ephesians, "Therefore watch, and remember that for three years I did not cease to warn everyone night and day with tears" (Acts 20:31).

If our Gospel contains no warnings, we're not preaching the "whole counsel of God." If we fail to heed the warnings God sends us, we're endangering our souls.

Walking This Pilgrim Pathway

For we walk by faith, not by sight.

2 Corinthians 5:7

Dr. J. Vernon McGee wrote about California: "I have a ranch out here. It's not what you would call a big ranch—72 feet wide and 128 feet deep. But I have my house in the middle of it, and I have … orange trees, avocado trees, tangerine trees, nectarine trees, and lemons…. The other day I just looked up and thanked the Lord that *He* gave me that place. It is the first place I have ever owned and paid for, but He gave it to me, and I thank Him for it. However, I told Him, 'Don't let me get in love with this place, or I won't want to leave it and go to a better place.' We are strangers and pilgrims down here, because we are walking by faith, looking to a better place."[17]

Possessions accumulate with time, but it's helpful to echo Dr. McGee's prayer: "Lord, don't let me get in love with this place." Faith is how we receive God's grace, and our greatest possessions are Christ, His Word, and the future He's planned for us. Don't fall in love with the world. Walk by faith on the pilgrim pathway.

---

17 J. Vernon McGee, *Hebrews Chapters 8-13* (Nashville: Thomas Nelson, 1991), 87.

Extravagant Love

*The Spirit of the Lord GOD is upon Me, because the LORD
has anointed Me to preach good tidings to the poor; He has
sent Me to heal the brokenhearted, to proclaim liberty to the
captives, and the opening of the prison to those who are bound.*

Isaiah 61:1

God's love for us is like an intricately cut diamond. The longer we examine each facet, the deeper our understanding of it. Jesus uses the father in the story of the Prodigal Son to describe His heart and affection for the lost. When the prodigal returned home, the father could have cut him off from the family. This was the acceptable course of action against a person who had brought such shame upon his family. It was naive of the son to think he could return home, even as a servant.

But this father does the unexpected. When he sees his son in the distance, he runs to him, embracing and kissing him. The father is more concerned with having his son return than with hearing why he returned. He is given a robe, a ring, and shoes—these are visible signs to the community that the son is a part of his family.

We serve a loving God: He searches for us and runs to us. He embraces us and adopts us into His family. When God's love touches our lives, we are inspired to seek and love the lost as Jesus did.

BLINDED BY PRIDE

When Jesus heard it, He said to them, "Those who are well have no need of a physician, but those who are sick. I did not come to call the righteous, but sinners, to repentance."

MARK 2:17

Children will sometimes fake an illness to get out of school and may even convince themselves they are sick. The Pharisees had the opposite problem. They convinced themselves they were better than others and avoided those they saw as lower than themselves.

Jesus confused them. His authority and healing power could have allowed Him to choose His associates and to gain status in the synagogue. Instead He was moved with compassion toward those who called upon Him: the sick, destitute, and unclean.

Pride makes us blind to the work of God. We forget His sovereignty. Pride also blinds us to our own need for a Savior, and we withhold grace from those we feel do not deserve it. It is important to confess our pride or we will end up like the Pharisees, taking God's grace for granted and missing opportunities to lead others to Christ. If we are not careful, pride will distance us from others and from God.

BLESSED

Blessed are the pure in heart, for they shall see God.

MATTHEW 5:8

"Back to the basics." We hear that phrase a lot—so many things in life can be "fixed" when we return to basic principles. That lesson was at the heart of Jesus' Beatitudes (Matthew 5:3-11). Nine times He said, "Blessed are [those] . . ." referring to people who put the kingdom of God first.

Blessedness is more than happiness. It is akin to the Hebrew concept of *shalom*, or peace, the contented, stable, peaceful relationship one has with man and God. Blessedness is an Old Testament concept that was picked up by Jesus in the Sermon on the Mount. In Psalm 1—the psalm chosen to introduce Israel's hymnbook—the psalmist begins just as Jesus did: "Blessed is the man who . . . ." The psalmist says we are blessed when our "delight is in the law of the LORD." That is, we are blessed when our thoughts and actions are consistent with God's values and priorities as found in Scripture. It's the same message Jesus gave to His audience: Center your heart on God, and you will know Him now and forever.

It's good to be happy in this world, but even better to be blessed by God. Blessing comes from getting back to spiritual basics.

The Power of "No"

My son, if sinners entice you, do not consent.

Temptation has been around since the days of Adam and Eve, but it's never been as virulent as today. Sexual temptation, especially, has been intensified by technology, and it tends to reach people earlier in life. Still, we read in 1 Corinthians 10:13 that no temptation has overtaken us except what is common to humanity; and God is faithful to provide pathways of escape. He did this for Joseph in Genesis 39. When tempted by Potiphar's wife, Joseph was able to say "No" because he had established his convictions before the crisis. His moral principles were set in advance, so Joseph instinctively resisted the lure of lust.

Temptation has many guises, but God gives power over all forms of temptation. Our greatest weapons are: (1) a preset determination to obey God; (2) memorized Scripture on needed topics; and (3) prayer. Jesus told us to watch and pray so we don't fall into temptation (Matthew 26:41).

Don't wait until the moment of crisis. Plan ahead, hide God's Word in your heart, and pray in advance for victory, holiness, and a life pleasing to God.

STAND FOR RIGHTEOUSNESS

Therefore you are inexcusable, O man, whoever you are who judge, for in whatever you judge another you condemn yourself; for you who judge practice the same things.

ROMANS 2:1

We are all disappointed when someone we know, or *thought* we knew, shocks us by being involved in an immoral or illegal activity. Our disappointment is the deepest when the guilty party has previously stood for the very opposite behavior he has been found guilty of. It seems harder to forgive when the H-word "hypocrisy" is involved.

Judging another person for some act while practicing the same thing ourselves is plainly hypocritical. Jesus said it bluntly: "Hypocrite! First remove the plank from your own eye …." So what should we do? Should we never stand and speak for righteousness for fear that we might one day commit the very sin we stand and speak against? Should we never call out sin when necessary? No, we should always stand and speak for righteousness—but with a serious measure of grace, knowing that, "There, but for the grace of God, go I" (1 Corinthians 15:10; see 1 Corinthians 10:12). And if we do fail or fall, we must repent with equal grace and humility.

When others fail, let us forgive them and pray that God will keep us from the same end.

JULY 11

GOD'S EQUALITY

They, measuring themselves by themselves, and comparing themselves among themselves, are not wise.

2 CORINTHIANS 10:12

*T*he *Washington Post* ran a column entitled "Do Your Employees Think You Play Favorites?" According to the author, 28 percent of federal employees believe their supervisor has engaged in favoritism, and over half believe favoritism has influenced the decisions of adjacent supervisors. The article suggested supervisors ask themselves: Are you spending more time with some employees than others? Are your decisions clear? Are your employees clear about their standing on the team?[18]

The apostle Paul warned against favoritism and against comparing ourselves to one another. God's plan for each of us is unique and specifically designed for each of us alone. God sees everyone equally and judges impartially. He wants to spend time with all His children; He wants to bless each of us richly; and He loves all of us with infinite love. We're also equally responsible to give Him our hearts and our lives in constant and ever-renewed yieldedness. We are equally sinful, equally loved, equally forgiven, and equally vital to the cause of Christ.

---

18 Tom Fox, "Do Your Employees Think You Play Favorites?" *The Washington Post,* http://www.washingtonpost,com/blogs/onleadership/wp/2014/01/30 (accessed May 5, 2014).

DAVID JEREMIAH

GLOBAL PEACE

Therefore, having been justified by faith, we have peace...

ROMANS 5:1

One evening in 2013, residents of a town in the Philippines made a gallant effort to set a Guinness World Record for the number of sky lanterns illumined in one place. Over 100,000 people created a sea of lights that shimmered like the stars. The slogan for the event was: "World Peace Through Inner Peace." Organizers wanted to advance their belief that meditation could bring about personal peace; and if everyone possessed inner peace, it would lead to global peace.

There was logic to their slogan, but something was missing. Without Christ, there is no inner peace. Perhaps meditation and other psychological techniques can lower our blood pressure or stave off panic attacks; but enduring inner peace is a gift of God's grace, and it comes only from a personal commitment to Christ. When we receive God's grace, we receive His peace.

Jesus said, "Peace I leave with you, My peace I give to you; not as the world gives do I give to you. Let not your heart be troubled, neither let it be afraid" (John 14:27). He will keep you in perfect peace as your mind is fixed on Him (Isaiah 26:3).

JULY 13

DIVINE DEPENDENCE

Draw near to God and He will draw near to you.

JAMES 4:8A

Emergency medical care for wounded soldiers is amazing. Soldiers who, in a previous era, would have died on the battlefield are now surviving. But they often recover with life-changing and often debilitating results. Soldiers who have survived the loss of one or more limbs awake from their surgeries with a new realization: "I'll never be able to do this on my own."

Strong, self-sufficient soldiers have to accept the humbling reality that they need others around them to help them adapt to a new life. If there is a silver lining in such an experience, it is learning the lesson afresh that we were not created by God to live life alone—even the healthiest among us are dependent. Jesus said as much when He told His disciples, "Without Me you can do nothing." That was not a statement of ego on Jesus' part; it was a way of stating the truth that man was created to live in dependence upon God. And God gives the grace needed to live such a life of leaning on Him (James 4:6).

If you feel the need for God in your life, that's exactly how you are supposed to feel. You were never intended to do life on your own.

CALL THE REPAIRMAN!

For the eyes of the LORD run to and fro throughout
the whole earth, to show Himself strong on behalf
of those whose heart is loyal to Him.

2 CHRONICLES 16:9

Quick, call the repairman! Something's wrong with our TV sets. Suddenly all over the world they're exploding in radioactive levels of profanity and toxic sewage, contaminating houses and homes like leaking reactors. It's so bad, even *Time* magazine posed the question, "Is there an epidemic of nudity on prime-time TV?"[19]

As we lament the proliferation of immorality all around us, we're tempted to despair. But it helps to consider the greatest heroes of the Bible. They too lived in declining societies, and they lamented the falling standards of their day. Even in the book of Genesis, the heroes of the faith—men like Abel, Enoch, Noah, Abraham, and Joseph—faced the challenge of living godly lives in a shifting culture and amid collapsing standards of morality.

When culture changes around us, God's standard of living does not. Even when we're engulfed by evil, the eyes of the Lord range to and fro throughout all the earth to strengthen those whose hearts are fully committed to Him.

It's not the repairman we need. It's the Redeemer.

19 Gary Susman, "Is There an Epidemic of Nudity on Prime-Time TV?" *TIME*, June 10, 2013.

MULTIPLIED GRACE

This is a faithful saying and worthy of all acceptance, that Christ Jesus came into the world to save sinners, of whom I am chief.

1 TIMOTHY 1:15

The apostle Paul is often called "the apostle of grace" because his writings are filled with references to the grace of God. "Grace" appears 83 times in Paul's epistles, especially when he wrote about his past and present.

First there's the grace of forgiveness. Paul referred to himself as the "chief" of sinners. For him, his pre-Christian life of persecuting the Church of Jesus Christ was beyond the pale (1 Corinthians 15:9). He never seemed to get over the fact that the grace of God was greater than all his previous sins (Romans 5:20). Regardless of our past sins, we each feel the same way: How could God forgive all I have done and said? But He does.

Then there's the grace of endurance. Even as a mature Christian, Paul suffered in various ways; and he was not shy about asking God to relieve his suffering. On at least one occasion, God granted him grace to endure rather than removing the cause of his suffering (2 Corinthians 12:7-10). Regardless of our present situation, that same grace is sufficient for our every need.

God knows every detail of your past sins and present situation. And His grace is sufficient for both.

Lost and Found

*For the Son of Man has come to seek and
to save that which was lost.*

Luke 19:10

Jesus said His mission was "to seek and to save that which was lost" (Luke 19:10). The Jews to whom He said those words were confused. How could they be lost? After all, they were the chosen people of God.

People today who hear the biblical term "lost" have an equally hard time comprehending the meaning. Lost from who or what? In the Jews' case, God had rebuked the spiritual leaders of Israel, her shepherds, for allowing their "sheep" to wander off into carnality and captivity. He said through the prophet Ezekiel, "I will seek what was lost and bring back what was driven away" (Ezekiel 34:16). The Jews were lost because they had wandered away from God, and they needed to be found. That's what Jesus meant in the three parables He told about the lost sheep, the lost coin, and the lost son (Luke 15:3-32). Jesus was fulfilling God's promise to seek "the lost sheep of the house of Israel" (Matthew 10:6; 15:24).

But His mission was extended to all of God's creation—to reconcile the world back to God (2 Corinthians 5:18-20). If you are apart from Christ, you are lost. But Christ has come to seek and save you today.

COMMUNITY

Finally, all of you be of one mind, having compassion for one another; love as brothers, be tenderhearted, be courteous.

1 PETER 3:8

One of the most distinctive changes between the Old Testament and the New Testament was terminology. In the Old Testament, God and Israel's relationship was theocratic: God was King and Israelites were His subjects as defined by divine covenants. But in the New Testament the relationship became familial: God is Father and Christians are His children (Romans 8:12-17). The phrase "children of God" occurs ten times in the New Testament, not at all in the Old Testament.

Families live "communally"—that is, they hold things in common. The body of Christ, therefore, is a family community that shares in the grace and gifts of God equally. And the New Testament is filled with images of what that community of believers should look like. It should share in love, unity (comm*unity*), forgiveness, tenderheartedness, compassion, courtesy, generosity, and more. Family members are to love one another as God the Father loves the family (Ephesians 4:32).

Consider how you might strengthen the ties that bind you closer to your brothers and sisters in Christian community—in your own family and the family of God.

Get Some Rest

And He said to them, "Come aside by yourselves
to a deserted place and rest a while."

Mark 6:31

The disciples endured a stressful period in Mark 6. At the start of the chapter, they were caught in a riot in Nazareth. In mid-chapter, they went out two-by-two to practice their ministry skills. Then John the Baptist was executed. By the time we get to verse 31, we're told "There were many coming and going, and they did not even have time to eat." That's when Jesus gave them a command: "Come with Me by yourselves to a quiet place and get some rest."[20]

Our Lord often said, "Come *to* Me," but here He said, "Come *with* Me." Never leave Jesus behind when you take a break or a vacation. Your soul needs rest as well as your body. And notice the words "by yourselves." Don't drag the world around with you. Turn off your phone and ignore your email. Find "a quiet place," not a loud and pulsating spot. And note those final words: "Get some rest."

God doesn't want you to live in perpetual weariness. He wants you to take care of yourself so you can better serve Him.

20 New International Version

ABBA FATHER

*In this manner, therefore, pray: Our Father
in heaven, hallowed be Your name.*

MATTHEW 6:9

English "father" was *vader* in Dutch, *fadēr* in early German, *vater* in later German, and *fader* in Middle English. And all those words were built on Latin *pater,* which was very close to Greek *patēr.* But all those Western spellings were a radical departure from Aramaic, the language Jesus spoke. He would have pronounced "father" as *abba,* derived from Hebrew *ab.*

In fact, Jesus' use of "father" represented a major shift in how the Hebrews used the term—almost exclusively to refer to human fathers. God was rarely called Father by the Jews (Isaiah 63:16; 64:8; Jeremiah 31:9; Malachi 2:10), but Jesus called God "Father" (*Abba*—Matthew 11:26) and taught His disciples to do the same (Matthew 6:9). But this was not the formal, Victorian "father" of the English language. This was the *abba* of the Hebrew family unit—the "papa" or "daddy" used by children the world over today (Mark 14:36). Jesus introduced a new way to relate to God—a familial way of fondness and closeness.

However you view and address your earthly father, feel free to address your heavenly Father the way Jesus did—as *Abba* Father.

Daily Grace

Catch us the foxes, the little foxes that spoil the vines, for our vines have tender grapes.

Song of Solomon 2:15

The small problems of life aren't always small. Consider what happened at the McMillen Community Center in Fort Wayne, Indiana, when a little squirrel managed to get into the place. The building was under construction and due to open within weeks. The furry guy chewed into some wiring and caused a power surge that fried three HVAC systems and destroyed the building's heating, ventilation, and air conditioning units. The damages exceeded $300,000.

Perhaps you're not facing traumatic, life-altering events right now; but the little foxes are trying to ruin the vines, and the little squirrels are short-circuiting your happiness. God's grace is endless and amazing, but it also comes in small doses and daily allotments. The same grace that keeps us from losing our souls in hell also keeps us from losing our temper in the office. The same grace that transports us to heaven also gives us composure when our flights are delayed or the traffic is jammed up.

God's grace is infinite, but accessible. It's an ocean of grace, but it also falls in gentle drops at our feet. It's more than enough for the little problems you'll face today.

THE BEST LAID SCHEMES

*A man's steps are of the LORD; how then
can a man understand his own way?*

PROVERBS 20:24

Robert Burns was plowing a field one day when he inadvertently destroyed a mouse's nest. Seeing the destruction at his feet, the poet realized his plowing had upended all the plans the mouse had made for winter. It was late in the season, and now the mouse, which had carefully prepared for the coming snows, was in a fight for survival. That's what led Burns to write "To a Mouse," which includes one of the most famous lines in poetry: "The best laid schemes o' mice an' men gang aft agley [go often awry]."

Without a firm belief in God's personal guidance of our lives, our plans would go often awry. Without warning, our world can be upended and our best-laid schemes derailed. But the Bible assures us of God's watch-care over our days and His guidance of our lives. He leads us in paths of righteousness. Psalm 32:8 promises, "I will instruct you and teach you in the way you should go; I will guide you with My eye."

God's plan for our lives is good, and His plans for us never go awry.

SEEKING THE LOST

But we had to celebrate and be glad, because this brother of yours was dead and is alive again; he was lost and is found.

LUKE 15:32, NIV

Some things only work in pairs: shoes, socks, gloves, the two parts of scissors, the two wings of a bird, the two sides of a coin. And that applies to Jesus' mission in the world: seeking and finding. It makes no sense that Jesus Christ would come into the world to seek those who are lost and not find them.

Jesus was criticized by "Pharisees and scribes" for socializing and sharing meals with "sinners" (Luke 15:1-2). Earlier, Jesus had answered their objections in a word: "I have not come to call the righteous, but sinners, to repentance" (Luke 5:32). "Sinners" were those who needed to be found—those He came seeking. To amplify the point, He told three stories about "finding." A single sheep was lost and found, a coin was lost and found, and a son was lost and found (Luke 15:3-32). He meant that He associated with sinners—and found them—because they knew they were lost; they knew they needed finding, unlike the Pharisees.

If you have been found by Jesus, it is because He came seeking you. If you want Him to find you, tell Him you are lost and want to be found.

SAY "YES" TO CHRIST

For the grace of God that brings salvation has appeared to all
men, teaching us that, denying ungodliness and worldly lusts,
we should live soberly, righteously, and godly in the present age.

TITUS 2:11-12

The same grace that brings us salvation gives strength to live biblically in this age. We need grace-based living, but that can only happen as we focus our thoughts on God's Word and live it out. A study by the Evangelical Alliance found that many Christians struggle with making time for prayer and Bible study. Sixty percent of those born before 1960 said they read their Bibles daily; only 31 percent of younger Christians did the same.

As Christians, we're to live a different lifestyle than the world by loving God and loving others. As we grow in grace, we should understand God's Word more, respect others, care for the poor, tend to the widows, and keep ourselves unspotted by the world. Pastor Tony Evans wrote, "Grace-based Christians obey because it's their delight … To grace-based Christians, the spiritual life is the lifting of a burden."[21]

The same grace that helps us say "Yes" to Christ helps us say "No" to the world.

---

21 Tony Evans, *The Grace of God* (Chicago: Moody Publishers, 2004), 12.

Do Something

*But when [Jesus] saw the multitudes, He was moved
with compassion for them, because they were weary
and scattered, like sheep having no shepherd.*

Matthew 9:36

While walking in the crowded streets of the Old City of Jerusalem, an American Christian tourist saw the poorest person he had ever seen—a tiny woman with bare, dirty feet; she was clothed only in a threadbare black garment which she used to cover her face. After she vanished into the crowds, he prayed that God would let him see her again so he might give her the foreign coins in his pocket. Before too long, he was amazed to see her coming toward him. He stopped her, frightening her, and held out a handful of coins and gestured for her to take them, which she did. Although he couldn't see her face, he could tell that her eyes were grateful as they parted ways.

He had no idea who the woman was—Arab, Christian, Jew, or other. And he knew he would never see her again. But he knew she was desperately poor and that he, with his sunglasses, camera, and nice clothes, was rich by comparison. She had nothing; he had everything. And he had to meet at least part of her need.

Having the life of Jesus in us means having His hands and heart toward those in need. We can't do everything, but we can do something.

An Attitude of Gratitude

And he appointed some of the Levites to minister before the ark of the LORD, to commemorate, to thank, and to praise the LORD God of Israel.

1 Chronicles 16:4

Churches come in all sizes. Some have no paid staff at all. Others may employ a vast team of people in many roles. How big is your church's staff? Have you ever known a church hiring someone just to be thankful? When King David set up the worship leaders for the tabernacle, he appointed certain Levites just to continually thank and praise the Lord. Thanksgiving was their job.

What if our churches hired a person whose only job was to go around with a thankful attitude and to motivate others to have the same? We could call them Pastors of Gratitude. How would that look on their business card?

God wants to hire all of us for that job. It's His will for us to be grateful Christians. When we feel that old spirit of complaining start to bubble up in our hearts, we need to remind ourselves to take time to thank God for His blessings. It helps refocus our minds and put things back in perspective, lifting the spirits of those around us. And that is pleasing to Him.

David Jeremiah

OBTAINING PROMISES

…who through faith… obtained promises.

HEBREWS 11:33

The Bible is full of promises, but how are they obtained? Can we purchase them like items in a store? Can we earn them like wages in a factory? Can we win them like dollars in a lottery? If you have a perplexity in your life presently, there's surely a promise in the Bible meeting your need. If you're worried about the future, there's a word from God to give you confidence. But how do you occupy that promise?

Through faith! It's like salvation. Christ has already purchased what we need, and it's available by grace. Our job is to receive it by faith, which means trusting Him to do just as He has said. God has given us the gift of faith that we can take what's unseen and make it part of who we are.

Hebrews 11 gives lots of examples of that, including Abraham (see Hebrews 11:8-18). He didn't know where he was going or how to find the land promised him, but he took every forward footstep with the assurance that God could and would unerringly guide him. We can do the same and through faith obtain the promises.

ON PAR

*Better is a dry morsel with quietness, than
a house full of feasting with strife.*

PROVERBS 17:1

Tom Parr was born in 1483 and lived a simple life in the British countryside, subsisting on green cheese, onions, bread, buttermilk, and mild ale. He didn't smoke and rarely drank. He got married at eighty and fathered two children, both of whom died in infancy. At 100, he fathered a child out of wedlock. He remarried at 122. When he was 152, news of his advanced age spread abroad. He sat for a portrait (now in the National Portrait Gallery in London), and King Charles I invited him to the palace.

Tom packed his bags and traveled to London where he was served more alcohol and rich food than he had ever consumed. Unfortunately, the change in his diet and the foggy air weren't good for him. He abruptly died and was buried in Westminster Abbey, where you can still visit his grave.

We might dream of being pampered and invited to the palace; but on par, a simple life seems best. "Better to be of a humble spirit with the lowly, than to divide the spoil with the proud" (Proverbs 16:19).

JULY 28

FIT FOR THE MASTER'S USE

*Therefore if anyone cleanses himself from the latter,
he will be a vessel for honor, sanctified and useful
for the Master, prepared for every good work.*

2 TIMOTHY 2:21

The Smithsonian Institution has 137 million items, including the Wright Brothers' airplane and the *Spirit of St. Louis.* They have Dorothy's ruby slippers and Julia Child's kitchen. But there are about 20 items in a category by themselves. These odd instruments are called "What-is-its?" No one knows the purpose for which they were made. One device is composed of hand-blown globules linked together on a suspended axis above a circular mirror. No one can figure out its purpose.[22]

There are a lot of "What-Is-It" people in the world too. They are intricately made, but seem to have no known purpose. They may be beautiful, but in terms of being useful for anything beyond their own entertainment and pleasure, they are a "What-Is-It."

The Bible tells us to be people of purpose, fit for the Master's use. We are created in Christ Jesus to do good works, which God prepared in advance for us to do. Don't be idle. Do something for the Lord today. Be a vessel of holiness and honor, useful to Him.

22 "Can You Name These 'What's-Its'" by Richard Dempewolff in *Popular Mechanics,* February 1978, 90.

THE HOUND OF HEAVEN

*There is none who understands; there
is none who seeks after God.*

ROMANS 3:11

There is a seeking instinct hardwired into human beings. When a hiker is lost in the wilderness, when a child doesn't return from school on time, when a fishing party fails to return to port, when an airliner vanishes over the ocean without a trace—the human instinct to seek and save those who are lost is inevitable. Individuals, groups, armies, and nations commit limitless resources to seeking.

But there is one case in which humans don't seek as they should. We don't seek after God. Solomon wrote that we have an eternal sensibility in us (Ecclesiastes 3:11), and Paul wrote that our lack of seeking God is inexcusable (Romans 1:20). But there is also a powerful, sinful inclination that argues against any innate desire to seek after God (Romans 3:10-18). If that is true, how do any of us find God? We don't find God; He finds us. From heaven, "the grace of God that brings salvation has appeared to all men" (Titus 2:11). God sent His Son into the world so that the world through Him might be saved (John 3:16-17). None of us are saved by our efforts but by the grace of God (Ephesians 2:8-9).

Thank God today that He is a seeking God who looked for, and found, you.

Expressions of Gratitude

One of them, when he saw that he was healed, returned, and with a loud voice glorified God, and fell down on his face at His feet, giving Him thanks.

Luke 17:15-16

Last spring, a dog became stranded in the water at the bottom of a canal in Romania. A passerby, seeing the pooch whimpering and trying to climb to safety, scaled down the wall, jumped into the water, pulled the dog out by the scruff of its neck, and carried it back up to dry land. The dog ran away and shook itself; but then it quickly returned, ran to its rescuer, and showered the man with lots of nuzzles and licks. The video of the grateful canine became a sensation.

Sometimes we can learn a lot from our four-footed friends. Jesus once healed ten lepers, but only one came back with thanksgiving—and he was a Samaritan. Everyone who is in Christ has been rescued. We've been healed. We're the most blessed people on earth. Some days may be harder than others, and some seasons of life might be tumultuous. But gratitude isn't situational. It isn't based on what we have or where we are, but on our relationship with the God who pulled us out of deep waters, set our feet on a rock, and put a new song of praise in our mouths.

FIVE PEOPLE TO LOVE

Let brotherly love continue.

HEBREWS 13:1

According to Hebrews 13:1, we must live in brotherly love. We're to love everyone with the love of Christ; but Hebrews 13:1-8 gives us five people we must love in particular.

(1) The stranger. Verse 2 says: "Do not forget to entertain strangers, for by so doing some have unwittingly entertained angels."

(2) The prisoner. Verse 3 says: "Remember the prisoners as if chained with them."

(3) The person to whom you are married. Verse 4 says: "Marriage is honorable among all."

(4) The Lord Himself. Verses 5 and 6 say: "Let your conduct be without covetousness… for He Himself has said, 'I will never leave you nor forsake you.'"

(5) The church worker, your pastor, or teacher. Verses 7 and 8 tell us, "Remember those who rule over you, who have spoken the word of God to you, whose faith follow, considering the outcome of their conduct."

In which of those five areas are you strongest? Weakest? Let's take Hebrews 13:1 seriously and let brotherly love continue.

AUGUST

God's Guidebook

*However, when He, the Spirit of truth, has
come, He will guide you into all truth.*

John 16:13a

Driving the 469 miles of the Blue Ridge Parkway is an explorer's delight. From northern Virginia to the Tennessee-North Carolina border, there are wonders around every bend in the mountainous road. You may see wildlife, a pioneer cabin, gorgeous vistas, a country church, a stream or waterfall—the beauty never ends. The Parkway is not for the hurried; it is for the expectant—those eager for new experiences and discovery.

And the same is true for the Christian life—if, that is, we take seriously the foundational biblical truth that our God is a guide through life. Even though we do not know what is around every bend in the road, God does. There are encounters, discoveries, people, events, opportunities, blessings, and challenges to be found. Instead of being shocked at a circumstance or event, we should look at our path through the lens of heaven. There is a time, season, and purpose for everything (Ecclesiastes 3:1-8). There is something to rejoice in, give thanks for, and pray about around every curve (1 Thessalonians 5:16-18).

Today, trust that the Holy Spirit is guiding you into all truth. Live with eyes and arms open to embrace what you discover.

AUGUST 2

THE PLACE OF GRACE

Let us therefore come boldly to the throne of grace, that we may obtain mercy and find grace to help in time of need.

HEBREWS 4:16

Most people are familiar with the story of the Wizard of Oz. Dorothy and her three companions follow a yellow brick road to the Emerald City to ask the Wizard of Oz for what they need: Dorothy needed to get home to Kansas, the Scarecrow needed a brain, the Tin Man needed a heart, and the Cowardly Lion needed courage. They discover, of course, that the Wizard is a fraud.

But the idea of approaching a throne for help is much older than *The Wizard of Oz.* The writer to the Hebrews encouraged his readers to "come boldly to the throne of grace" to find "mercy" and "grace to help in time of need." What else would one expect to receive at a throne of *grace* but grace? And therein lies an important theological and practical truth: Regardless of what we think we need in terms of help, we really only need one thing: the grace of God. When God pours out His grace, we receive what He knows we need: provision, endurance, wisdom, patience, strength, resistance, courage, and more.

If you are facing a need right now, regardless of the specifics, go to the throne of grace and ask God for that which you are certain to receive: the grace of God.

FUTURE PLANS

For I know the thoughts that I think toward
you, says the LORD, thoughts of peace and not
of evil, to give you a future and a hope.

JEREMIAH 29:11

If you have 20/20 vision, you can see what a normal person sees on a chart when standing 20 feet away. If you have 20/40 vision, it means that you, while standing 20 feet from the chart, can see what a normal person can see from 40 feet away—meaning your eyesight is imperfect. The expression "hindsight is 20/20" means that everyone sees the past clearly. What seems fuzzy before it happens is always clear after the fact.

We humans might have 20/20 hindsight, but God also has 20/20 foresight. That is, His view of the future is just as clear as His (and our) view of the past. We try our best to see the future clearly—we pray, do our research, seek counsel, and prepare. But only God knows the future. That is the heart of biblical prophecy. God knows and declares, through His prophets, "the end from the beginning ... *things* that are not *yet* done" (Isaiah 46:10). God's heart is to give His people "a future and a hope" (Jeremiah 29:11).

You know your past today, and God knows your future. If you trust Him with what has already happened, trust Him as well with things to come.

DAVID JEREMIAH

AUGUST 4

OUR NIGHT LIGHT

The day is Yours, the night also is Yours; You have prepared the light and the sun.

PSALM 74:16

The book of Psalms is full of nocturnal verses. Psalm 1 tells us to meditate on God's Word day and night. Psalm 16:7 says, "My heart also instructs me in the night seasons." According to Psalm 30, "weeping may endure for a night, but joy *comes* in the morning." Psalm 77 reminds us to sing at night, and Psalm 92 speaks of God's faithfulness to us every night.

Psalm 134, one of the shortest chapters in the Bible, was written to priests on the graveyard shift: "Behold, bless the LORD, all *you* servants of the LORD, who by night stand in the house of the LORD! Lift up your hands *in* the sanctuary, and bless the LORD. The LORD who made heaven and earth bless you from Zion!"

Sometimes our "nights" are metaphorical as we go through dark seasons in life. But sometimes they're literal, for we often have trouble sleeping, sometimes due to anxious care. Remember, you can lift up your hands in the night seasons as well as in the light, for both the day and night belong to the Lord.

My Strong Refuge

*Be my strong refuge, to which I may resort
continually; You have given the commandment to
save me, for You are my rock and my fortress.*

Psalm 71:3

When our lives progress according to our plans, we feel confident and secure. We value our independence and sense of control. This sense of security dissipates when we face trials, difficulty, or loss. Instead of feeling secure, we become acutely aware of our vulnerability. As our plans unravel, we realize the limitations of our control and power. As Christians, we may wish for an exemption from suffering, but this was never promised to us. In the midst of our insecurity, we have a choice.

We can be like trees whose roots grow deep into the ground to withstand the winds shaking them, or we can allow the circumstances to separate us from God, our strength and foundation. He is the only one who can provide the power and peace we need to survive trials. The security offered by other sources is temporary. God alone is steadfast and constant.

Start a list of God's attributes and the ways in which He has worked in your life. This can serve as a reminder when you face trials. When we remember who God is and His faithfulness to us in the past, we are encouraged to continue depending on Him as our strong refuge in the midst of new challenges.

EXPERT COUNSEL

*Happy is he who has the God of Jacob for his help, whose
hope is in the LORD his God, who made heaven and earth,
the sea, and all that is in them; who keeps truth forever.*

PSALM 146:5-6

Who will help me? Our natural response to challenges is to react in our own strength. We strategize and try to think our way to a solution. When that fails, we turn to those around us. Have you experienced this? What did you do?

While these methods sometimes work, we have forgotten our most powerful ally. This simple refrain from a children's song reminds us, "He's got the whole world in His hands." True wisdom and help come from the One who not only holds the world, but created it. If we are struggling to trust God's insight and sovereignty, all we need to do is spend time in His creation. The details, structure, and creative coloring of each plant and creature point to God's power.

Instead of running to God as an afterthought, we can start with Him. We are His creation and He knows what we need. God knows more about you and your situation than any other being, including you. He is also the only one who can control the outcome. When we realize this, we will seek His expertise and help first. As we surrender ourselves and our situation to His expertise, we gain the hope and confidence of knowing that He is in control and that He loves to help us.

DEVOTED

Ezra had devoted himself to the study and observance of the Law of the Lord, and to teaching its decrees and laws in Israel.

EZRA 7:10 (NIV)

Are you familiar with phrases about having our *daily devotions?* Where did that term originate? We don't know when the word *devotions* was first used for our periods of Bible study and prayer, but it's appropriate. The word *devotion* means "earnest affection for a person or a cause." It's a better term than the word *commitment*. We can be committed to a cause out of sheer duty; but to be devoted implies commitment plus affection.

When we're devoted to learning God's Word, it helps to have the right study tools. The primary point is having a Bible; and a good study Bible is indispensable. Many Christians also use a personal notebook to record their thoughts. A concordance (either online or in book format) can help locate all the occurrences of particular words in Scripture. And a simple one-volume commentary can yield helpful insights on difficult passages.

As our children head back to school, it's time to don our backpacks and enroll in the Ezra School of Bible Study—devoting ourselves to the study and observance of God's Word and to teaching it to others.

A CONFIDENT PROMISE

Nevertheless we, according to His promise, look for new heavens and a new earth in which righteousness dwells.

2 PETER 3:13

Consider how you feel when you're in a relationship with a person—spouse, friend, coworker, boss—who has *never* been untrue in word or deed. The longer that person goes without betraying your trust, the higher your confidence soars. But should something untrue be said or done, your confidence crashes. It can take a long time to restore trust.

We serve a God who has never been untrue in word or deed. In fact, Jesus called Himself "the truth," personifying the quality that is an attribute of God (John 14:6). While man is constantly redefining truth—Pontius Pilate famously asked, "What is truth?" (John 18:38)—Jesus and the psalmist declared that God's Word is truth (Psalm 119:160; John 17:17). And God's promises are part of His Word (2 Peter 1:2-4). Jesus said that the Christian's place in eternity, in God's family, is eternal—that is a promise that will be eternally true (John 10:28). Nothing can separate the Christian from the love of God in Christ (Romans 8:38-39).

Whatever your need today—provision, protection, perseverance—cling to the promises from the One who has never been untrue.

A SPIRITUAL LESSON

When he had consulted with the people, he appointed those
who should sing to the LORD, and who should praise the
beauty of holiness, as they went out before the army.

2 CHRONICLES 20:21

Cliff Barrows, worship leader for the Billy Graham Crusades, tells how his father, an avid Gideon, traveled to Rangoon years ago. The area was under oppression and Gideon Bibles had been removed from hotels. While there, he met with local Gideons who were trying to restore the Bibles. During the meeting, Barrows had difficulty following the discussion because two men were singing hymns just a few yards away. Finally he asked, "Why are those men singing while we're trying to have this meeting?" The local Gideon replied, "Because this room is bugged, and the singing confuses the enemy who is trying to listen to us."

"There's a spiritual lesson in that," says Cliff. "When we sing, it confuses the enemy and allows the Lord's work to proceed."[23]

When we're discouraged, attacked, or faced with unanswered prayers, singing a song of triumph brings us back into focus, allowing us to express our thanks to God for who He is.

23 Robert J. Morgan, *Then Sings My Soul: Book 3* (Nashville: Thomas Nelson, 2011), 282.

DAVID JEREMIAH

A Costly Sacrifice

*On the next day, when [the Samaritan] departed, he
took out two denarii, gave them to the innkeeper, and
said to him, "Take care of him; and whatever more
you spend, when I come again, I will repay you."*

Luke 10:35

What is the most you have ever given, spontaneously, to a
person in need? A dollar? Five, ten dollars, or more? How
about the equivalent of what you earn in two days? There are 260
working days in the year (52 weeks x 5 days per week). Divide 260
into your annual salary and see what you come up with. Would
you give that much money to a person in need—*someone you
didn't know?*

That's what the "good Samaritan" did who stopped to help a
man who had been beaten and robbed on the road from Jerusalem
to Jericho. The Samaritan tended to the injured man's wounds,
then took him to an inn and gave the innkeeper two denarii—
the equivalent of two days' wages—to look after the injured man
(Matthew 20:2). He even promised the innkeeper he would cover
any additional expenses incurred when he passed that way again.
Writing a check for two or three hundred dollars today sounds
like a lot. And it is! But love and compassion are costly and
require sacrifice.

Giving until it hurts means we have crossed the line between
convenience and sacrifice.

WHY WE WORSHIP

Give unto the LORD the glory due to His name;
worship the LORD in the beauty of holiness.

PSALM 29:2

Some things in life are negotiable, others are not. Civil laws are non-negotiable. The physical laws of the universe, like gravity, are non-negotiable. Going to the gym, raking the leaves, purchasing a desired item—these, and other things in life, are negotiable. That means we can allow our feelings to help determine our course of action.

Non-negotiables in the kingdom of God are expressed as commands. Sometimes we are told they are laws, as in the Ten Commandments (Exodus 20:1-17), and other times their status as commands is implied by how they are written. As suggested by Hebrew grammar, worshiping God is not negotiable: "worship the Lord" is an imperative form (1 Chronicles 16:29; Psalm 29:2; 96:9). We think of worship as an emotional act born out of love and gratitude—those are good reasons to worship God. But what if we don't feel love and gratitude? At that point we worship God because of "the splendor of His holiness" (NIV). That is, we worship Him because He deserves to be worshiped as our Creator-God.

Don't let feelings be an obstacle to worship. Worship God because of Who He is and what He deserves—and feelings will follow.

HOMEWORK

Now a certain Jew named Apollos, born at Alexandria, an eloquent man and mighty in the Scriptures, came to Ephesus.

ACTS 18:24

There's a never-ending debate among educators about homework. While schools are assigning more and more homework in earlier and earlier grades, a rash of recent reports have questioned its value. We'll leave that discussion to parents and educators; but when it comes to studying the Good Book, there's no question. Like Apollos, we need to be mighty in the Scriptures, and that requires homework—daily times of Bible study.

Dr. William Henry Griffith Thomas, an Anglican preacher of an earlier era, wrote: "The Bible is the Word of God, the revelation of His Will to man. It follows that we ought to know this revelation and heed its message. Knowledge demands study, earnest, faithful, patient, constant ... Knowledge, however, presupposes very much more than reading; it calls for *study*. And not study only, but a genuine application of mind, heart, and conscience to the substance and teaching of Holy Writ.... Bible study involves hard work, because it demands *thought*."[24]

Have you set aside a daily time for your "homework"? If so, enjoy it today. If not, begin today!

---

24 W. H. G. Thomas, *Methods of Bible Study* (New York: Association Press, 1911), 1-2.

The Unexpected

O God, You are my God; early will I seek You; my soul thirsts for You; my flesh longs for You in a dry and thirsty land where there is no water.

Psalm 63:1

In June 1995, the Emir of Qatar, Sheikh Khalifa bin Hamad al-Thani, was deposed in a coup by his own son, the Crown Prince of Qatar. The Sheikh was in Switzerland when the coup occurred, but he vowed to return and regain the throne. (He didn't; his son remained the new leader of the nation.)

The Emir of Qatar was no doubt embarrassed by his grown son's behavior; parents tend to think that post-adolescent children will be friends for life. But trouble can come at unexpected times. The same thing happened to King David of Israel near the end of his life when his son Absalom rebelled against him (2 Samuel 15). David was brokenhearted over his son's actions and poured out his heart to God in the Judean Desert (Psalm 63). Even in the midst of heartache David vowed to seek God, to rejoice in Him, and to seek refuge "in the shadow of [His] wings" (verse 7). Whether we are young, middle-aged, or older, we should be prepared for trouble. We are born for it, Job said, "as the sparks fly upward" (Job 5:7).

Whether you are in the desert or green pastures today, put your hope in God. What surprises us is no surprise for Him.

DAVID JEREMIAH

AUGUST 14

SLEEP WELL

When I remember You on my bed, I meditate
on You in the night watches.

PSALM 63:6

Scientists and researchers aren't sure why we sleep. When we don't sleep, we are tired, less alert, irritable, and have poorer memory. So we sleep to prevent those things from happening. We do know this: The mind is active while we sleep. Many believe it is helpful to give the mind positive and peaceful thoughts while drifting off to sleep.

And what could be more positive and peace-inducing than thoughts of God's love and care? Meditating on Scripture before going to sleep is encouraged by verses like Hebrews 4:12: "Scripture is alive and active, able to separate soul from spirit, able to reveal the thoughts and intents of the heart" (paraphrase). Why not give our mind "food for thought" that is alive and active, truth the Holy Spirit can use even as we sleep to create ideas, desires, insights, and motivations for our life? And if we awake from sleep in the night with a troubled heart, a whispered prayer to God for rest and peace is better than tossing and turning (Philippians 4:6-7).

Give your mind and body the rest it needs by sleeping peacefully in the knowledge that God is at work in you for His own good pleasure (Philippians 2:13).

THE JOB'S TOO SMALL

*Before you were born I sanctified you; I
ordained you a prophet to the nations.*

JEREMIAH 1:5

In her book, *It's My Turn*, Ruth Bell Graham recalls growing up as a missionary kid in China. An oil company, she said, wanted someone to manage a new division. They located a man who met their qualifications, a 28-year-old missionary living in the city where the company was opening its office. The oil company offered the young missionary over ten times his current salary. When he declined they raised the offer. He declined again, and yet again. Finally the agent asked, "What will you take?"

"It's not a question of salary," replied the missionary. "The trouble is with the job. The job is too little. I feel that God has called me to preach the Gospel of Christ. I would be a fool to quit preaching in order to sell oil."

"Such were the giants," recalled Mrs. Graham, "among whom we grew up."[25]

God has a calling on your life, and any other pursuit is too small. Let His will be first and His plan foremost in your life. Give Him all your life all the time, starting now.

---

25 Ruth Bell Graham, *It's My Turn* (Old Tappan, NJ: Fleming H. Revell Co., 1982), 20-21.

YOUR RESURRECTION BODY

*…the Lord Jesus Christ…will transform our lowly body
that it may be conformed to His glorious body.*

PHILIPPIANS 3:20-21

Although we're inwardly renewed by the Lord day by day, we're nonetheless outwardly perishing (2 Corinthians 4:16). Our aging bodies experience pain, illness, and death. But one day, God's children will be changed in the twinkling of an eye. Our resurrected bodies will be raised, glorified, and transformed into the pattern of the body of the risen Christ. That means: (1) Our bodies will be physical, real, and recognizable (Luke 24:36-43). (2) Our racial and gender identities will likely continue into heaven (Revelation 7:9). (3) We will be incapable of dying (1 Corinthians 15:50-54). (4) We'll be free from pain and tears (Revelation 21:4). (5) We may have extra dimensional qualities like those of Jesus who could move in and out of locked rooms (Luke 24:30-31). (6) We'll forever be in the prime of life, like the Lord at His Resurrection.

We'll have indestructible bodies in an ideal environment, and so shall we ever be with the Lord. These truths may not relieve your physical pain or disability right now, but perhaps they'll encourage you to look forward to what God has planned.

In Every Condition

*Your sandals shall be iron and bronze; as
your days, so shall your strength be.*

Deuteronomy 33:25

Reverend John Rippon served as pastor of Carter's Lane Baptist Church in London for 63 years. Perhaps his greatest legacy was in the hymnals he compiled with the help of his worship minister, Robert Keene. In one of those hymnbooks, a new song appeared. The author simply identified himself as "K," but most scholars believe the "K" stands for Keene. The title was "How Firm a Foundation," and the stanzas were all adapted from Bible verses. Stanza two, inspired by Deuteronomy 33:25, says: "In every condition, in sickness, in health; in poverty's vale, or abounding in wealth; at home or abroad, on the land, on the sea, as thy days may demand, shall thy strength ever be."

When we're sick, we should ask God for healing. The apostle Paul did so when afflicted by a thorn in his flesh. But whether we're healed physically or not, the Lord wants us to trust Him for our daily strength. In His grace, God sometimes grants rapid or immediate physical healing. In His love, God always desires our best and asks us to trust Him.

*Even down to old age all My people shall prove
My sovereign, eternal, unchangeable love.*

AUGUST 18

UNDIMINISHED

Surely goodness and mercy shall follow
me all the days of my life.

PSALM 23:6

William Wilberforce, the English politician whose commitment to Christ fueled his career, is remembered for his campaign to abolish slavery in the British Empire. What isn't well known is the financial disaster that befell him after he retired from politics. His son invested the family fortune in a failed dairy farm, and the Wilberforce family lost everything—even their beautiful home, Highwood Hill. "What I shall most miss will be my books and my garden," Wilberforce wrote. But his biographer said, "As he prayed and reflected during walks along garden paths that were not his own, he arrived at the belief that this turn of events was in some way part of God's plan for his life." Wilberforce learned to count his blessings and concluded that his heavy loss had actually led to "the solid and great increase of [their] enjoyments."[26]

When we go from prosperity to poverty, it doesn't change who God is. His resources are undiminished, and His promises to care for us are unaffected. Good comes from adversity, and goodness still follows every day until we go to dwell in the house of the Lord forever.

---

26 Kevin Belmonte, *William Wilberforce* (Grand Rapids: Zondervan, 2007), 318-322.

AUGUST 19

RESTORATION

Vindicate me, O God, and plead my cause against an ungodly nation; oh, deliver me from the deceitful and unjust man!

PSALM 43:1

Taking the Hill is an hour-long documentary focusing on the recovery of Vietnam veterans. Halfway through the movie, Raul Ries confessed, "I didn't think God could forgive me." Soldiers returning from war often have secrets and shame that haunt them forever—until they discover that God will still hear their prayers.

Even King David of Israel learned that lesson. Early in his life he wasn't guilty of sin, but he was definitely discouraged because of persecution by his attackers. And he cried out to God for deliverance and vindication. But later in life, he *was* guilty of sin. Even then, he found the ears of God still open to his cries for cleansing and restoration (Psalm 32, 51). Discouragement isn't always a result of sin. It can just be the result of the stress of life. And if we have called on God for strength before, we think He can't possibly be willing to meet our need again.

But the Bible is clear: God's grace is greater than all our sin, shame, discouragement, or fear (Romans 5:20b).

WISE INVESTING

The law of Your mouth is better to me than
thousands of coins of gold and silver.

PSALM 119:72

Writing 200 years after Christ, Bishop Cyprian of Carthage said of the Scriptures, "(They) are nothing else than divine commands, foundations on which hope is to be built up, buttresses by which faith is to be strengthened, nourishment wherefrom the heart is to be comforted, helps whereby to steer our way, ramparts whereby salvation is to be preserved; and thus, while they instruct the teachable minds of believers on earth, they also lead them onto the heavenly kingdom."[27]

There has never been a book like the Bible—inspired by God and penned by men, deep enough to study for a lifetime but concise enough to hold in our hands. Every page is a treasure. Psalm 19 says the Word of God is more desirable than fine gold. Proverbs 3:15 says it's more precious than rubies. And Psalm 119:72 says it's better than thousands of coins of gold and silver.

When you invest yourself in the Bible, you're the richest person on earth.

---

27 T. Herbert Bindley, *St. Cyprian on the Lord's Prayer: An English Translation with Introduction* (London: Society for Promoting Christian Knowledge, 1904), 25.

BLESS THOSE WHO CURSE YOU

And do not be conformed to this world, but be transformed by the renewing of your mind, that you may prove what is that good and acceptable and perfect will of God.

ROMANS 12:2

The media is filled with stories of people who retaliate against those who transgress against them, even to the point of pulling a car over to berate another driver who may have somehow offended them. We can read similar stories in the Bible dating back to the days of Cain and Abel.

Under the Mosaic Law, retaliation was limited to the offense committed against a person: an eye for an eye, a tooth for a tooth, and a life for a life (Deuteronomy19:19-21). But in the New Testament, the Lord made it clear that this law no longer stood true: "Beloved, do not avenge yourselves, but *rather* give place to wrath; for it is written, 'Vengeance is Mine, I will repay,' says the Lord" (Romans 12:19).

As Christians we are called to refrain from any revenge or retaliation, as commanded by the Lord Himself, and to love our enemies, doing good to those who have hurt us (Matthew 5:44). Regardless of the pain you've been through or the wrong done to you, "Do not be overcome by evil, but overcome evil with good" (Romans 12:21). The Lord will be the ultimate judge who will settle all scores—not us.

AUGUST 22

GONE, GONE, GONE, GONE

*Purge me with hyssop, and I shall be clean; wash
me, and I shall be whiter than snow.*

PSALM 51:7

Have you ever bundled up for a walk through the snow on a sunny day? If so, you know you need to grab your sunglasses along with your scarf because the reflection of the sun on the snow is blinding. Underneath the snow there may be dirt and mud, potholes, and decaying leaves. But all is covered, hidden, and washed white by the dazzling blanket of snow. It's as pristine as sheer light.

That's a picture of God's forgiveness. Two verses in the Bible talk about how His love covers a multitude of sins (1 Peter 4:8 and James 5:20). The blood of Christ cleanses us from all sin, covers a multitude of failures, and washes us whiter than snow. Perhaps you remember the little Sunday school song that said: *Gone, Gone, Gone, Gone! Yes, my sins are gone. / Now my soul is free, and in my heart's a song. / Buried in the deepest sea, Yes, that's good enough for me. / I shall live eternally, Praise God! My sins are gone!*

That's the way God's children should feel today—whiter than snow.

FOXHOLE PRAYERS

*So when they heard that, they raised their
voice to God with one accord . . .*

ACTS 4:24A

While the saying appears in various forms in war correspondence through the years, it was general-turned-president Dwight Eisenhower who put it in words that were made a part of the public record: "There are no atheists in foxholes." His remarks in a broadcast from the White House became a public recognition of what most people know instinctively: The more serious the trouble, the more likely we are to call out to God.

Yes, it's an instinctive response and one well understood based on the biblical record. We are created in God's image (Genesis 1:26-27) and have eternity in our hearts (Ecclesiastes 3:11). When we are threatened, like small children we intuitively call out for the One we know cares for us. Christians have learned that God welcomes our prayers. Jesus taught us to ask, seek, and knock (Matthew 7:7-8); Paul said to bring all our requests to God without ceasing (Philippians 4:6-7; 1 Thessalonians 5:17-18); and Hebrews 4:16 tells us to call on God boldly for mercy and grace—two things every discouraged person needs.

If you are in a "foxhole" today, call upon God. Even if you have never called on God before, today is a good day to begin.

The Covering Presence

*And the cloud of the LORD was above them by
day when they went out from the camp.*

Numbers 10:34

In the old missionary biography *A Thousand Miles of Miracle in
China*, Archibald Glover tells of his family's deliverance during
the Boxer Rebellion in China at the turn of the twentieth century.
At one point while traveling to safety, the family was captured
at a wayside inn with no way to escape. "[We prayed] He would
not permit the officials … or our captors in the room, to touch a
hair of our head, and that no power might be given them against
us…. There was dead silence as the prayer went up." Later, about
midnight, the orders came: "Kill them at once." One of the captors
lit a lamp and the fumes of some narcotic began filling the room.
The Glovers passed out, and the guards were too insensible to
obey their orders. One of the guards later said, "These people have
been praying to [their God]; and we could do nothing against
their prayers."[28]

Our pathways often twist through stormy landscapes; but when
we look back, we'll see a thousand miles of miracles and answered
prayers. We'll grow stronger along the way, and we'll praise Him
more heartily. Over the storm clouds is the Covering Presence.

28 Archibald E. Glover, *A Thousand Miles of Miracle in China*, 3d ed. (London: Hodder and Stroughton, 1907), 258-263.

Ever-Present Help

*Your servant has killed both lion and bear; and this
uncircumcised Philistine will be like one of them,
seeing he has defied the armies of the living God.*

1 Samuel 17:36

When the shepherding lad, David, went to check on his
brothers in the army, he was alarmed to find them paralyzed
with fear because of the threats of a Philistine giant named Goliath.
The whole army seemed stupefied, from King Saul down to the
lowest ranks. David offered to take on the giant, but his brothers
were scornful and Saul was doubtful. "You are a youth," Saul said.
But David told him how he had killed the lion and the bear that
had threatened his flocks. In verse 37, he said, "The LORD, who
delivered me from the paw of the lion and from the paw of the
bear, He will deliver me from the hand of this Philistine."

And God did.

Our Lord's past performance of faithfulness is an ever-present
comfort during times of distress. One of the reasons God allows
trials is to strengthen our faith for the future. Don't waste
yesterday's lessons by forgetting the deliverance of God. The same
God who delivered you from the lion and the bear will give you
victory and grace today and tomorrow.

GREATER WORKS

Most assuredly, I say to you, he who believes in Me,
the works that I do he will do also; and greater works
than these he will do, because I go to My Father.

JOHN 14:12

The world's population was around 200 million in the first century. For Jesus to reach all those people individually would have been humanly impossible. Even with the assistance of 12 helpers (Luke 9:1), even with 70 helpers (Luke 10:1), human limitations would have caused the Great Commission to fail.

Jesus lived His life by the power and wisdom of the Holy Spirit, who was given to Him by the Father without limit (John 3:34). No number of men and women operating in their own strength could accomplish the Great Commission in their own fleshly power. So Jesus returned to heaven and sent the Holy Spirit to fill and empower His helpers so they could do even greater works (more works) than Jesus Himself did in His three years of ministry on earth. Indeed, He said it was to His disciples' advantage that He should leave them and send the Holy Spirit in His place (John 16:7).

If you are facing a task you feel is impossible, remember that Jesus sent His Spirit to enable you to do what He Himself would do if He were here—and more.

Mindful of You

When I consider Your heavens, the work of Your fingers,
the moon and the stars, which You have ordained,
what is man that You are mindful of him?

PSALM 8:3-4A

When the ancients looked up at the heavens, they didn't know what they were seeing. We may know more about the universe than they did, but we still know relatively little. The *observable* universe is thought to be 92 billion light-years in diameter—and one light-year is 6 trillion miles. So do the math: 92 billion times 6 trillion equals . . . well, it equals a long way from one side of the observable universe to the other. And what about the *unobservable* part?

Based just on what they saw and understood of the heavens, the ancient biblical writers were overwhelmed with their smallness measured against its immensity. And they were amazed that God invested time and attention in them. When we have problems in life, they seem very large—and they are. But when we consider that God is powerful enough to have created the universe, we realize He is more than capable of meeting our needs.

God cares about you and your needs. Bring them to Him in a spirit of worship and thanksgiving, knowing that He is mindful of your place in His creation.

JOURNALING

Write in a book for yourself all the words
that I have spoken to you.

JEREMIAH 30:2

As our children head back to school, it's a good time to talk with them about good penmanship—and to practice it ourselves. Every Christian should be reading one book—the Bible—and writing two. The first is a daily journal. Though not everyone finds this helpful, it's hard to object to keeping a small notebook (either literally or electronically) beside our Bibles so we can jot down the daily insights that come from our Bible study.

The other book is an autobiography. Somewhere and somehow we should begin recording our testimony for those who will come after us. It might be a document you work on whenever you have a chance; or it might be a few handwritten stories you file away in the desk or in your family Bible.

When we're dead and gone, our voices will no longer be heard on earth; but if we leave behind an account of our testimonies, we can minister to the next generation. Why not start your journal and a simple record of your life today? Make a record of God's faithfulness to you!

COUNSELOR AND KING

For unto us a Child is born, unto us a Son is given;
and the government will be upon His shoulder.
And His name will be called Wonderful, Counselor,
Mighty God, Everlasting Father, Prince of Peace.

ISAIAH 9:6

One of the embarrassing facts about King David's affair with Bathsheba was that she was the granddaughter of Ahithophel the Gilonite, one of David's most trusted counselors (2 Samuel 15:12). Seeking counsel from Ahithophel was "as if one had inquired at the oracle of God" (2 Samuel 16:23).

Kings had counselors, even if they didn't always follow their advice. The sage—the wise man—was an important part of God's economy in Israel along with prophet, priest, and king. But counselors were fallible; their advice was not perfect, so kings had more than one. But the prophet Isaiah foresaw a day when One would come who was both king *and* counselor, One who would be a counselor to those He ruled. That person was the Messiah, Jesus of Nazareth. After giving Israel counsel for three years on earth, He returned to heaven and sent the Holy Spirit to continue His ministry of Counselor to His people (John 14:16, 26; 15:26; 16:7, HCSB).

If you need counsel, start with the One who is both Counselor and King—the One who is the source of both wisdom and power.

Penned Prayers

The LORD God is my strength; He will make my feet like deer's feet, and He will make me walk on my high hills.

Habakkuk 3:19

When was the last time you wrote a prayer with pen and ink? We have many methods of prayer, and we should try all of them. But we have two great encouragements to add written prayers to the mix—our Bibles and our hymnals.

In the Bible, many of our heroes wrote out their prayers. Study the Psalms, for example, and notice how many are written prayers. The prophets, such as Jonah and Habakkuk, left us with recorded prayers on the printed page. The apostle Paul composed prayers for most of his congregations.

In the hymnbook, many of our great songs are prayers written to God and designed to be read and sung to Him. Think of the hymn, "How Great Thou Art." The words aren't written *about* God but addressed *to* Him: "O Lord my God, when I in awesome wonder…."

Sometimes we have trouble focusing our thoughts in prayer or harnessing our emotions. In such times, it's often helpful to write out a prayer and perhaps then share it verbally. God can read as well as He can hear; He knows your scribbling as well as He knows your soul.

Places

From that time Jesus began to show to His
disciples that He must go to Jerusalem . . . .

Matthew 16:21

According to the 2011 U.S. Census, a typical American moves his place of residence 11.7 times in his lifetime—about once every seven years. But when it comes to changing our "place," there is more than geography to consider.

Our life consists of many different "places": work, recreation, relationships, education—even mental, spiritual, or emotional places ("I'm in a really great place right now!"). "Place" is one of those parts of life that needs to be always before the Lord for His confirmation or correction. God may want us to serve or help someone, which will require us to change our place. Or He may want us to leave a place that is having a negative impact on our life. He may even want us to remain there and be an agent of godly change in a place that doesn't acknowledge Him. Christ made His disciples into apostles by sending them from where they were into the world (Matthew 28:19-20). We should be ready for Him to change our place in life as well.

Where are you this summer—physically, emotionally, spiritually, and mentally? Ask God to confirm the place where you are or give you grace to change if needed.

David Jeremiah

SEPTEMBER

FEAR NO EVIL

*Why should I fear in the days of evil, when
the iniquity at my heels surrounds me?*

PSALM 49:5

Revelation devotes several chapters to the coming days of evil and tribulation. Reading these passages, we sense the time drawing near. We're astounded at the evil of our days and prone to worry about the evils to be unleashed on earth.

But remember, the times have always been evil. Genesis 6:5 says of mankind in Noah's day, "Every intent of the thoughts of his heart *was* only evil continually." Moses described his people as, "this evil generation" (Deuteronomy 1:35). Isaiah called the people of his day "a brood of evildoers" (Isaiah 1:4). Jesus referred to His generation as evil (Matthew 12:39). Paul told people in his age to redeem the time "because the days are evil" (Ephesians 5:16).

Perhaps the evil is worse now; we're closer to the end than we've ever been before. But evil has been around since the Garden of Eden, and God's plan for victory was designed before the world began. The Bible tells us to fear no evil. Because Christ triumphed, we will also overcome evil in the end. Trust Christ in this evil age and redeem the time for the days are evil.

FATHER OF LIGHTS

Every good gift and every perfect gift is from above,
and comes down from the Father of lights.

JAMES 1:17

One of the greatest speeches in sports history was given seventy-five years ago. It was short—277 words, spoken by a shy man whose head was bowed in modesty. He held his baseball cap in one hand and wiped tears with the other. Those in the stands knew Lou Gehrig was ill, but didn't know the nature of his disease. He didn't tell them. He simply began: "Fans, for the past two weeks you have been reading about a bad break I got. Yet today I consider myself the luckiest man on the face of the earth." For the next few minutes, he told the crowd how thankful he was for his life, his wife, his parents, his teammates, even his mother-in-law. The simplicity of his words earned him the title, "The Luckiest Man."

As Christians, we don't think of ourselves as lucky but as blessed. Occasionally we have bad breaks, but we have a good God who bestows good things. He doesn't demand gratitude, just as most restaurants don't demand tips. We give it willingly. It's how we remember we're the most blessed people on the face of the earth.

WHEN HEARTS COME TOGETHER

From the end of the earth I will cry to You, when my heart is overwhelmed; lead me to the rock that is higher than I.

PSALM 61:2

In November 2004, two North Carolina buddies, Dale Beatty and John Gallina, were wounded when their vehicle hit an anti-tank mine in Iraq. John received severe head and back injuries. Dale lost both legs below the knee. Neither man let their injuries stop them. Returning home, they formed an organization to provide accessible housing solutions for disabled veterans. Their story has widely appeared in the media, and they've been called part of "the new greatest generation." Their slogan: "When hearts come together, great things happen."[29]

We can't always control what happens to us, but we are responsible for our response. It takes time to work through painful and injurious episodes in life; but nothing is wasted in the providence of God. He knows how to take every burden and bring from it a blessing. Obstacles are stepping stones, not roadblocks.

In times of loss, it's necessary to grieve, process the pain, ask questions, and allow ourselves to cycle through natural human emotions. But all the while, we can cry to the Lord. When overwhelmed, we can pray, "Lead me to the rock that is higher than I."

29 Purple Heart Homes, http://www.purplehearthomesusa.org (accessed July 29, 2014).

SOONER THAN EXPECTED

*Blessed is he who reads and those who hear the
words of this prophecy, and keep those things
which are written in it; for the time is near.*

REVELATION 1:3

An economist released a book last year predicting the collapse of the global monetary system, but in a recent interview he confessed he got something wrong. "The tempo of events is faster than expected," he said. "Therefore some of these catastrophic outcomes may come sooner than I wrote about."[30] That's how Christians feel about world events. Rogue nations are acquiring nuclear weapons. Terrorism is a constant threat. Government surveillance is relentless. Middle East tensions are rising. Missionary work is expanding. And morals are collapsing like dominoes.

What a great time to read and study the book of Revelation! When we read the Bible's concluding book, we're motivated by its promise of blessing—Christ's return. He is coming swiftly. He is coming surely. He is coming suddenly. And He is coming for us.

If you're anxious about the state of the world, that's understandable. But trade your anxiety for the blessing of hearing the words of Scripture, keeping them in faith and obedience, and remembering the time is near.

30 "'Death of Money': Author Rickards predicts collapse of global monetary system," www.trunews.com/death-money-author-rickards-predicts-collapse-global-monetary-system/ (accessed June 23, 2014).

THE FINE LINE

Listen to Me, you stubborn-hearted, who
are far from righteousness: I bring My
righteousness near, it shall not be far off.

ISAIAH 46:12-13

Are you stubborn? If so, is your stubbornness a good quality or a bad one? When stubbornness means dogged determination to do the will of God, it's good. Perhaps a better term would be *perseverance*—a quality the Bible upholds as the core of character (Romans 5:4). But when stubbornness is another word for self-will, it's a destructive force. The Bible says, "For rebellion *is as* the sin of witchcraft, and stubbornness *is as* iniquity and idolatry" (1 Samuel 15:23).

There's a fine line between stubborn self-will and godly perseverance; and often the Lord uses crises in our lives to move us from one to the other. Take the patriarch Jacob for example. His story in the book of Genesis is filled with selfish and stubborn choices, which caused pain to himself and others. But by the end of the story, God had used a series of crises in his life to turn his stubbornness into sanctified perseverance.

We can't avoid pressure in life, but we should always remember that whatever crisis we face is God's way of reshaping our stubborn hearts into models of perseverance and character.

DAVID JEREMIAH

CHARACTER COUNTS

*And [God] said, "Your name shall no longer be
called Jacob, but Israel; for you have struggled with
God and with men, and have prevailed."*

GENESIS 32:28

Given names (first names) came first in history, with surnames (last names) being added later. It's easy to see how some name combinations were formed: John the miller became John Miller; Thomas the blacksmith (or ironsmith) became Thomas Smith; Joseph the farmer became Joseph Farmer. Surnames were also derived from geography, nature, and character traits.

That last category—character traits and responsibilities—describes how many biblical names were assigned or changed. For example, Jacob ("tripper" or "supplanter") received his name because he grasped his firstborn twin brother Esau's foot when they were born. And later, Jacob "tripped" Esau up by stealing his birthright and blessing from their father Isaac. But then God humbled Jacob in an encounter and changed his name to Israel—"he who struggles with God." Characteristically, Israel the nation took Israel the patriarch's name, and rightfully so: Israel as a nation has struggled all its life with God, and remains in that struggle today.

If God ascribed a name to you, based on character, what would it be?

Priorities

And this is eternal life, that they may know You, the only true God, and Jesus Christ whom You have sent.

John 17:3

We hear a lot about priorities in life and there are many. Every area of life—family, work, personal—has its own set of priorities. But is there one that stands above all others? It could be said that attaining eternal life is more important than any other goal in life. After all, eternal life was the gift of God in the beginning, and it is what was lost due to sin. So reestablishing that status could be seen as Priority One in life.

"But I have already achieved that priority," you say. "After all, Jesus said that knowing the Father and the Son is eternal life. I know the Father through faith in Christ and have eternal life." Yes, knowing Christ is where eternal life begins; but by its very definition it never ends. All of our earthly, temporal life should be lived in light of the eternity we possess and the presence of God we anticipate. We should be living *now* the same way we will live in heaven *forever*.

As the season changes, ask whether your life is changing as well. Is your life taking on more and more of a Christlike quality every day—becoming less temporal, more eternal?

THE REALITY OF THE DEVIL

*...that serpent of old, called the Devil and
Satan, who deceives the whole world.*

REVELATION 12:9

In his recent newspaper column, "My Answer," evangelist Billy Graham responded to a critic who belittled the biblical teaching of Satan by calling the devil "some imaginary supernatural being." Graham pointed out that the Bible clearly teaches the devil is real and far more powerful than most of us realize. "Remember," he said, "Satan is for death, not life; chaos, not order; despair, not hope."

Jesus certainly believed the devil was real; He battled him in the desert. Peter believed in the reality of Satan, for he called him "a roaring lion seeking whom he may devour" (1 Peter 5:8). Paul warned about the devil, telling us not to be ignorant of his schemes (2 Corinthians 2:11).

Satan is real; he is dangerous and hungry for power. We need to be aware of his plans and reject his attempts to confuse us. The best way to resist the devil is by drawing near to Christ. Jesus is Victor. Jesus is Lord. Jesus is our Triumph today and forever.

EDUCATIONAL ENCOUNTER

Also God said to [Jacob]: "I am God Almighty. Be fruitful and multiply; a nation and a company of nations shall proceed from you, and kings shall come from your body."

GENESIS 35:11

The list of those whom God saved out of carnality and rebellion into a life of spiritual maturity is long. But that's the whole point isn't it? God's goal is to transform us into the image of Christ (Romans 8:29)—and He will use all means necessary (Romans 8:28).

Who would have thought that, in his younger days, a scheming man like Jacob would become the father of twelve sons from whom would arise the multitudes in the nation of Israel? And yet that is what God did through a painful encounter with Jacob (Genesis 32:22-30). In fact, Jacob lived with a limp after that encounter, and his descendants refused to eat the meat in an animal's hip socket in memory of Jacob's encounter and transformation (Genesis 32:31-32). In short, God will do whatever it takes to conform us to the image of His Son—even allow us to experience pain and live with reminders of our "educational encounter" with Him.

Let God have His way in your life today. The sooner we say "Yes, Lord" to Him, the sooner we become like Him.

DAVID JEREMIAH

HIS SUPREME WAYS

Even if you should suffer for righteousness' sake, you are blessed.

1 PETER 3:14

The movie *Chariots of Fire* was written about the trials and triumphs that Scottish Olympic sprinter Eric Liddell faced in representing his country and representing His Lord in the 1924 Olympic Games in Paris. He was quoted as saying, "I feel God's pleasure when I run," but he also felt compulsion about keeping the Sabbath for the Lord, and his best race, the 100 meter race, was scheduled for a Sunday. So, Liddell withdrew from that race to the dismay of many of his countrymen and entered the 400 meter race. As he readied for the race, an American trainer slipped him a piece of paper that said, "Those who honor Me I will honor" (1 Samuel 2:30). To the surprise of all, Eric won the 400 meter race. God honored him with a gold medal.

Eric was quoted as saying, "It has been a wonderful experience to compete in the Olympic Games and to bring home a gold medal. But since I have been a young lad, I have had my eyes on a different prize. You see, each one of us is in a greater race than any I have run in Paris, and this race ends when God gives out the medals." Liddell, the child of Scottish missionaries to China, followed his parents in that calling. He served as a missionary teacher for the rest of his life in China. He died there in a Japanese internment camp in 1945 at the age of 43. His last words were "It is surrender…" His life belonged to God.

BIBLICAL BOLDNESS

...and then the end will come.

MATTHEW 24:14

In *The Global War on Christians,* John L. Allen Jr. calls persecution against Christians "the most dramatic religion story of the early twenty-first century, yet one that most people in the West have little idea is even happening ... Christians today indisputably are the most persecuted religious body on the planet."[31] Allen goes on to catalogue blood-chilling stories of believers being oppressed, imprisoned, vilified, and slain around the world each day.

And yet the church is growing. Reports from Latin America, Asia, and Africa tell of incredible numbers coming to Christ. Even in the West, there are signs of revival and a resurgence of evangelism as Millennials search for an alternative to the emptiness of secularism.

In His sermon on the Signs of the Times, Jesus said, "You will be hated by all nations for My name's sake... And this gospel of the kingdom will be preached in all the world" (Matthew 24:9, 14). The persecution of Christians has never been worse, but the proclamation of Christ has never been greater—just as Jesus predicted. It's time for biblical boldness.

---

31 John L. Allen Jr., *The Global War on Christians* (New York: Crown, 2013), introduction.

BEHIND THE SCENES

Then it came to pass, when Pharaoh had let the people go, that God did not lead them by way of the land of the Philistines, although that was near; for God said, "Lest perhaps the people change their minds when they see war, and return to Egypt."

EXODUS 13:17

On the way *out of* Egypt, God protected Israel from *military* danger by sending them deep into the Sinai Peninsula (Exodus 13:17-18). And God sent them *into* Egypt to protect them from a *moral* danger in the land of Canaan (Genesis 38).

Without going into the unsavory details, some in Jacob's family—specifically, Jacob's son Judah—became involved in serious immorality because of his family's close proximity to Canaanites. It became apparent that if Jacob's sons and their families were to remain faithful to the Lord, they needed to leave Canaan until they were morally and spiritually stronger. So God sent a famine on Canaan, arranged for his son Joseph to provide a place of refuge for Jacob's family in Egypt, and kept them there for 400 years, separated from the Egyptians in a corner of the land (Genesis 46:31-34).

Don't be too quick to judge inconvenient circumstances in your life. God may be at work behind the scenes to protect you from something more serious.

NOW OR LATER

But Peter and John answered and said to them,
"Whether it is right in the sight of God to listen to
you more than to God, you judge. For we cannot but
speak the things which we have seen and heard."

ACTS 4:19-20

A well-known maker of automobile oil filters became famous for their slogan introduced in 1971: "You can pay me now, or pay me later.®" The point was, it's better to spend a little money on regular maintenance *now* than a lot of money on repairs *later*. The "now or later" principle applies to many areas of life—even the spiritual life.

During the coming Tribulation, God will send two witnesses into the world to testify for Him (Revelation 11:1-13). They will faithfully prophesy for God until they are eventually killed. But the world will be astounded when they are raised from the dead and taken into heaven. God always honors and rewards faithfulness in the face of persecution. It is better to pay whatever price is needed today to remain loyal to Christ than to risk the eternal cost of separation from Him.

The time to make decisions about loyalty to Christ is today, not tomorrow when we are faced with the temptation to deny Him. Consider today what kind of witness you will be for Christ until He returns—one who is faithful to Him or one who denies Him.

THE LAST WORD

You shall not bear false witness against your neighbor.

EXODUS 20:16

There are at least two ways to be untruthful about another person. One, it is possible to tell a lie—to say that someone did or said something that he didn't. The other way is *not* to tell the truth when you know someone is under a false impression. Staying quiet in the presence of a lie can be as wrong as telling the lie.

Ten of Jacob's sons, who were also brothers of Joseph, the eleventh son, were guilty on both counts. First, they misrepresented what happened to Joseph; they pretended they didn't know how Joseph's torn, bloody coat got that way. They even pretended not to know if the coat was Joseph's. Then, when Jacob reached a wrong conclusion about Joseph's fate—that he had been killed by a wild animal—the brothers remained silent, knowing that they had sold Joseph, alive and well, to Midianite traders. Not to worry—God always gets the last word when it comes to truth as He did in Joseph's case (Genesis 39:19-23; Matthew 12:36).

First, purpose never to traffic in falsehoods yourself. Second, purpose never to remain silent in the presence of a lie (Ephesians 4:15). The false reports of man are always subject to the final reports of God.

READY TO SPEAK

*And Paul said, "I would to God that not only you, but
also all who hear me today, might become both almost
and altogether such as I am, except for these chains."*

ACTS 26:29

The American pop artist Andy Warhol wrote in 1968, "In the
future, everyone will be world-famous for 15 minutes." From
that statement came the now famous reference to "15 minutes of
fame"—a moment when someone finds himself in the spotlight.
What would we do or say if we suddenly found ourselves with a
captive audience?

That is, if you had one thing you could tell the world, what
would it be? The spotlight can cause some people to lose their
nerve and freeze—but not the apostle Paul. On the several
occasions he found himself standing before authorities with a
captive audience, he never failed to declare the Gospel of Jesus
Christ and encourage those listening to believe in Him (Acts
21:27–22:21; 23:1-11; 24:10-21; 26:1-29; 28:17-31). And the same
thing will happen in the coming Tribulation when, because of
modern technology, the whole world will hear the testimony of
God's two faithful witnesses (Revelation 11:1-13).

Regardless of the size and place of the opportunities God gives
you, be prepared to speak of the hope that lies in you (1 Peter 3:15).

GOD'S AMAZING LOVE

*For whom the LORD loves He corrects, just as
a father the son in whom he delights.*

PROVERBS 3:12

Most Bible readers know that the story of Joseph and the
family of Jacob moving to Egypt takes up the last major
section of Genesis: chapters 37-50. We meet Joseph as a teenager
in Genesis 37 and see him buried at the end of his life in Egypt in
Genesis 50. The story flows smoothly except for one part: Genesis
38. If you connect the last verse of Genesis 37 with the first verse
of Genesis 39, the story flows beautifully. But Genesis 38 has
nothing to do with Joseph and appears to be just a snapshot of
Jacob's family in Canaan.

Since God inspired the writing of Scripture (2 Timothy 3:16;
2 Peter 1:20-21), we know that Genesis 38 is there for a reason.
And the reason is this: It explains *why* God sent Joseph to Egypt
to prepare a place for Jacob's family to live in isolation from the
world. It reveals the serious moral compromises Jacob's family was
making in Canaan that could have ruined the future of Abraham's
descendants. It proves that God loves His people enough to
protect and preserve them through drastic measures if needed.

And God loves us that much as well. He loves us enough to
do what we may be unwilling to do ourselves to protect our
spiritual life.

PLANS

A man's heart plans his way, but the LORD directs his steps.

PROVERBS 16:9

Think for a moment about all the plans you have in place right now: You plan to finish reading this devotional; you plan to take care of chores and tasks this weekend; you plan to do certain things next week; you plan to accomplish some family objectives this fall; you plan to take a vacation, get involved in a committee at church, retire, enjoy your senior years, and spend eternity with Christ. We live with plans—from the small to the sacred and everywhere in between.

Scripture commends plan-making—especially Proverbs (3:5-6; 16:1-4, 9; 19:21; 20:24). Proverbs even commends the ants for "planning" for the winter by storing up food in the summer (Proverbs 6:6-8). Yet for human planners, there is one caveat when it comes to making plans: God's plans always take precedence over ours. Every plan we make should carry the conscious addendum, "As the Lord directs." In a parable the apostle James taught, planners are told to say, "If the Lord wills . . ." (James 4:15).

So, make your plans for this weekend, this fall, and the coming year. Just allow God to direct your steps. And trust that if He changes your plans, it is a chance to walk by faith (2 Corinthians 5:7).

DEFEATING TEMPTATION

*And He was there in the wilderness forty days,
tempted by Satan, and was with the wild beasts;
and the angels ministered to Him.*

MARK 1:13

Comedian Flip Wilson made this line famous: "The devil made me do it!" The characters in Wilson's comedy routines often blamed the devil for leading them into trouble. While comedians are not usually a go-to source for biblical theology, Flip Wilson was partly right. The devil can't *make* anyone do anything, but he can definitely tempt us and influence our choices. But we have defensive measures.

Jesus' encounter with Satan in the Judean wilderness is a proof-text for the fact that Satan can tempt the child of God. This happened at the very beginning of Jesus' public ministry when a failure on His part would have been catastrophic. Satan tempted Jesus three different times with three different enticements. But each time, Jesus rebuffed the offers and remained true to God's Word and God's will (Matthew 4:1-11). Unsuccessful, Satan "departed from [Jesus] until an opportune time" (Luke 4:13).

James writes that if we do what Jesus did—submit to God in obedient faith and resist the devil—Satan will flee from us (James 4:7). When we live clothed with the armor of God in obedient faith (Ephesians 6:10-18), Satan will be defeated.

ENTICEMENTS

*. . . [Potiphar's wife] caught [Joseph] by his garment,
saying, "Lie with me." But he left his garment
in her hand, and fled and ran outside.*

GENESIS 39:12

Singer-songwriter Kate Campbell sings about temptations: "There's vices and voodoo always enticing you, from the day that you're born 'til the day you leave this world. The devil's got a line for you for sure and 10,000 lures. . . . He's a master of disguise, he'll reel you in with power, roaming to and fro seeking whom he may devour."[32]

One of the devil's "10,000 lures" he cast toward Joseph in Egypt was the wife of Joseph's master, Potiphar. But Joseph refused to take the bait. He had been absolutely loyal to Potiphar and had gained his complete trust. Not only did Joseph refuse to dishonor God by yielding to sin, he also refused to dishonor the trust Potiphar had extended toward him (Genesis 39:8-9). He was willing to do whatever it took to remain pure in the sight of both God and man. And God blessed Joseph's commitment.

The first thing to be aware of is what both the songwriter and Scripture writer have said: There will always be enticements to sin. Committing to resist the lure is the first step toward not being caught in the devil's trap.

---

32 Kate Campbell and Mark Narmore ©1999 Large River Music (BMI) / Starstruck Angel Music, Inc. / Mitchelltown Music (BMI)

Elephant Tracks

And the God of peace will crush Satan under your feet shortly.
The grace of our Lord Jesus Christ be with you. Amen.

Romans 16:20

Tor Bowling, 27, an engineer, quit his job to see the world; but earlier this year in Thailand he got more than he bargained for. While hiking in the Phu Luang Wildlife Sanctuary, he encountered an elephant charging at him like a freight train. Bowling instinctively stepped forward and held up his hand in a halting motion. The elephant stopped, turned, and fled in the opposite direction.

At times, Satan charges us like a stampeding elephant or a roaring lion. He can be intimidating. He may even appear to be winning. He reduced Job to the ash heap, sifted Peter like wheat, caused Christ to die for our sins, and hindered Paul from visiting the Thessalonians. According to the book of Revelation, he will dominate the entire world during the Tribulation.

But when we hold up the cross, Satan's power is broken. His defeat is certain, and the God of peace will crush him under our feet shortly. Until then, we have all we need for victory—the grace of our Lord Jesus Christ.

FRIENDS

*The LORD repay your work, and a full reward
be given you by the LORD God of Israel, under
whose wings you have come for refuge.*

RUTH 2:12

Aristotle made the following observation about friendship: "My best friend is the man who in wishing me well wishes it for my sake."

The Bible often exhorts us to care for one another. In the book of Ruth, for example, Boaz extended kindness toward Ruth; and she thanked him in return, saying, "What have I done to deserve such kindness? … I am only a foreigner."

"'Yes, I know,' Boaz replied. 'But I also know about everything you have done for your mother-in-law… May the LORD, the God of Israel, under whose wings you have come to take refuge, reward you fully for what you have done'" (Ruth 2:10-12, NLT). This story has gratitude all around—Ruth to Naomi, Boaz to Ruth, Ruth to Boaz—and is a great example to us.

Do you have a friendship that needs tending? Mend it with thanksgiving.

THE GREAT COUNTERFEITER

For we do not wrestle against flesh and blood, but against principalities, against powers, against the rulers of the darkness of this age, against spiritual hosts of wickedness in the heavenly places.

EPHESIANS 6:12

When you think of counterfeiting, don't just think of money. Fraudsters are creating knockoff *websites* that imitate those of real companies. Customers are tricked into purchasing inferior products on these fraudulent Internet pages, thinking they're shopping on the genuine website.

Counterfeiting in all its forms is a devilish crime. Satan is the original counterfeiter, and his goal is to duplicate everything God has made and to trick us into buying the bogus article. The Bible says of false teachers: "Satan himself transforms himself into an angel of light. Therefore it is no great thing if his ministers also transform themselves into ministers of righteousness, whose end will be according to their works" (2 Corinthians 11:14-15). During the Great Tribulation, the devil, the Antichrist, and the False Prophet will even try to trick the world into following a counterfeit trinity.

Satan can imitate God, but he cannot duplicate Him—God is the only One who can deliver us from our pain and suffering. Let's look to Jesus, put on His armor, and resist the wiles of the great counterfeiter—the devil.

BELATED REWARDS

Though it tarries, wait for it; because it will surely come.

HABAKKUK 2:3

One day in 1977, Ken Littleboy saw a head bobbing up and down in the adjacent canal. Leaping over a couple of fences, he jumped into the water. A three-year-old had fallen in while feeding swans. "I thought he was a goner," said Ken, who pulled him from the canal and turned him over. "Water came out of the child's mouth, and he started breathing." Decades passed, and recently Ken received a thank-you card. It was from Peter King, now forty, who explained that he had been mistakenly told years ago that his rescuer had died. Discovering Littleboy was still alive, King wasted no time penning what he called a "very long overdue thank you."[33]

Just as it's never too late to thank someone who helped you, in the same way God's affirmation sometimes takes a while to reach us. Sometimes we have to wait on Him to reward our efforts. Think of Joseph's long wait in prison, prior to the throne. Think of Abraham's long wait for a son, prior to Isaac's birth.

Though it may seem overdue, righteousness is always rewarded. Don't be impatient with God. He'll never forget to reward your efforts for Him.

---

33 Ken Jordan, "Hero who saved 3 year old boy from drowning receives thank-you card-37 YEARS later," *Mirror,* July 16, 2014.

Clouds in the Eastern Sky

*This same Jesus, who was taken up from you into heaven,
will so come in like manner as you saw Him go into heaven.*

Acts 1:11

When Jesus led His disciples to the Mount of Olives and ascended into heaven before their eyes, two angels were standing nearby. The apostles were stunned to see their Lord disappear into the clouds, but the angels reassured them that Jesus would return one day "in like manner as you saw Him go into heaven." What does that mean?

It means: (1) Jesus will descend to the earth just as He ascended. (2) The location will be the same. According to Zechariah 14:4, "His feet will stand on the Mount of Olives." (3) His return will be physical, visible, and observable. (4) His coming will be in the clouds. Just as a cloud hid Jesus from view in Acts 1:9, so He will come in the clouds of glory (Mark 13:26). (5) His coming will be in the presence of angels (Matthew 25:31).

Are you ready for that day? He will come physically, visibly, in the clouds of glory, to the Mount of Olives east of Jerusalem. And we shall behold Him, face to face, in all of His glory. Think of *that* the next time you see a cloud in the eastern sky.

The Big Idea

Then God blessed [Adam and Eve], and God said to them,
"Be fruitful and multiply; fill the earth and subdue it; have
dominion over the fish of the sea, over the birds of the air,
and over every living thing that moves on the earth."

Genesis 1:28

When a new employee reports for his first day on the job, he may be given a summary statement of his responsibilities: "You'll be overseeing all of the company's graphic designs for our advertising and website." Or, "You'll be responsible for the parts made on this machine." Details will follow, but the "big idea" is most important.

The very first thing God said to Adam and Eve was their job description, summed up in one word: stewardship. Man's chief responsibility toward God is to be a good steward of God's revelation, creation, resources, and spiritual and physical gifts. Then, and now, a steward is a manager who serves his master's wishes. The apostle Paul saw himself as a steward of the revelation of God's grace and noted the primary requirement of all stewards: faithfulness (1 Corinthians 4:1-2).

Consider what God has given you: salvation, His Spirit, the Bible, property, money, a family, children, relationships, gifts and abilities. Ask God today for grace to be a good steward of all that comes from Him.

No Happy Medium

So Saul died for his unfaithfulness which he had committed against the Lord, because he did not keep the word of the Lord, and also because he consulted a medium for guidance.

1 Chronicles 10:13

King Saul is a tragic example of a promising leader whose life ended in failure. One of his final mistakes was consulting a medium for guidance. It's remarkable how many people still do that. Bible teachers rightly warn us to avoid anything remotely connected with the occult, such as Ouija boards, séances, fortune-tellers, and so forth. Don't call the psychic hotline or consult the horoscopes in the newspapers. Avoid entertainment that majors on these elements.

We should even go a step further and ignore superstitions. Don't worry about black cats, broken mirrors, four-leaf clovers, or spilled salt. Don't follow old wives' tales.

Be a student instead of the Scriptures. Isaiah 8:19-20 says, "And when they say to you, 'Seek those who are mediums and wizards, who whisper and mutter,' should not a people seek their God? Should they seek the dead on behalf of the living? To the law and to the testimony!"

Make sure you're covered with the blood of Christ and trusting the Word of God. Greater is He who is in you than he who is in the world (1 John 4:4).

SOMETHING ABOUT THAT NAME

*You shall call His name Jesus, for He will
save His people from their sins.*

MATTHEW 1:21

In biblical times the name *Jesus* was common, which speaks to His humanity. He was called Jesus of Nazareth, a real man from an ordinary town. But there was nothing ordinary about His mission. The name *Jesus* is the New Testament version of the Old Testament *Joshua,* which means *Jehovah Saves.* His name thus embodies His mission – "to seek and to save that which was lost" (Luke 19:10).

Many of us are immediate-thinkers instead of ultimate thinkers. As long as everything's going all right today, we're satisfied. We don't bother to think of ultimate consequences. But the Bible warns that sooner or later, those without Christ must stand before God and give an account of their thoughts and actions and moral behavior. Jesus came to save us from the consequences of our own sins and from the wrath of God. That's the significance of the name *Jesus.* He has the power to deliver us from any habit, from any sin, from any chaos. And He has the power to deliver us from death, judgment, and hell.

Praise Him for His name—Jesus, for He saves His people from their sins.

SEPTEMBER 28

THE KING'S VISIT

So they told him that Jesus of Nazareth was passing by.

LUKE 18:37

King George III took every opportunity to leave London for his royal home at Windsor Castle. Sometimes while there, he'd take off by himself on long walks. Occasionally he'd surprise the neighbors by popping over to their homes. One day George walked into a barn where a woman was milking a cow. She had no idea who he was. The king asked her where all the other laborers and farm hands had gone. They had all gone to see the King, she said, adding, "I wouldn't give a pin to see him. Besides the fools will lose a day's work by it, and that is more than I can afford to do. I have five children to work for."

Taking some coins from his pocket, George gave them to her. "Well, then," he said, "you may tell your companions who were gone to see the King, that the King came to see you."[34]

That's what happened when Jesus came to earth. The King of kings and Lord of lords came to see us. In fact, He is with us always. Every day Jesus is near, we can enjoy His fellowship, and He leaves blessings in His wake.

34 Christopher Hibbert, *George III* (London: Penguin, 1999), 198.

LOTS OF SMILES

...not lagging in diligence, fervent in spirit, serving the Lord.

ROMANS 12:11

Many years ago a Scottish boy named Samuel Smiles was too spirited to be a good schoolchild, causing his teacher to tell him he would never be fit for anything but sweeping streets. But Smiles had two qualities that served him well. He wanted to improve himself and he could persevere. As he went through life, he read a lot and applied himself. In 1859, he wrote a book on improving oneself. It was called *Self Help*, and it became a sensation. Samuel Smiles virtually launched the genre of self-help books.

"The greatest results in life are usually attained by simple means and the exercise of ordinary qualities," he wrote. "They who are the most persistent, and work in the truest spirit, will usually be the most successful.... Great results cannot be achieved at once; and we must be satisfied to advance in life as we walk, step by step."

Smiles probably got his advice from the Bible, which tells us to serve the Lord daily with diligence and fervor of spirit. Whatever we do, we're to do it with all our hearts as unto the Lord. A persevering attitude will bring a lifetime of results and lots of smiles.

ABIDING

As the branch cannot bear fruit of itself, unless it abides
in the vine, neither can you, unless you abide in Me.

JOHN 15:4

Ruth Bell Graham once compared the Holy Spirit's work in our lives to sap in a grapevine. In John 15, Jesus said, "I am the vine, you *are* the branches. He who abides in Me, and I in him, bears much fruit; for without Me you can do nothing" (verse 5). Sap is the circulatory system of the plant. Its unseen flow draws no attention to itself but keeps the relationship healthy between branch and vine. That's what produces the fruit.

Abiding in Christ means living in unhindered fellowship with our Lord, walking with Him, talking with Him, confessing our sins, and being filled with His Spirit. The Holy Spirit then has free recourse to take the life of Jesus and replicate it in us. He takes the work of Christ and accomplishes it through us. He enables us to bear fruit, more fruit, and much fruit (see John 15:1, 2, 5). He produces the fruit of the Spirit (Galatians 5:22-23).

When we bear fruit, it's evidence the Lord is in us and the Holy Spirit is doing His work through us.

OCTOBER

ADVICE ON GIVING

My son, …honor the Lord with your possessions.

PROVERBS 3:1, 9

When William Colgate left home at age sixteen, a canal boat captain asked where he was going. "I don't know," replied William. "Father is too poor to keep me at home any longer." William said he had no skills except making soap and candles.

"Well," said the man, "let me pray with you." The two knelt and prayed, then, rising up, the man said: "Be a good man; give your heart to Christ; give the Lord all that belongs to Him of every dollar you earn; make an honest soap; give a full pound; and I am certain you will yet be a prosperous and rich man."

When William arrived in New York, he dedicated himself to Christ, joined a church, and began tithing from the first dollar he earned. Late in his life, he had become so successful he devoted a major portion of his income to the Lord. His name is famous to this day. Colgate-Palmolive is one of America's oldest and most successful Fortune 500 companies today.

You never know the good that comes from giving, whether it's a word of advice to a teenager or a tithe of our income. The returns are enormous.

DIVINE GPS

*O Lord, I know the way of man is not in himself; it
is not in man who walks to direct his own steps.*

JEREMIAH 10:23

The introduction of GPS in recent years has put a new spin on finding directions. Our phones, tablets, and dedicated GPS devices can connect with orbiting satellites to determine where we are and tell us how to get where we want to go. We have to take the steps ourselves, but the directions come from over our heads.

This is not an entirely new idea, of course. The psalmist David said that God has ordained our days—and so, the steps in those days—before they come to pass (Psalm 139:16). Solomon wrote that "a man's heart plans his way, but the Lord directs his steps" (Proverbs 16:9). And the prophet Jeremiah wrote that "a man's life is not his own; it is not for man to direct his steps" (Jeremiah 10:23, NIV, 1984). The point of these verses is not that God micromanages our individual steps through life. Rather it is the sense found in *The Message*: ". . . mere mortals can't run their own lives, that men and women don't have what it takes to take charge of life" (Jeremiah 10:23).

Who hasn't felt that way? We need God to guide our steps and walk us through this thing called life. Based on these verses ask God to guide you today and every day. Divine guidance beats all others.

October 3

Renewable Energy

But those who wait on the Lord shall renew their strength;
they shall mount up with wings like eagles, they shall
run and not be weary, they shall walk and not faint.

ISAIAH 40:31

When we pump a barrel of oil or extract a ton of coal from the ground, it comes from a finite supply. The world's underground deposits—though vast—are reduced by that barrel or ton. When we capture the same amount of energy in a solar panel, a wind turbine, or a waterfall, it doesn't reduce the sun or the wind or the river one bit. That's why it's called renewable. But the politics and economics of it are another story, and political campaigns are won or lost on issues of energy policy.

On a personal level, we have a constant source of renewable energy to keep the lights burning in our hearts. Isaiah 40:31 says, "Those who wait on the Lord shall renew their strength; they shall mount up with wings like eagles."

When you face a problem that drains your energy, get alone with the Lord and give it to Him. Entrust it to Him in a conscious act of faith. Wait on His resolution in hopeful faith. You'll be amazed at how you're inwardly strengthened by the process. That's renewable energy that works!

OCTOBER 4

GREAT DAY IN THE MORNING

*Now in the morning, having risen a long while
before daylight, He went out and departed to
a solitary place; and there He prayed.*

MARK 1:35

Yes, we can pray without ceasing and practice the presence of the Lord all day long (1 Thessalonians 5:17). But there's something about the morning hours that are perfectly primed for prayer, and it's a shame to start the day without a specific regular prayer time with the Lord.

The psalmist said, "My voice You shall hear in the morning, O Lord; in the morning I will direct it to You, and I will look up" (Psalm 5:3). When the Tabernacle was set up, Aaron was told to burn fragrant incense on the altar every morning when he tended the lamps (Exodus 30:7). The priests were to begin each day with morning sacrifices (Leviticus 6:12). The patriarch Job began each day by offering sacrifices early in the morning for his family (Job 1:5). Mary Magdalene rose early in the morning to tend to the Master's tomb, but instead she came face to face with the Master.

Everyone's schedule is different. But as much as possible, start the day face to face with the Master. Begin every day in fellowship with the Lord. You'll find it's a great day in the morning.

OCTOBER 5

NOTHING HIDDEN

And there is no creature hidden from His sight,
but all things are naked and open to the eyes
of Him to whom we must give account.

HEBREWS 4:13

The front (obverse) of the great seal of the United States appears in many settings associated with the President. The back (reverse) side was never made into a seal, but its design can be seen on the back of the United States one-dollar bill. A distinctive feature is the unfinished pyramid with an eye appearing in glory above the pyramid. Such an image of an eye has been used in history to represent God's omnipotence and providence—the fact that He sees and watches over all things.

It is certainly a biblical image. The writer of 2 Chronicles 16:9 says "the eyes of the Lord" survey all the earth, while the psalmist says "the Lord looks from heaven [and] He sees all the sons of men" (Psalm 33:13-14). The writer to the Hebrews put it more dramatically: "And there is no creature hidden from His sight"—suggesting that mankind would prefer to hide some things from God. The writer also suggests that hiding is a bad idea since we "must give account" to Him who sees everything.

Today, consider the "everythings" of your life. Is there anything you hope God doesn't see? Ask God for grace to live a life you will be glad for Him to see.

DAVID JEREMIAH

OCTOBER 6

SEEKING AND FINDING

*If you seek [wisdom] as silver, and search
for her as for hidden treasures . . .*

PROVERBS 2:4

At Sutter's Mill in Coloma, California, the California Gold
Rush began in 1848. By 1849, 300,000 "Forty-Niners" were
streaming across the country to strike it rich in California. Some
even sailed from the East Coast, going around the tip of South
America to reach California—a five to eight month journey. Fifty
years later, the frenzy was repeated as 100,000 prospectors left
everything to join the Klondike Gold Rush in Canada.

People will often spare no expense to increase their *wealth*,
but the same is not always true concerning *wisdom*. Solomon
used the image of searching for "silver" and "hidden treasures"
to illustrate the effort required to gain wisdom. Prospecting for
gold and silver was hard work—with no promise of reward. By
contrast, Solomon says that those who seek diligently for God's
wisdom "will understand the fear of the Lord, and find the
knowledge of God. For the Lord gives wisdom; from His mouth
come knowledge and understanding" (Proverbs 2:5-6).

Seeking God's wisdom will result in finding something more
precious than gold and silver—guaranteed! If we're going to
search on our knees, let it be for wisdom rather than for gold.

AT HOME WITH THE LORD

*We are confident, yes, well pleased rather to be absent
from the body and to be present with the Lord.*

2 CORINTHIANS 5:8

The apostle Paul had an unusually optimistic view about death. He wrote, "To die is gain…. (I have) a desire to depart and be with Christ, which is far better" (Philippians 1:21-23). In 2 Corinthians 5, he said, "How weary we grow of our present bodies. That is why we look forward eagerly to the day when we shall have heavenly bodies… We look forward with confidence to our heavenly bodies, realizing that every moment we spend in these earthly bodies is time spent away from our eternal home in heaven with Jesus…. We are not afraid, but quite content to die, for then we will be at home with the Lord" (verses 2-8, *The Living Bible*). Perhaps Paul's anticipation was heightened by the time he was "caught up to the third heaven… into Paradise and heard inexpressible words…" (See 2 Corinthians 12:1-6).

While we don't want to leave this planet before God's purposes for us are finished here, it's healthy to cultivate the mindset of the biblical writers, not fearing death but being "confident, yes, well pleased rather to be absent from the body and … present with the Lord."

DAVID JEREMIAH

SAILING THROUGH LIFE

*For prophecy never came by the will of man, but holy men
of God spoke as they were moved by the Holy Spirit.*

2 PETER 1:21

The next time you are near a lake or a seashore, spend some time observing the movements of sailboats on the water. Though some larger sailboats have small motors to use in case of an emergency, for normal use they are totally dependent on the wind. Their pilots can change the direction of the boat to a degree, but it is the wind that is in charge.

Sailboats existed for thousands of years before the apostle Peter's day; as a fisherman, he knew the value and power of the wind. So when he wrote about how God inspired the Old Testament prophets to write their books, he used an image akin to sailing: "[men] spoke from God as they were carried along by the Holy Spirit" (2 Peter 1:21, NIV). Just as the wind carries along a sailboat, so the Holy Spirit was the power and resource behind the writers of Scripture (2 Timothy 3:16). But the same image applies to our daily life as Christians. When we are filled with and yielded to the Spirit, He is the power who silently guides us through life. Yes, our hand is on the rudder, but it is the wind of the Spirit that fills our sail.

Recommit yourself today to being "filled with the Spirit" (Ephesians 5:18). Trust Him to guide and empower you.

BETTER TO GIVE

And remember the words of the Lord Jesus, that He said, "It is more blessed to give than to receive."

ACTS 20:35

There is one teaching of Jesus that is not recorded in any of the four Gospels—and it is an important one that can be applied every day: It is more blessed to give than to receive. Giving is a God kind of act, a *godly* act. It is nowhere demonstrated more clearly than in John 3:16: "For God so loved the world that He *gave* His only begotten Son."

Giving involves loss. When we give something to another person we forfeit the right to keep it for ourselves. We place the need or want of another person ahead of our own (Philippians 2:4). When the Father *gave* His Son to humanity as a Savior, He gave up the privilege of fellowship with the Son in heaven for our sake; He put our needs above His own desires. Giving is a daily way to imitate God. We can give a gift, we can give our time, we can give up our place in line to someone who is in a hurry, we can give a personal possession to someone in need, we can give a room in our home to someone in need of temporary shelter, we can give a meal, we can give a hug, a smile, or a kind word. There is no end to the ways we can imitate God by giving.

Watch for a time and place today to do the "better" thing—to give as God gives. And if someone gives to you, receive the gift with thanksgiving and humility.

DAVID JEREMIAH

CALLED BUT SCARED

*So the Lord said to [Moses], "Who has made man's
mouth? Or who makes the mute, the deaf, the
seeing, or the blind? Have not I, the Lord?"*

EXODUS 4:11

Sometimes we get asked to do things that are clearly beyond our ability: donate a million dollars, sing a solo, or run a marathon for charity. Some people can do those things, but most cannot. More often, God puts opportunities in front of us for which we are, in fact, qualified—but we are afraid of failure; we are afraid the challenge is beyond our ability. And sometimes it is. But it is in those moments of life that we recognize our dependence on God.

Moses was brilliant, highly educated, seemingly a born leader, experienced—and scared. When God called him to confront Egypt's Pharaoh and lead the Hebrew slaves to the Promised Land, Moses dug in his heels. One of the objections this highly literate man gave was his lack of eloquence—his inability as a public speaker. God had to remind Moses that it was He who created man's ability to speak: "Now therefore, go, and I will be with your mouth and teach you what you shall say" (Exodus 4:12).

If you believe God has called you to your current place in life (spouse, parent, employee, volunteer), but you feel inadequate, remember: "He who calls you is faithful, who also will do it" (1 Thessalonians 5:24).

Joyful Surprise

Your kingdom come. Your will be done
on earth as it is in heaven.

Matthew 6:10

Edwin Muir was a Scottish poet who faced double calamities in March 1939. His wife grew seriously ill, and at the same time Europe was seized by global war. One night as he undressed for bed, Muir began reciting a set of words for the first time in many years: "Our Father, who art in heaven, hallowed be Thy name…" As he continued saying this prayer, he began calming down. "My soul grew still," he said. "Every word had a strange fullness of meaning which astonished and delighted me…. I was sleepy; but as I stood in the middle of the floor half undressed saying the prayer over and over, meaning after meaning sprang from it, overcoming me again with joyful surprise."

We can discover the same. The Lord's Prayer is a model for all our prayers. It starts with praise, makes a series of requests that are important to God, a series of requests that are important to us, and ends with a doxology.

If you're distressed about anything today, try meditating on and praying through the Lord's Prayer of Matthew 6:8-13. You'll be overcome with joyful surprise.

A HIDDEN GULLY

*Therefore submit to God. Resist the devil
and he will flee from you.*

JAMES 4:7

Does temptation grab your mind and pull you away from the Lord? Consider this testimony from a young missionary in China, James Fraser. During one period he was assailed with stubborn temptations and evil thoughts. "These thoughts were present with me even when I was preaching," he said. "I went out of the city to a hidden gully on the hillside, one of my prayer haunts, and there voiced my determined resistance to Satan in the matter. I claimed deliverance on the ground of my Redeemer's victory on the Cross. I even shouted my resistance to Satan and all his thoughts. The obsession collapsed then and there, like a pack of cards."

Fraser went on to say, "James 4:7 is still in the Bible. Our Lord cried…with a loud voice at the grave of Lazarus. He cried with a loud voice on the cross. In times of conflict I still find deliverance through repeating Scripture out loud, appropriate Scripture, brought to mind through the Holy Spirit. It is like crashing through opposition. Resist the devil and he will flee from you."

And draw near to God, and He will draw near to you.

SO CLOSE, YET SO FAR

*The Lord God planted a garden eastward in Eden,
and there He put the man whom He had formed.*

GENESIS 2:8

Last year a remarkable photograph appeared in California newspapers. It showed a humpback whale and her calf surfacing beside a small sailboat. The whales were playing and eating fish. Just behind the whales sat a man on the cab of his boat in the open air. He was so close he could have almost touched the creatures. But he didn't even notice them. He was too busy looking at the screen of his phone, apparently absorbed in texting.

We inhabit a beautiful universe and we shouldn't miss it. The Garden of Eden is gone, but much of the original beauty of God's creation shines through. Beneath our feet are remarkable blades of grass. Before our eyes are trees, each unique, filled with birds of many sizes and songs. Above our heads are endless formations of clouds. Every morning and evening we're greeted with a fresh sunrise and sunset.

Let's get our noses out of our busyness long enough to smell the roses, spot the whales, and rejoice in God's creation. Enjoy the world today, and sing the mighty power of God that made the mountains rise.

DAVID JEREMIAH

HOW BIG IS GOD?

*Now to Him who is able to do exceedingly abundantly above all
that we ask or think, according to the power that works in us.*

EPHESIANS 3:20

If for some reason it was your job to design the universe, how big
would you make it? You probably would not design the universe
to look like the one God created. Consider this: The distance from
planet Earth to the observable "edge" of the universe is 46 billion
light years—and one light year is about six *trillion* miles. So the
distance from Earth to the edge of the universe is 46 billion times
six trillion miles. It is thought there are more than 100 billion
galaxies containing anywhere from 10 million to one trillion
stars each.

God doesn't think small. We don't know why God created such
a huge universe—we only know that He did. If the creation is
BIG, that means the Creator is BIGGER. When it comes to us and
our needs, God is always bigger—not just big, but *bigger*. God is
able to do "exceedingly abundantly above all that we ask or think."
Whatever you think would represent a blessing in your life, God
is able to do more. Our challenge is to allow our faith to see God
for who He really is.

If you have a need today that seems bigger than anyone's ability,
remember what God did when creating the universe. God is
bigger than all our needs—bigger than we could ask or think.

LIKE A TREE

He shall be like a tree planted by the rivers of water,
that brings forth its fruit in its season, whose leaf also
shall not wither; and whatever he does shall prosper.

PSALM 1:3

The Holy Land was never completely forested like portions of Europe and North America, but there were more trees there in biblical days than there are today. One of the most useful was the date palm which grew in the Jordan River valley—a tall, branchless tree with clusters of sweet dates at its crown. Jericho was known as "the city of palm trees" (2 Chronicles 28:15). Was this the tree the psalmist referred to in Psalm 1:3?

The tree the psalmist pictures is planted by a river, is fruitful in its season, and never withers because its roots run deep. That is the image of a person the psalmist is describing—and who would not want to be such a person? There are two requirements: Such a person must distance himself from the ways, words, and walk of the sinful and scornful, and must delight "in the law of the Lord," meditating on it "day and night." In New Testament terms, Jesus put it this way: abide in Him (not the world) and let His Word abide in us (John 15:7).

Develop these goals for every day: flee from sin; and cling to the Savior and His Word.

Don't Be a Skeptic

Then Zechariah said to the angel, "How shall I know this?
For I am an old man, and my wife is advanced in years."

Luke 1:18, NABRE

The *Oxford English Dictionary* says the phrase "too good to be true" was used as early as 1580. Since then, the phrase has been changed to a warning: "If it sounds too good to be true, it probably is." Regardless of when the phrase was first written down, humans have always been a skeptical lot—even when talking to God.

Zechariah, the priest who became the father of John the Baptist, should have known better than to question the angel Gabriel who had just announced that Zechariah and Elizabeth would have a baby boy. Zechariah's skepticism was based on the same reasoning as father Abraham's: "We're much too old!" (Genesis 17:17, paraphrase). But what about us? We have read the stories of Abraham, Moses, Gideon, Zechariah, and others—how God was faithful to fulfill His promises—and yet we still sometimes wonder if God will be faithful to keep His Word. We are skeptical about God's goodness, His ability, His timing, His intention, His forgiveness, and more. We have been given great and precious promises which we have every reason to believe (2 Peter 1:4).

If you are trying to decide whether to trust God today, don't be skeptical. Take Him at His Word and rest in His promise.

A TIME FOR EVERYTHING

To everything there is a season, a time for
every purpose under heaven.

ECCLESIASTES 3:1

A song by the late folk artist Pete Seeger holds a unique record: the number one American song with the oldest lyrics. In this case the lyrics were written by King Solomon nearly 3,000 years ago. The song is "Turn! Turn! Turn! (to Everything There Is a Season)"—written by Seeger in the late 1950s and covered by the rock group, The Byrds, for whom it became a number one hit in 1965.

The song uses Solomon's words almost verbatim from Ecclesiastes 3:1-8 (with the addition of "turn, turn, turn"). Ecclesiastes 3:1 was Solomon's "big idea"—there is a time and purpose for all the seasons of life. He then listed examples: times for birth and death, planting and reaping, destroying and building, mourning and dancing, and more. This was not a fatalistic statement on Solomon's part—that life will be what life will be. Rather, it was a realistic statement: God is sovereign over all the affairs of men and it does no good for us to rail against God or what He allows to happen in His Providence. Rather, we should yield to God's sovereign will and trust Him.

Regardless of what time or season you are in now, give thanks to God for it and for all things, "for this is the will of God in Christ Jesus for you" (1 Thessalonians 5:18).

A TRANSFORMED LIFE

*[The man healed of blindness] answered and said,
"Whether He is a sinner or not I do not know. One
thing I know: that though I was blind, now I see."*

JOHN 9:25

I magine a person who has an encounter with Jesus Christ whose life is radically changed—but who knows almost nothing of the Bible and very little theology as a brand new Christian. And imagine that new believer is challenged by a committee of famous theologians who quiz him on the validity of his belief in Christ. How should an unschooled new believer respond to the investigating committee?

Perhaps the example of the man healed by Jesus of blindness is worth noting (John 9:1-41). People who knew the man Jesus healed took him to the Pharisees who promptly declared the healing invalid—that is, not from God because Jesus had been known to break Sabbath laws and traditions. A thorough investigation followed. The Pharisees questioned the man and his parents, trying to convince them that Jesus was a sinner. Exasperated, the once-blind man said, "All I know is that once I was blind, but now I can see!" (paraphrase) That is the answer that no critic can take away: Jesus Christ changed my life.

You don't need to be a theologian to tell friends what Christ has done for you and can do for them. A transformed life says it all.

WHO INVENTED RADAR?

The fool has said in his heart, "There is no God."

PSALM 14:1

The science of radar began in the 1880s when a German physicist determined that radio waves could bounce off of solid objects. By World War II, several nations had super-secret programs for developing radar technology. The ability to detect incoming planes helped save the British Islands.

Long before radar, there were bats. As bats fly through the air, they emit high-pitched sounds, far above the hearing capabilities of humans. The sound travels through the air, bounces off objects, and echoes back in the big ears of the creature. The bat's brain instantly processes the information and determines its flight plan. God was the original inventor of radar as He installed it into the structure of His strange little creatures.

What if you claimed that the science of radar happened without physicists, scientists, and engineers? What if you said the great dishes aimed at the sky in radar installations around the world simply grew from rocks and evolved from the ground on their own? Someone might call you a fool. Nothing so complex happens by random accident. It requires an intelligent designer. It requires a creator.

OCTOBER 20

THE MIRACULOUS AND THE MUNDANE

He does great things past finding out,
yes, wonders without number.

JOB 9:10

In his book about miracles, journalist Tim Stafford admits that it's hard to define the miraculous. Every sunrise is beautiful and every baby's birth is astonishing. "If they happened once in a generation," said Stafford, "we would drop everything and stare at them in sheer amazement. If no one had seen a sunrise, and then one morning you did, it would strike you speechless."

We don't use the word "miracle" for a sunrise or a baby's birth because if everything is a miracle then nothing would be a miracle. Miracles are "distinct kinds of marvels." Nevertheless, Stafford observes, "The non-miracles that God does every day should astonish us." Things like the nuclear fusion of the sun and the electrical flashes of the human brain occur constantly but are constantly amazing.

In the works of God, the lines between the miraculous and the mundane aren't as great as we think. Everything God does is wonderful and should elicit awe, thanksgiving, and reverence. He does great things all the time, yes, wonders without number.

Look around you today and praise Him.

THE RIGHT TRACKS

*Don't get off track, either left or right, so as to
make sure you get to where you're going.*

JOSHUA 1:7, THE MESSAGE

Last year a subway operator in New York pulled onto the wrong tracks as he left the Canal Street Station. He headed uptown on the downtown rails. The dispatcher frantically tried to radio the train but the crew didn't hear the emergency broadcasts. The driver continued for several stops until he saw the headlights of a southbound train coming toward him. Both trains managed to stop in time or it could have been a disaster. Interestingly, the passengers had no idea they were on the wrong tracks. They sat there napping or reading their newspapers or listening to their earphones, oblivious to the potentially fatal mistake.

God has a specific strategy for your life and for mine. He saw us before we were born and scheduled each day of our lives before we began to breathe (See Psalm 139:16). How sad that so many people never get on the right tracks.

Commit yourself to Jesus Christ and determine to do His will each day. Seek Him in His word and obey it. Live for Him so that when your train pulls into the heavenly terminal, you'll hear Him say, "Well done, good and faithful servant."

THE WOUNDED WORSHIPER

*Bless the Lord, O my soul; and all that is
within me, bless His holy name!*

PSALM 103:1

When World War I erupted, a Scottish fellow named Duncan Campbell enlisted in the British Army. He was a Christian believer. The fighting around him was terrible, and in the midst of the carnage his horse was shot from under him. Duncan himself was severely wounded. He was laid across the back of a horse and taken to a hospital where he expected to die. But a nurse from the Highlands sat down beside his bed and started singing the hymn, "There is a fountain filled with blood drawn from Emmanuel's veins, and sinners plunged beneath that flood lose all their guilty stains."

Duncan's spirit rallied, and he began testifying and quoting Psalm 103. Instantly the presence of God came into the room, and seven nearby wounded soldiers were converted to Christ. That began a long ministry of evangelism and revival wrought through the life of Duncan Campbell, who is remembered as one of Scotland's greatest modern revivalists.

Our spirits can revive in our darkest moment by the power of Emmanuel's blood. Because of Christ, we can say whatever the circumstances: "Bless the Lord, O my soul!"[35]

35 Andrew A. Woolsey, *Channel of Revival* (Edinburgh: The Faith Mission, 1982), 51-53.

HIDDEN CONTENTS

So now, brethren, I commend you to God and to the word
of His grace, which is able to build you up and give you
an inheritance among all those who are sanctified.

ACTS 20:32

An employee at the thrift store in Ellsworth, Maine, picked up a book while sorting merchandise. It didn't feel right, and the employee opened it to find a secret compartment with a .31 derringer-style pistol. They quickly turned over the book to the police. It's frightening to think what could have happened had that book ended up in a home with small children.

Lots of books contain dangerous content. We have to be very careful about what we read and about the books our children read. Many books are filled with persuasive lies, humanistic thinking, profanity, and narrative pornography. Even schoolbooks demand scrutiny from discerning believers.

There's one book we can always trust, and it's filled with dynamite—the power of the Word of God. Whenever we prayerfully read its content, we are built up and better informed about our inheritance in Christ. The Bible is a double-edged sword, piercing to the division of soul and spirit. It affects our heads and also our hearts (Hebrews 4:12).

Be careful what you read, and be careful to read God's Word daily.

FREE FROM PAIN

I acknowledged my sin to You, and my iniquity I have not hidden. I said, "I will confess my transgressions to the Lord," and You forgave the iniquity of my sin.

All of us can testify to the "before and after" of relief from physical pain. It might happen quickly—an aspirin and a good night's sleep relieves a headache—or it might be a long-term process—a painful broken bone gradually heals. However long the transition takes, we know how good it feels to be relieved of pain.

Guilt can be as painful spiritually as an ailment can be physically. The guilt of sin, whether by omission or commission, can be removed. And when guilt is removed, the accompanying pain of fear, stress, despair, or shame is removed as well. The psalmist David described the pain of his unconfessed sin (Psalm 32:3-4) and implied the removal of that pain when he "confessed [his] transgressions to the Lord" (verse 5). We don't know if this psalm was written in the aftermath of his adultery and conspiracy to murder (2 Samuel 11-12); but if it was, he had lived almost a year with the pain of his guilt. He saw confession to God as the path to the restoration of his joy (Psalm 51:12).

If you are living with an unconfessed sin, ask God to cleanse you and deliver you from pain to relief (1 John 1:9).

PROGRESS?

*And the Lord said, "Indeed the people are one and they all
have one language, and this is what they begin to do; now
nothing that they propose to do will be withheld from them."*

GENESIS 11:6

In Genesis 11, the Babelites began building a tower to reach the
heavens, wanting to make a name for themselves and act as
their own gods. The Lord acknowledged the potential of human
enterprise when He said, "After this, nothing they set out to do
will be impossible for them!"[36] The Lord created us in His image,
with incredible creativity and capacity to advance. But our vast
achievements in the column of human progress are dangerous,
unless under the Lordship of Christ.

There's a story of four brothers with special abilities. One could
take a bone and create flesh around it. The next could cover the
flesh with beautiful hair or fur. The third could fashion it into an
upright form. The fourth could give it life. Going into the forest
they found the bone of a lion. Each brother did his part. They
were soon killed and eaten by the lion they had created.

That's the danger of our technologies and advancements unless
we approach all of life with the attitude of Colossians 1:18: *In all
things He must have the preeminence.*

36 New Living Translation

DAVID JEREMIAH

FLEEING AND JOINING

*Let love be without hypocrisy. Abhor what
is evil. Cling to what is good.*

ROMANS 12:9

Christianity is known for its emphasis on love: God so loved the world, love your neighbor, love your enemies, and more. But there are times when we are told to hate—specifically, we are told to hate what is evil while we cling to what is good.

The two words Paul uses in Romans 12:9 for "hate" (or "abhor") and "cling" are instructive. Indeed, they are almost opposites. The word for "abhor" is used only once in the New Testament—here in this verse. "Abhor" is a better translation than "hate" because it carries the idea of revulsion—of shrinking back with disgust and detest. It is an active word, not passive; we are to actively pull away from that which is evil. "Cling," on the other hand, is a word that means to glue something, to join to something else. Once joined, we are to "cling" to—to stay joined to—that which is good. So when it comes to evil, we are to back away in disgust, but we are to glue ourselves to that which is good—and stay joined to it.

Think about your own life—your practices, your thoughts, your entertainment choices, your words. Is there somewhere you need to back away, and somewhere else you need to cling more tightly?

OCTOBER 27

LOVE AND FRAGRANCE

*Thus says the Lord of hosts: "In those days ten men
from every language of the nations shall grasp the
sleeve of a Jewish man, saying, 'Let us go with you,
for we have heard that God is with you.'"*

ZECHARIAH 8:23

Scripture is filled with the working out of redemption: Noah and his family beginning again after the Flood, Abraham being the father of a nation through whom all the world would be blessed, rulers from other nations flocking to Jerusalem during Solomon's reign, and the prophet Zechariah foretelling a day when Gentiles will follow Jews into Jerusalem because they have heard that God is there.

In the New Testament, there are markers of this plan as well: Jews from the Mediterranean nations witness the coming of the Spirit at Pentecost; Jesus sends His apostles into the world to preach the Gospel of reconciliation and redemption. But there are other ways the knowledge of God will be spread. Jesus said His followers' love for one another would be a sign to the world; Paul said Christians will be "the fragrance of Christ among those who are being saved and among those who are perishing" (2 Corinthians 2:14-15).

Ask God to give you the kind of love and fragrance that will signal the presence of God to those who do not yet know Him.

NO SEPARATION

*For I am persuaded that [nothing] shall be able to separate
us from the love of God which is in Christ Jesus our Lord.*

ROMANS 8:38-39

In 1929, the Hungarian writer Frigyes Karinthy used one of his short stories to set forth the idea of "six degrees of separation"— the idea that everyone in the world is linked to everyone else by no more than six "degrees," or contacts or relationships (a friend of a friend, and so forth). In 1929, before the Internet, that was a revolutionary idea. Today, in the age of "friending" on social media, it seems more possible.

The apostle Paul had a more revolutionary idea: There is only ONE single relationship—between us and God. He wrote, "For there is one God and one Mediator between God and men, the Man Christ Jesus" (1 Timothy 2:5). Paul also wrote that there is no separation between Christians and the love of God because God is love and Christ is God. He lists some obstacles we might worry about, dismisses them all, and concludes that "nothing shall be able to separate us from the love of God which is in Christ Jesus our Lord."

If you are connected to God through Christ, you are also connected to His love, for "God is love" (1 John 4:8, 16). If you want to know God's love, come to know God through faith in Jesus Christ.

LET HIM LEAD

*The Lord is my shepherd; I shall not want. He
makes me to lie down in green pastures; He leads
me beside the still waters. He restores my soul.*

PSALM 23:1-3A

When we consider how to stay calm and peaceful in our chaotic world, we might think of David, the psalmist and king of Israel. He didn't write Psalm 23 as an idyllic picture of his life. After all, this was a man who had faced a giant, done battle with the Philistines, dodged the spear and sword of Saul, been betrayed by his own son, and brought serious trouble upon his own head by his own sinful actions. David led anything but an idyllic life.

The key to reconciling Psalm 23 with David's tumultuous life—and ours—is in the words he chooses. To be led into green pastures suggests that some pastures aren't always so green. To reference still waters is to say that sometimes the waters of life are not so still. To describe his soul as being restored implies that his soul *needed* restoring, that it had been in turmoil and needed quieting. Every shepherd wants the best for his sheep, but the best isn't always available. But when life is challenging, our Shepherd can be counted on to lead us into a place and time of restoration and healing.

If you are in need of such refreshment today, let your first thought be to seek it from the Good Shepherd. He knows what you need (John 10:14).

LIVING LIKE JESUS

. . . how God anointed Jesus of Nazareth with the Holy Spirit and with power, who went about doing good and healing all who were oppressed by the devil, for God was with Him.

ACTS 10:38

Sometime this week you will likely be asked, "How was your day?" or "What did you do today?" The answers to those questions range from A to Z; our lives are filled with busyness and activity leading often to a collapse at the end of the day.

Have you considered what Jesus did all day while on earth? The closest description we have is found in Acts 10:38: He went about "doing good" and freeing those who were oppressed by the devil. That is, He preached and demonstrated the reality of the kingdom of God (Mark 1:14-15; Luke 8:1). He went about bringing light into a spiritually dark world (John 1:5-9). He went about destroying the works of the devil (1 John 3:8). When we are asked to describe our day, are we able to describe it in similar terms? We are not called to work miracles and confront the devil in the same ways Jesus did, but we are called to let our light so shine before men that they might know the reality of God (Matthew 5:14-16). We are called to manifest the presence and power of the kingdom of God as we share the Gospel in word and deed.

— Ask God to help you manifest the kingdom of God in whatever you do and say today.

THE GREATEST VIRTUE

*He who covers a transgression seeks love, but he
who repeats a matter separates friends.*

PROVERBS 17:9

We occasionally learn of a crime that someone had concealed years before. Perhaps the guilty party hid it, or perhaps someone was trying to protect another person. Regardless of the reason, such acts of "covering a transgression" are not what Solomon had in mind in Proverbs 17:9.

When he talks about covering a transgression, he is referring to a wrong done to you personally (or to another). Instead of telling others about the wrong, you choose to cover it rather than reveal it to those who have no need to know. Telling others is likely to "separate friends." What is the motivation for covering a transgression? The pursuit of love, Solomon says. He put it this way in Proverbs 10:12: "Love covers all sins." As Paul wrote in 1 Corinthians 13:13, "the greatest of [all virtues] is love." If we suffer a wrong and want to pursue the highest virtue in response, we should do whatever will advance love—which includes forgiveness, reconciliation, mercy, and not damaging the reputation of the offender.

If you have been offended or wounded by another, let love be the guide for your response. Love others as Christ has loved you (Ephesians 4:32).

DAVID JEREMIAH

NOVEMBER

TEN WORDS

*The discretion of a man makes him slow to anger,
and his glory is to overlook a transgression.*

PROVERBS 19:11

Anger is a strange emotion that's sometimes appropriate but more often self-destructive. The dictionary defines it as a strong feeling of displeasure and belligerence aroused by a wrong. But sometimes it's the anger itself that's wrong, and one angry word or deed can easily damage the people or things we love.

People have been working on anger management from the beginning of time. Thomas Jefferson is reported to have advised his readers to count to ten when angry, and when very angry to one hundred. Mark Twain said, "When angry, count four; when very angry, swear." Mrs. Fulton Oursler, wife of the famed writer, said she used to count to ten when becoming provoked. But then she realized there was more power in repeating the first ten words of the Lord's Prayer: "Our Father which art in heaven, Hallowed be Thy name."

Well, here are ten more words that will help you when angry. Memorize them, take them seriously, post them on the bulletin board of your mind, and let them become a rule for your life: *The discretion of a man makes him slow to anger.*

A HAPPY COUNTENANCE

Be of good cheer. Rise, He is calling you.

MARK 10:49

Our English word *cheer* comes from a Latin word, *cara*, meaning *face* or *head*. By the late fourteenth century, the word was coming to refer to a positive mood as reflected on the face. Cheerfulness is joy showing up on the face. That's biblical, for Proverbs 15:13 says, "A merry heart makes a cheerful countenance."

Jesus is the one who brings cheerfulness into our hearts and onto our faces. In Matthew 9:2, He told the paralytic who had been lowered from the roof: "Son, be of good cheer; your sins are forgiven." In Matthew 9:22, He said to the woman with the issue of blood: "Be of good cheer, daughter; your faith has made you well." When the disciples were in the storm, Jesus walked across the water to them, saying, "Be of good cheer! It is I; do not be afraid" (Matthew 14:27). In the Upper Room He told His disciples, "Be of good cheer, I have overcome the world" (John 16:33).

Let *cheer* be your word for the day from the Bible; work on a happy countenance. It's the best cosmetic available.

Take It by Faith

I am the vine, you are the branches. He who abides in Me, and I in him, bears much fruit; for without Me you can do nothing.

John 15:5

The world's largest furniture retailer, a company founded in Sweden, is known for selling furniture that has to be assembled by the purchaser. The instruction books that accompany their products are precise—woe to any who ignore the steps or skip ahead. Having to start over is all it takes to learn: Trust the instructions; take it by faith even if you think you can do it yourself.

That principle applies to the spiritual life as well. In John 15:5 Jesus makes an amazing statement: "Without Me you can do nothing." The image of the vine and branches lends support—we know a branch can't bear fruit without staying connected to the vine. But how far should we take Jesus' agricultural analogy? Is it really true that we can do nothing in life apart from Him? Conversely, are you prepared to doubt what Jesus has said? The problem is, once we live or act apart from Christ, the deed is done. We will never know how it might have been different had we relied on, and remained connected to, Him in all things.

Even though it looks like you can live your life apart from Christ, it is better to take Jesus' words by faith and follow His instructions. There are no do-overs; once done, life is done.

NOVEMBER 4

ALL YOUR HEART

Trust in the LORD, and do good; dwell in the land, and feed on His faithfulness. Delight yourself also in the LORD, and He shall give you the desires of your heart.

PSALM 37:3-4

There are times in life when we can lean on our own understanding to solve a problem. For example, we can figure out a new digital device by experimenting, looking online, and reading the owner's manual.

But there are also plenty of times when our reasoning, intelligence, diligence, and understanding are simply not adequate. For example, why has our child been diagnosed with a life-threatening illness? Why have I been released from a job I enjoyed and in which I felt secure? Why has a family member been unwilling to commit her life to Christ after years of prayer and witnessing? There is no manual that explains the answers to these dilemmas—not even the Bible. But it is not without instruction and guidance. The Bible says to "trust in the Lord with all your heart." When human understanding is not enough, it is time to commit the problem to God: "Lord, I have done everything I know to do. I commit this matter into Your hands. I trust You with all my heart. I know You care about this situation, so I trust You to work above and beyond my abilities" (Ephesians 3:20).

If you are in a situation that is beyond your ability today, trust in the Lord with all your heart—He will make your path straight (Proverbs 3:6).

REMEMBER WHEN YOU PRAY

But without faith it is impossible to please Him, for he
who comes to God must believe that He is, and that
He is a rewarder of those who diligently seek Him.

HEBREWS 11:6

"Honey, would you have time after work to pick up the dry cleaning on your way home?"

"Bob, are you heading to the break room? Could you bring me a bottled water on your way back?"

We make many requests of others during the day, most of which we already know the answers to. We hardly think about asking for others' help. In fact, faith rarely enters the equation, and we don't make our requests "diligently."

But does that casual approach influence the way we seek God and ask for His help? Most of the time, what we are asking from God is not something we automatically know the answer to. Such requests are made as a matter of trust in Him and His will. For that reason, the writer to the Hebrews says we must ask in faith. We must seek God believing He is the God of the Bible. We must seek Him diligently—that is, with strong faith. That faith is demonstrated by our coming "boldly to the throne of grace" (Hebrews 4:16). Not boldly as in arrogantly, but boldly as in expectantly; boldly as in full of faith in God and His goodness.

Before you pray today, remember who God is; remember to pray in faith, believing; remember to pray diligently.

BEING IMMOVABLE

*Those who trust in the Lord are like Mount Zion,
which cannot be moved, but abides forever.*

PSALM 125:1

Mount Zion ("citadel") was one of the hills upon which Jerusalem was built. The Jebusites who originally occupied that hill swore to David that it was impregnable, that David's men would not be able to conquer it. But David did conquer it and established his throne upon it and the slightly higher hill to the north, Mount Moriah, where Solomon eventually built the temple.

Later in Israel's monarchy we find the psalmist saying the same thing about Mount Zion that the Jebusites said, that it would never be shaken or conquered. The permanence of Mount Zion became an image of the faithful Israelite who trusts in God: "Those who trust in the Lord are like Mount Zion." It wasn't so much that Mount Zion itself might never be shaken (see Zechariah 14:4), but that the God whose kingdom is established on Mount Zion can never be shaken. It is the presence of God that makes the image of Zion an enduring one.

It is the presence of God in our life that makes us as strong as Mount Zion, that makes us unshakable in the face of trouble or attack. If the ground around you is trembling, if spiritual enemies are on the horizon, trust in the Lord and you will not be moved.

THE LULL BEFORE THE STORM

And all these, having obtained a good testimony
through faith, did not receive the promise, God
having provided something better for us, that they
should not be made perfect apart from us.

HEBREWS 11:39-40

Ramon Lull was born in 1232 into a wealthy family on an island off the coast of Spain. His early life was spent in debauchery, but during his thirties Lull had a powerful and life-changing dream. He saw the Savior hanging on the cross with blood trickling from His hands, feet, and brow. As a result of that dream, Lull gave his life to Christ and devoted himself to the ministry of reaching Muslims with the Gospel. He continued his missionary work until he was 82, when he was beaten to death with sticks and stones by an angry Islamic crowd. Lull paved the way for all subsequent ministries to the Muslims.

Today millions of Christian believers are suffering a storm of persecution in Muslim lands, yet the Gospel presses on to the ends of the earth. Until Christ returns, God will raise up a band of faithful followers in every generation. Become a student of Christian history and learn the story of the expansion of the Gospel. Read missionary biographies. Be among those inflamed with the global adventure of missions. Let's carry the torch of God's love to the ends of the earth.

RESONANCE

Though I speak with the tongues of men and of angels, but have not love, I have become sounding brass or a clanging cymbal.

1 CORINTHIANS 13:1

Actor Richard Burton was famous for his melodious baritone voice; and when we hear someone like that, we sometimes wonder how such a voice could have been used for the kingdom, had it been dedicated to God. How about you? Do you wish your gifts were greater? Do you envy someone whose natural talents seem stronger than yours?

Don't worry about it. You could have the voice of Richard Burton, the vocabulary of Winston Churchill, the winsomeness of Ronald Reagan, the cadence of Martin Luther King, the wit of Charles Spurgeon, the wisdom of Socrates, and the dramatics of Sophocles all rolled up into one. But a single drop of spiritual power is greater than all. Zechariah 4:6 says, "Not by might nor by power, but by My Spirit."

Paul said, "My speech and my preaching were not with persuasive words of human wisdom, but in demonstration of the Spirit and of power" (1 Corinthians 2:4). The greatest orations are worthless compared to a stammering Spirit-filled soul. Only Jesus Christ speaking through us by His Spirit can yield effective results for the kingdom. Everything else is a clanging cymbal.

BOTH GOD AND MAN

Jesus Christ our Lord, who was born of the seed of David according to the flesh, and declared to be the Son of God with power according to the Spirit of holiness.

ROMANS 1:3-4

If someone asks you to describe Jesus, you can accurately sum Him up in four words: *Both God and Man.* The golden-mouthed preacher of Constantinople, Chrysostom, put it this way: "I do not think of Christ as God alone, or man alone, but both together. For I know He was hungry, and I know that with five loaves He fed 5,000. I know He was thirsty, and I know that He turned the water into wine. I know He was carried in a ship, and I know that He walked on the sea. I know that He died, and I know that He raised the dead. I know that He was set before Pilate, and I know that He sits with the Father on His throne. I know that He was worshipped by angels, and I know that He was stoned by the Jews. And truly some of these I ascribe to the human, and others to the divine nature. For by reason of this He is said to have been both God and man."

What a Savior!

Praise Him today as the Word made flesh (John 1:14).

JESUS IN ME

*Be of the same mind toward one another. Do not
set your mind on high things, but associate with the
humble. Do not be wise in your own opinion.*

ROMANS 12:16

The apostle Paul never lived with Christ, learning from Him
during His earthly life. Paul's personal knowledge of Jesus
was based on visions (Acts 9:1, 23:11; 2 Corinthians 12:1-4) and
what he was told by the other apostles. And yet Paul's knowledge
of Christ was profound—it infiltrated what he wrote to the
early churches.

Paul's simple words to the Roman church in Romans 12:16—be
like-minded, not high-minded; associate with the poor and humble;
don't be conceited or wise in your own eyes—parallel the words
he used to describe Jesus in Philippians 2:5-11. After repeating
some of the same admonitions to the Philippians as he wrote to
the Romans, Paul says, in short, "be like Jesus." Jesus was humble,
leaving heaven to associate with poor sinners; He wasn't conceited
or wise in His own eyes; He considered our needs more important
than His own; He humbled Himself before the will of God.

Our calling as Christians is not so much to *imitate* Christ as to
allow the *indwelling* Christ to live His life through us (Galatians
2:20, 5:22-23). Yield yourself today to the Holy Spirit who is *in*
you to manifest Christ *through* you (Romans 8:14).

YOUR VERY BEST

*Let us therefore be diligent to enter that rest, lest anyone
fall according to the same example of disobedience.*

HEBREWS 4:11

Christians can sometimes be confused about the idea of
"work" in a religion that is based on "grace." Paul wrote
that we are saved by grace, not by works (Ephesians 2:8-9). Yet
there is work—diligent work—to be done by those who are saved
(Ephesians 2:10). And the New Testament writers spare no words
in saying the Christian life requires hard, diligent work—our very
best efforts for the sake of Christ and His kingdom.

The New Testament word "be diligent" (*spoudazo*) means to
make haste, to make every effort, to be eager, to do your very best.
And that is the attitude and approach we are to have in our service
for Christ. We are not saved by doing our best, but we express our
gratitude for our salvation by being diligent in our service. Think
of the apostles. We know more of Paul's labors than anyone else's,
but none of them could be accused of being lazy or careless.

How about your service for Christ? How would those around
you describe your approach? Diligent, giving your very best,
eager, making haste—or not? Make today a day of diligence for
the Lord, giving your best to Him who gave His all for you.

SPROUTING FAITH

*Most assuredly, I say to you, unless a grain of
wheat falls into the ground and dies, it remains
alone; but if it dies, it produces much grain.*

JOHN 12:24

Every gardener knows there are many places in which a seed will not sprout, the ultimate example being in the seed packet itself. Seeds are shipped in dry packets, and stored in dry jars and containers, because they will lie dormant and not sprout. In general, seeds need two things to sprout: warmth and moisture, both of which are provided by the earth.

A single seed in a packet or jar will remain as is—a single seed. But when that seed is dropped into the ground and dies— an image of death and burial—it has the potential for springing up, bearing fruit, and producing hundreds more seeds. This is a principle throughout nature, and Jesus applied it to the spiritual life as well. He spoke of His own coming death and resurrection to new life in these terms and applied the principle to all who would follow Him. We can't live for ourselves and live for Christ at the same time. We must "die daily," as Paul put it, by being a "living sacrifice" unto God (Romans 12:1; 1 Corinthians 1:31).

Commit yourself afresh today to live as a sacrifice to God in order to bring forth new life for Christ. Be willing to fall into the soil of faith in order to be raised to new life through the Spirit.

Actions Still Matter

Lord, who may abide in Your tabernacle?
Who may dwell in Your holy hill?

Psalm 15:1

Psalm 15:1 and other similar Old Testament verses could be interpreted as asking, "Who can be saved?" The reference to the tabernacle and God's "holy hill" (Mount Zion, or Jerusalem) helps us interpret the verse more correctly: "Lord, what must I do to merit Your approval and blessing?" Under the Old Covenant, adherence to the law was the measure—and the psalmist David lists ten characteristics of the person qualified to stand before God.

Walk blamelessly, act righteously, speak the truth, do not slander others, do no harm to a neighbor, don't speak poorly of others, detest wickedness, honor those who fear the Lord, keep your word, lend money without interest, and accept no bribes (Psalm 15:2-5a). How do we interpret these requirements in the New Testament? Jesus boiled all the law and prophets down to two: Love God and love your neighbor (Matthew 22:37-40), remembering that by the works of the law "no flesh shall be justified" (Galatians 2:16). In the New Testament, keeping God's commands is not the basis of salvation but the fruit of it.

With an emphasis on grace, it is easy to forget that our behavior and actions do matter in God's sight. Live consciously of that truth today.

David Jeremiah

Be Patient

*And let us not grow weary while doing good, for in
due season we shall reap if we do not lose heart.*

Galatians 6:9

A novice gardener may plant a number of different kinds of seeds in the garden and expect them all to germinate at the same time. Not so. Lettuce, sweet corn, and cucumbers will sprout in about three days; tomatoes, peppers, and celery take about a week. But you'll wait two weeks for parsley and parsnips to sprout. And they all bear fruit at different times as well. The secret is patience—to let nature take its course.

Paul used the "harvest law" as both a warning and an encouragement in Galatians 6:7-9. The warning is, "Do not be deceived . . . whatever a man sows, that he will also reap" (verse 7). And the encouragement is, "Let us not grow weary while doing good, for in due season we shall reap if we do not lose heart" (verse 9). Think of every thought, word, and deed in life as a seed that will produce a harvest of some kind. Therefore, it behooves us to sow (think, speak, act) wisely. When we sow righteously but see no immediate results, it is easy to think, "What's the point?" But Paul's admonition is to not "grow weary"; the harvest will come in due time.

If you are investing your very best for the kingdom of God, do not grow weary. Trust God that the seeds you are sowing will bear a harvest at the right time.

Into Your Hands

*Into Your hand I commit my spirit; You have
redeemed me, O Lord God of truth.*

Psalm 31:5

Martin Luther spent February 17, 1546, ministering in Eisleben, Germany. That evening he suffered chest pains. Doctors applied hot clothes to the area, and Luther fell asleep on a couch. He awoke at 10 and went to his bed. At 2 a.m., he suffered another attack and began praying, "Father, into Thy hands I commend myself… O my heavenly Father, one God, and Father of our Lord Jesus Christ, Thou God of all comfort, I thank Thee that Thou hast given for me Thy dear Son Jesus Christ, in whom I believe, who I have preached and confessed, loved and praised…. Let me commend my little soul to Thee."

A friend asked him, "Reverend Father, are you willing to die in the name of Christ and the doctrine which you have preached?" Luther replied: "Yes!" A few minutes later he was in heaven.

We can claim Psalm 31:5 every day, for our God is able to guide us with His counsel and afterward take us to glory (Psalm 73:24). Whatever the future holds, commit yourself to the Lord and commend your life into His hands.

EVERYWHERE IN BETWEEN

*You shall teach them diligently to your children, and shall
talk of them when you sit in your house, when you walk
by the way, when you lie down, and when you rise up.*

DEUTERONOMY 6:7

Someone coined a phrase to describe how the early church
in Jerusalem went about spreading the Gospel. It was called
"gossiping the Gospel"—integrating the Gospel into everyday
conversation. There were no tracts, books, or Bibles to hand
out. Rather, witnessing was a matter of word of mouth wherever
people went.

That idea is found in Deuteronomy 6:4-9 where Moses instructs
parents on how to pass on the requirements of the covenant, the
details of God's law, to their children. He said to talk to the children
in the house and in the street, when you're going to bed and
when you rise up—and everywhere in between. It was a common
Hebrew way of expressing the idea of totality—the two ends of
the spectrum included everything in between. But it doesn't mean
simply to teach children the contents of the covenant. It meant to
illustrate how the covenant applied to daily life—in the home, in
the street, in the market, and "everywhere in between."

How often in a day do you grasp the opportunity to integrate
God's truth into your daily conversations—especially with those
who are not believers?

JESUS ON PRAYER

*If you then, being evil, know how to give good gifts
to your children, how much more will your heavenly
Father give the Holy Spirit to those who ask Him!*

LUKE 11:13

It is part of the human condition to need reminding. We make notes, set our smartphones to beep at us, mark our calendars, and tell friends, "Don't let me forget to . . . ." That human condition answers an important question: "Why did Jesus talk so much about prayer?" The answer is obvious to honest persons: We need to be reminded that God welcomes our prayers.

Luke did his Gospel readers a favor by grouping some of Jesus' teachings on prayer together in Luke 11:1-13. This short section serves as a powerful reminder that we should not fail to pray. There are five parts: a notice of Jesus at prayer (verse 1), the prayer Jesus taught His disciples (verses 2-4), an illustration of the need for persistence in prayer (verses 5-8), a promise that prayers will be answered (verses 9-10), and a summary illustration about the reasonableness of expecting God to answer our prayers (verses 11-13). We have an example (Jesus), a model prayer, a reminder not to give up, a promise, and an appeal to reason.

If you find your prayer life flagging, take time to meditate on Jesus' teaching about prayer. And let His teaching have its intended result: pray (1 Thessalonians 5:17)!

WISDOM AND HOPE

*And in the days of these kings the God of heaven
will set up a kingdom which shall never be
destroyed . . . it shall break in pieces and consume
all these kingdoms, and it shall stand forever.*

DANIEL 2:44

One of the mysteries of the New Testament is that we know so little about Jesus' youth and education. We have one glimpse of a pre-teen Jesus astounding religious scholars with His knowledge and wisdom in the temple at age 12 (Luke 2:47). He gained wisdom the same way we can—by pursuing it through God and His Word (Proverbs 2:1-10).

For example, when Jesus came preaching "the gospel of the kingdom" (Matthew 4:23; 9:35), He was using language set forth by Daniel the prophet who recognized this coming kingdom of God in the dream of Nebuchadnezzar, king of Babylon (Daniel 2). Through a pagan king, God revealed that His kingdom would one day replace all earthly kingdoms and "stand forever" (Daniel 2:44). Jesus came announcing that kingdom, taught His disciples to pray for its arrival (Matthew 6:10), and said the promise of its coming would be preached to all the world (Matthew 24:14) before it would be finally established.

There are two lessons: First, study God's Word as diligently as Jesus did to gain wisdom and understanding. Second, don't despair at the state of the world; the kingdom of God is coming.

NOVEMBER 19

BE AWARE OF ANGELS

Are they not all ministering spirits sent forth to minister for those who will inherit salvation?

HEBREWS 1:14

The most recognizable painting of Jesus as the Good Shepherd was painted by the nineteenth century German artist Bernhard Plockhorst. A lesser known painting of his, but equally stunning, is called "Guardian Angel." It shows two small children picking flowers by the edge of a cliff; standing protectively behind them is an angel, guarding their safety.

The Bible doesn't use the term "guardian angel," but the notion is not entirely unbiblical. Hebrews 1:14 says clearly that angels are sent to minister to the people of God. After enduring 40 days of temptations in the wilderness, after the devil had departed, "angels came and ministered to [Jesus]" (Matthew 4:11). Then, near the end of His life, "an angel appeared to [Jesus] from heaven, strengthening Him" in the Garden of Gethsemane (Luke 22:43). And they were there at His birth (Luke 2:15), resurrection (John 20:12), and ascension (Acts 1:10). Angels are mentioned 52 times in the four Gospels, often by Jesus Himself.

There is a lesson for all Christians in the words of Hebrews 13:2: Be hospitable to strangers—you may be "entertaining angels." And they may be there to minister to you.

JUST BELIEVE

And [Abraham] believed in the Lord, and He
accounted it to him for righteousness.

GENESIS 15:6

If you had to describe the essence of what it means to be in a trusting relationship with God or another person, what one word would you choose? Perhaps "belief" would qualify. After all, it was a lack of belief that caused humanity to be separated from God in the beginning. If Adam and Eve had believed God's words about what they could and couldn't eat in the Garden of Eden, the arc of history would have been entirely different.

Therefore, it is significant that Moses used the word "belief" to describe Abraham's response to God's promises about his future descendants and their destiny as the people of God. Adam didn't believe God and he fell into unrighteousness; Abraham did believe God and God "accounted it to him for righteousness." Adam was the father of all who are born in unbelief (Romans 5:2), but Abraham was "the father of all those who believe" (Romans 4:11).

Our whole relationship with God can be distilled down to belief. Do we believe Him sin and our need for salvation? Do we believe Him about His love and forgiveness? Do we believe His moral and ethical precepts as found in Scripture? Do we believe Him enough to do His will instead of our own?

Who Is He?

Jesus said to him, "Have I been with you so long, and yet you have not known Me, Philip? He who has seen Me has seen the Father; so how can you say, 'Show us the Father'?"

JOHN 14:9

About 31.5 billion of the earth's people are categorized as "Christian" based on culture or family tradition, church attendance, or self-identification. But there is no way to know exactly how many of those people believe Jesus Christ is God in the flesh who came to earth with the authority to remove man's sins. Some people believe Jesus was a good man, a teacher sent from God, or an example to follow—but not that He was God.

The great apologist C. S. Lewis had something to say about Jesus being just a good man but not God: "A man who was merely a man and said the sort of things Jesus said would not be a great moral teacher. He would either be a lunatic—on a level with the man who says he is a poached egg—or else He would be the Devil of Hell. You must make your choice. Either this man was, and is, the Son of God: or else a madman or something worse. . . . let us not come with any patronizing nonsense about His being a great human teacher. He has not left that open to us."[37]

To take deity away from Jesus is to take the essence away from Christianity.

---

37 C. S. Lewis, *Mere Christianity* (New York: Simon & Schuster, 1952), 56.

DAVID JEREMIAH

Back to Basics

But [Job] said to [his wife], "You speak as one of the foolish women speaks. Shall we indeed accept good from God, and shall we not accept adversity?" In all this Job did not sin with his lips.

Job 2:10

Football coaches are often caught on video telling their players, "Do the basics! Block, tackle! Don't be creative—play basic football!" There is a need to remember the basics in the spiritual life as well—especially in the midst of difficult times.

One of the advantages of reading the Old Testament is we find basic truth about God in short bites. The New Testament expansion of these truths is important, of course. But in the Old Testament we often find the basics. Take Job's response to his devastating trials, for example. When his wife, in a moment of despair, encouraged Job to give up his loyalty to God in light of their troubles, Job refused by asking a basic question: Is it reasonable to accept the blessings God sends but not accept the trials He allows? There is an element of basic logic in Job's question. Today, we might say, "Hey—you can't pick and choose. Either you trust God for the good *and* the bad or you don't trust Him at all."

Paul expands on this theme in Romans 8:28-39, which we should know by heart. But for this important tenet, Job's basic question requires our honest answer.

PREREQUISITE FOR PRAYER

*But let him ask in faith, with no doubting, for he who doubts
is like a wave of the sea driven and tossed by the wind.*

JAMES 1:6

Everyone who goes through college, even high school, understands the meaning of prerequisites. There are some courses that must be taken before signing up for others: Algebra I before Algebra II, French I before Conversational French, basic computer programming before program design.

There are also prerequisites in the spiritual life—in prayer, for example. One of the most famous verses in the New Testament is James 1:5 about asking God for wisdom when going through trials. The prerequisite is found in verse 6: "But when you ask, you must believe and not doubt" (NIV). There is the prerequisite: faith. It is what Hebrews 11:6 calls for—faith that God rewards those who diligently seek Him. If faith is indeed a prerequisite for prayer, that means stopping before we pray to examine our faith. Do I believe the promise of James 1:5? Am I prepared to trust God for His answer? Do I believe God loves me as His child?

Without such faith, James says, we will be "driven and tossed" like a wave that is driven by the wind. Does God love me? Will He answer me? Settle the matter of faith before you pray, then pray believing—even if your prayer is for faith itself (Mark 9:24).

Today Is Gratitude Day

Thanks be to God for His indescribable gift!

2 Corinthians 9:15

We often say, "God bless you!" to others without thinking about what it actually means. When God blesses us, He speaks a word of care or favor over us (Psalm 29:11). And when we bless God, we do the same—we speak a good word about God's many attributes that benefit (bless) us (Psalm 26:12). So when the psalmist says, "I will bless the Lord [at all times]," he is saying, "I will continually speak of God's goodness, kindness, generosity, and other traits." That is, I will continually manifest an attitude of gratitude toward God for who He is and what He has done.

Do you see this background of blessing in Paul's words, "In everything give thanks" (1 Thessalonians 5:18)? Not just on Thanksgiving Day, but on every day, we should give thanks to God and bless His holy name for His many gifts of grace to us. Even on challenging days, we can be grateful for the fact that God is with us, causing all things to work together for good for those who love Him (Romans 8:28).

Let today be a day of thanksgiving for sure. But let every day be one in which you live with an attitude of gratitude toward Him.

SERVERS

The natives showed us unusual kindness....

ACTS 28:2

Ask almost any waiter, waitress, or server and they'll tell you: They dread the Sunday after-church crowd. Perhaps it's undeserved, but many churchgoers have the reputation of being demanding and stingy. Somehow, we have gotten a bad name in the restaurant community, at least on Sundays.

It behooves us to be kind to those who serve us. One of the ways we express our thanksgiving to God is by treating others with gratitude and kindness. Proverbs 19:22 says, "What is desired in a man is kindness."

Those who serve us—waiters, clerks, tellers, flight attendants, bellhops and skycaps, ushers, babysitters, valets, supermarket baggers, parking attendants, shuttle drivers, and so forth—often work long hours and receive minimal pay. Yet they bear the brunt of complaints. They often have to put up with arrogant, unkind, irritable clients.

Go out of your way to smile at the guy behind the counter. Be pleasant to the woman on the phone. Tip when appropriate. Be a pleasure to serve. Show unusual kindness. A dash of gratitude can brighten the skies of others and exemplify Christ to those who don't know Him, and encourage those who do!

DAVID JEREMIAH

Just Ask

*You lust and do not have. You murder and covet
and cannot obtain. You fight and war. Yet you
do not have because you do not ask.*

James 4:2

You spend hours tinkering with a plumbing fixture trying to figure out how to make a repair. Finally, you take a picture of the broken fixture with your smartphone, go to the hardware store, show it to the clerk, and hear this: "No problem—you just need to replace that with one of these." In other words, all you had to do was ask.

We've all had that experience. After investing hours or days searching for a solution to a problem, we finally discover that an expert could have helped us quickly and easily if we had only asked. James reprimanded his readers for using carnal means to accomplish their goals instead of turning to God first. In fact, it's likely that our modern saying, "All you have to do is ask," came from James' words: "You do not have because you do not ask." Instead of seeing God as our first choice, we often make Him our last resort. And we wonder why we don't have the comfort, guidance, or provision we so desperately need and seek.

If you have a need today, make God your first choice. He is a Father who loves to meet His children's needs—if they will just ask.

INFINITE FORGIVENESS

*In Him we have redemption through His blood, the
forgiveness of sins, according to the riches of His grace.*

EPHESIANS 1:7

Most of us would call this symbol—∞—a figure "8" turned
sideways, but math majors know it as the symbol for infinity.
Our English word "infinite" comes from the Latin *infinitus*, a
combination of *in* (not) and *finitus* (finished). Therefore, *infinity*
means "not finished" or never-ending.

Infinity isn't easy to grasp, but it is biblical. For instance,
Psalm 147:5 says, "Great is our Lord and mighty in power; His
understanding is infinite"—meaning His understanding is
limitless. The infinite grace of God is able to reach far beyond what
we ask or think in any situation. There are limits to our capacity
to reason or understand, and God's thoughts and ways are far
above our understanding. Consider the matter of forgiveness. If
we think there are limits to God's forgiveness of our sins, we need
to remember that God is able to exceed our limits in terms of
what we ask or think. The psalmist made this heartfelt cry: "If
You, Lord, should mark iniquities, O Lord, who could stand? But
there is forgiveness with You" (Psalm 130:3-4).

If you despair of asking God to forgive you "yet again" for your
sins, remember that His understanding—and His forgiveness—
are infinite.

Amazing!

When Jesus heard these things, He marveled at him, and turned around and said to the crowd that followed Him, "I say to you, I have not found such great faith, not even in Israel!"

Luke 7:9

These days it is easy to be amazed. With access to videos from all over the world via the Internet, we see things we have never seen before in all realms of life: science, sports, nature, even dogs riding skateboards and surfboards. "Wow, that's amazing!" has become a cliché—but only because it's most often true. We do live in an amazing world.

What do you think amazed Jesus? While there are many instances in the four Gospels of people being amazed at Jesus' words and works, there are only two times when we read of Jesus being amazed at something (or "marveling" at something). Both times, He was amazed at faith—once when He found it where He least expected it (Luke 7:9) and once where He didn't find it when He most expected it (Mark 6:6). Faith, or its absence, is apparently a subject of amazement to Jesus. He works in its presence (Luke 7) and doesn't work in its absence (Mark 6).

If you want to amaze Jesus and commend yourself to Him, pray with great faith. After all, without faith, it is impossible to please God (Hebrews 11:6).

BELIEVING IS SEEING

*Now faith is the substance of things hoped
for, the evidence of things not seen.*

HEBREWS 11:1

Before the pioneering work of British surgeon Joseph Lister, it was thought that "bad (infected) air" was the cause of disease spreading in hospitals. Surgeons routinely operated without sterile hands or instruments. Lister discovered that carbolic acid was an effective disinfectant for hands, wounds, and surgical instruments. His work increased the understanding of the role of germs in spreading and preventing disease.

Germs couldn't be seen, but their effects could be. Survival of patients was "the evidence of things not seen" (Hebrews 11:1). And that is what faith is. We cannot apprehend faith with our senses, but we can definitely see its evidence. We see the world that exists and believe God created it (Hebrews 11:3). We can see the changes in our lives and believe the power of God is responsible (John 9:25). We pray and believe God answers our prayers (James 1:6). Like Abraham, we trust God's words and believe we are made righteous in His sight (Genesis 15:6).

Don't let faith be a stumbling block. Faith is ultimately dependent on the object of faith—in our case, God and His words. Place your faith in the God you cannot see—believing is seeing.

FEELING VERSUS DOING

Love suffers long and is kind; love does not envy;
love does not parade itself, is not puffed up.

1 CORINTHIANS 13:4

It could be debated whether Elizabeth Barrett Browning answered the important question posed by the title of her famous poem: "How Do I Love Thee? (Sonnet 43)." The answers she gives are rather abstract, based more on feelings than actions: as far as the soul can reach, freely, purely, with passion, with the breath, smiles, and tears of life. These are beautiful thoughts, no doubt, but harder to measure than Paul's description of love in 1 Corinthians 13.

If Paul were to answer Ms. Browning's question, he might say, "I love you by being patient, being kind, by not being envious, self-promoting, or proud. I love you by being courteous, by meeting your needs ahead of my own, by not being easily provoked, by thinking the best of you. I love you by being truthful, long-suffering, positive, and hopeful" (see 1 Corinthians 13:4-7). Poetry often lifts us to the heights of feeling while practicality lowers us to the reality of doing. Both are important, but when we say "I love you," actions always speak louder than words.

God loved by giving sacrificially (John 3:16)—it's a good place for us to begin as well.

DECEMBER

FORGIVE AND FORGET

And forgive us our debts, as we forgive our debtors.

MATTHEW 6:12

Quick—without thinking: What was your family's telephone number when you were eight years old? How many of your first-grade classmates' names can you recite? Instead, what is your current phone number? What are the names of your family members? Obviously, the information we use and repeat consistently is the information we remember. We forget what we don't recall on a regular basis.

The same goes for those who have sinned against us, whose sins we have forgiven but have a hard time forgetting. You can't recall every wrong you have experienced in life because you don't think about or talk about them every day. And the same goes for those you do remember. If you have forgiven someone for their sin, there is no reason at all to continue to dwell on it. Dwelling on a sin daily means you'll never forget it and you'll never move on. We are to forgive others as God has forgiven us (Ephesians 4:32). The more we forget *about* something, the sooner we will forget it altogether.

First, forgive. Second, forget by choosing not to dwell on that which is forgiven and in the past. We have no right to keep in front of us what God has put behind Him.

TURN THE CARAVAN AROUND!

"In returning and rest you shall be saved; in quietness and confidence shall be your strength." But you would not.

ISAIAH 30:15

In Isaiah 30, the king of Judah sent a caravan of diplomats to Egypt to persuade Pharaoh's army to join a defense pact against the Assyrians. There was no prayer about the matter, no trusting in the Lord, nothing but a panicked delegation going down to Egypt. The prophet Isaiah used the occasion to preach a sermon, advising the caravan to turn around. "In returning and rest you shall be saved," he said. "In quietness and confidence shall be your strength."

But the people would have none of it.

The Lord wants our trust. How harmful when we fail to pray or to rely on Him. How sad to see panicked believers running to Egypt when the Lord Himself can fight on our behalf. He can meet the need. He can enable us to be more than conquerors through Jesus Christ our Lord.

Do you need to turn the caravan around? Maybe it's time to reverse course and seek the guidance and provision of the Lord.

In returning and rest you shall be saved; in quietness and confidence shall be your strength.

COLD FEET

Asa became diseased in his feet, and his malady was severe; yet in his disease he did not seek the LORD.

2 CHRONICLES 16:12

The story of King Asa occupies three chapters in 2 Chronicles. In chapter 14, we see him trusting the Lord, instituting revival, and rejoicing in victory. In chapter 15, he hears and heeds the prophetic message. But several years pass, and by chapter 16 Asa wants nothing to do with the Lord. His diseased feet couldn't find the right path. Somehow he had lost the fire and faith of his earlier walk with God.

Why? Perhaps he stopped reading his Scriptures. Maybe his life became too busy for prayer. He might have allowed resentments to fester in his heart. Perhaps he fell into sin and his conscience was gradually dulled.

Whatever happened, Asa serves as a warning to us. We must keep close to the Lord every day, being quick to confess and turn from all known sin. Our hearts should break when we do wrong, knowing it was our sins that nailed Jesus to the cross. We should keep a tender heart, one that is growing warmer, not colder. Ask God today for a tender conscience and a closer walk with Him.

ANGRY BIRDS

*...for the wrath of man does not produce
the righteousness of God.*

JAMES 1:20

Students at New Mexico State University had trouble walking to class last fall after hawks built nests in trees by the gym. The mother hawks considered pedestrians threats to their hatchlings, and several students sustained injuries from the dive-bombing birds. One person was struck hard enough to suffer post-concussion symptoms that included dizziness and nausea.

If there's anything worse than an unexpected encounter with an angry hawk, it's having a face-off with an angry person. We never know when we'll encounter an irritable or irate driver, customer, coworker, boss, or stranger. The air nowadays is filled with angry birds. Sometimes they even nest under our roofs. And sometimes the angriest bird is the one in the mirror.

But consider this. Our attitude toward others reveals our genuine attitude toward God. When someone is angry, it's often symptomatic of spiritual need. When we're out of sorts, it's a reflection of our spiritual health. In our approach to others today and in our responses, let's be as gentle as possible. Be patient. Angry reactions do not bring about the righteous results God desires.

THAT ABOUT WRAPS IT UP

For all seek their own, not the things which are of Christ Jesus.

PHILIPPIANS 2:21

Gift wrapping is an art. Some people create packages so beautiful that recipients hate to tear off the paper, but many of us are slightly embarrassed by our gift-wrapping skills. Our presents suffer from jagged edges, crumpled corners, and patches of tape.

As a person, how are you wrapped? John Ruskin quipped, "A person all wrapped up in himself makes a very small package." If we're others-centered, we'll be a blessing; but if we're clothed in selfishness, we'll be of limited value to others.

Writing to the Philippians, Paul said of Timothy, "I have nobody else with a genuine interest in your well-being. All the others seem to be wrapped up in their own affairs and do not really care for the business of Jesus Christ. But you know how Timothy has proved his worth, working with me for the Gospel like a son with his father" (Philippians 2:20-22, Phillips).

When we're wrapped up in our own affairs, it's a sign we're not as Spirit-filled as we should be, and we're not being the blessing we could be. Let's not be like "all the others." Let's be Timothys—all wrapped up in Christ!

THE YULE LOG

Your wife shall be like a fruitful vine in the very heart of your house, your children like olive plants all around your table.

PSALM 128:3

"Yule" was an Old English word for Christmas Day, possibly derived from a Viking word, *jól*, referring to a 12-day festival. Somewhere, the tradition of cutting a large, hard log to burn in the family fireplace during Christmas—a Yule log—became a tradition. And while fewer houses today are built with wood-burning fireplaces, the notion of the family hearth at Christmas is a well-established one. Families gravitate to the warmth and light of the fireplace at Christmas as a place to bind hearts together.

The Bible, of course, doesn't speak of fireplaces or Yule logs, but it does speak of family. Just as the fireplace in the center of the house is a gathering place for families, so should godliness, the Word of God, and the love of Christ be the center of every family— and especially at Christmas. While a Yule log is temporary and generated by man, the Spirit of God provides permanent warmth and light wherever He is welcomed.

Around a fireplace or in some other way, gather your family and loved ones together this Christmas to bask in the glow of Christmas love that only Christ can give.

THINGS WE CAN'T CHANGE

The LORD is my strength and song, and
He has become my salvation.

PSALM 118:14

We accept narrowness in many areas of life without raising a question: We are allowed to drive only on one side of the road; we can only access the Internet through prescribed protocols; the law of gravity cannot be repealed; the length of a single night and day lasts a set amount of time; the distance between two geographical points remains constant.

We live within those fixed constraints daily without ever seriously objecting. But when it comes to salvation, we are not so easily convinced. We don't like the idea that God has prescribed only one avenue for salvation—through the person and work of Jesus Christ. We want to make accommodations for all the other world religions, suggesting they are all "different roads leading to the same place"—yet without any reference to Jesus Christ and His atonement for mankind's sin. Our objections leave out the most important fact: God is God and we are not. Just as we cannot change His law of gravity, neither can we change His "law" of salvation.

To reject God's Savior is to reject God's salvation. To accept both is to honor Him as Lord and God.

DAVID JEREMIAH

Speak the Truth

*But, speaking the truth in love, [we] may grow up
in all things into Him who is the head—Christ.*

Ephesians 4:15

Author and radio humorist Garrison Keillor is known for his take on facing reality: "Sometimes you have to look reality in the eye and deny it!" He was being funny, of course, but we laugh because we know we are tempted to do just that. Ever since the Garden of Eden, people have preferred making up alternative versions of reality instead of dealing with the truth.

It was Jesus who said, "The truth shall make you free" (John 8:32). He was talking about serious issues concerning salvation and His own identity, but the principle extends to all areas of life. Only when we know the actual truth—not a version of the truth, but the *true truth*—can we then respond in a real way. Knowing the truth may require forgiveness or reconciliation or restitution, but it is those acts that repair the past, bring healing in the present, and make the future possible. It is impossible to build a strong house on a foundation of denial or lies.

Revealing the truth, especially when it has been intentionally concealed, can be hard, if not painful. But it is how we grow up; it is how we are set free. If revealing the truth is painful, concealing it is even more so.

DELIGHTING IN GOD'S WILL

*I delight to do Your will, O my God, and
Your law is within my heart.*

PSALM 40:8

Esteemed theologian Bruce Waltke has written, "Why would a God who wants us to do His will hide it from us? . . . Our theology tells us that God loves us enough that He sent His Son to die on the cross to pay the penalty for our sins. So does it make sense that He would play some sort of game with His children, hiding His will? Is it logical that the God who says He has a plan for each life would conceal that plan so that His work cannot go forward through His people?"[38]

No one would suggest that God the Father hid His will from His own Son, Jesus. There was never any doubt in Jesus' mind about God's will for His life—including the painful conclusion of God's will (Matthew 16:21; Luke 19:10; John 3:14). Even though there were countless "diversions" along the way, Christ's life had a specific path and conclusion that Jesus recognized as God's will (Matthew 26:39, 42). Just as the Spirit led Christ (Matthew 4:1), so Paul says that the children of God are led by the Spirit of God as well (Romans 8:14).

Just as Jesus found delight and contentment in fulfilling God's will for His life, so we can find that same contentment in our life as we trust His Spirit to guide us.

38 Bruce K. Waltke, *Finding the Will of God* (Gresham, OR: Vision House Publishing, Inc., 1995), 7, 27.

TROUBLE AND PURPOSE

But as for you, you meant evil against me; but
God meant it for good, in order to bring it about
as it is this day, to save many people alive.

GENESIS 50:20

An operating room in the midst of a serious surgery can be a disconcerting sight. Yet it is all for a purpose. There is a greater good and higher purpose—correcting a problem that will lead to a long and fruitful life. The discomfort is planned and carried out on purpose, but it is only temporary.

Just so, God planned 400 years of discomfort for His people, the descendants of Abraham, in order to prepare them for their role as a light to the Gentiles. God planned this period of seclusion in Egypt and revealed it to Abraham years before it happened (Genesis 15:13-16). God was not punishing the descendants of Abraham, but rather protecting them when they were the family of Jacob in Canaan and in danger of being corrupted by pagan practices. In the midst of their 400 years in Egypt, the Hebrew slaves might have resented their situation—some lived and died in Egypt without knowing the greater purpose.

But God is always working out His will for people and nations. Don't let the troubles of the moment hide the glory of His purpose.

NO TURNING BACK

Then Jesus said to His disciples, "If anyone desires to come after Me, let him deny himself, and take up his cross, and follow Me."

MATTHEW 16:24

Many of us grew up singing a little chorus of commitment that said, "I have decided to follow Jesus." This hymn reportedly came from the nation of India and has its roots in an incident that occurred in the mid-1800s. A Welsh missionary had won a man to the Lord in the state of Assam. This man was saved along with his family. Persecution quickly ensued, and the village chief demanded the convert renounce his faith. But the man replied, "I have decided to follow Jesus." Amid continuing threats, he said, "Though no one joins me, still I will follow."

The man and his wife were executed, but their witness later led to the conversion of many in their town. Some years later, the Indian evangelist Sadhu Sundar Singh put the words to music.

As pressure mounts on Christians in the West and around the world, we need to remind ourselves of this simple song. We must continue to live in righteousness for God even if we're the only ones we know doing so. We must say: "The cross before me, the world behind me. No turning back, no turning back."

YOUR TREASURE—FAMILY

When he was still a great way off, his father saw him and had compassion, and ran and fell on his neck and kissed him.

LUKE 15:20

In February of 2014, John Allen, a British lawyer living in Holland, smiled across the supper table at his wife and three sons, ages eight to fourteen. Someone snapped a picture. They were happy. A family vacation to Indonesia was in the works.

Five months later the five Allens boarded Malaysia Airlines Flight MH17, but somewhere over Ukraine the plane was blown out of the sky. The whole family perished in an instant along with their fellow passengers.

We can't comprehend the evil and calamity in the world that cause events like this to occur. Such tragedies deeply upset and depress us, but they also represent a poignant reminder. Take every opportunity to cherish your loved ones. If you're peeved with a family member, forgive them. If you've neglected them, give them a call. If you've rebelled against your dad or mom, go home with the humble attitude of a repentant prodigal. If you've been tense with your kids, give them an extra hug. If you live far away, work harder to stay in touch. Whatever it takes, take care of your family as well as you can. It's at the core of God's plan and provision for the world.

TRUST GOD'S PROVISION

And Elijah said to her, "Do not fear; go and do as you have said, but make me a small cake from it first, and bring it to me; and afterward make some for yourself and your son.

1 KINGS 17:13

The widow glanced at all she had left: a handful of flour and a little oil. As she went outside to gather sticks for her and her son's last meal, she was preparing herself for the end. When she met the prophet Elijah and he requested water and bread, she explained her situation.

Elijah encouraged her to look beyond her circumstances to God's provision, "Do not fear" (1 Kings 19:13). As she prepared Elijah's meal that day and each day that followed, she had a choice to either trust God's provision or to protect the little she had.

When God prompts us to serve, it's easy to focus on our resources instead of God's glory. It's easy to list our lack of resources as an excuse or to mistakenly take the glory for ourselves when we have the resources. We forget that everything we have comes from God. His glory is tangible and real. Elijah asked the widow to set aside fear and to serve based on the God she was serving.

God is powerful and all glory belongs to Him. He changes circumstances and redeems even the darkest of circumstances. In the midst of situations the world sees as hopeless, we can cling to Elijah's words, "Do not fear."

CHRISTMAS STOCKINGS

*So He called His disciples to Himself and said to them,
"Assuredly, I say to you that this poor widow has put in
more than all those who have given to the treasury."*

MARK 12:43

A poor man, the father of three beautiful daughters, had no money to provide for their marriages or their futures. Hearing this, Saint Nicholas secretly put a bag of gold in the daughters' stockings, which were hanging by the fireplace to dry overnight. Upon rising, the family was overjoyed. Ever since, children have hung up stockings on Christmas Eve in hopes of a visit from Saint Nicholas.

That's the closest we can come to the origin of Christmas stockings. Regardless of the origin of the practice, one thing is evident: Christmas stockings can only hold small gifts. Indeed, what would fit in a child's stocking was the extent of the earliest Christmas gifts from parents to children. And therein is the lesson: It's the little things that matter most at Christmas. Jesus Himself revealed the true meaning of value when He commended a widow in Jerusalem for putting two pennies into the temple treasury.

As you plan your Christmas giving this year, keep "value" in mind. Gifts wrapped in Christmas love are the most valuable of all.

PROACTIVE LOVE

*Therefore, whatever you want men to do to you, do
also to them, for this is the Law and the Prophets.*

MATTHEW 7:12

The Golden Rule is found, in varying forms, in all religious and cultural traditions, many predating the time of Christ. Ethicists call it the "rule of reciprocity"—letting how we desire others to act toward us be the guide for how we act toward them. But when Jesus Christ stated His version of the Golden Rule, He gave it a twist that had been missing in other cultures.

Prior to Jesus, the rule of reciprocity had been stated in negative terms only. For instance, the Jewish book of Tobit said, "Do to no one what you yourself dislike." In other words, prior to Jesus, the Golden Rule focused on what *not* to do to others. But when Jesus stated it, He put it in positive terms: "Whatever you want men to do to you, do also to them." Instead of only withholding negative actions, Jesus said to demonstrate positive actions: Be proactive in your behavior toward others by loving them the same way you would want to be loved. He said such a proactive posture was a good way to summarize the whole Old Testament: "the Law and the Prophets."

*Not doing bad things is commendable, but doing good
things is even better. Doing both is to love as God loves.*

DAVID JEREMIAH

"WHATEVER HE SAYS TO YOU, DO"

Then Pharaoh said to all the Egyptians, "Go to Joseph; whatever he says to you, do."

GENESIS 41:55

In Genesis 41, God raised up Joseph to refocus and reprioritize the nation of Egypt during a prolonged period of drought and famine. During a national crisis, Joseph knew what to do, and everyone looked to him for answers. When the people cried to Pharaoh, he simply replied, "Go to Joseph; whatever he says to you, do."

That reminds us of another Bible story. In John 2, the wedding party in Cana faced a similar crisis—though far less serious. They ran out of wine during their festivities. Mary the mother of Jesus took things in hand. Speaking of her Son, she echoed the words of Pharaoh: "Whatever He says to you, do it" (John 2:5).

We all face shortages at one time or another. It might be lack of funds, lack of energy, lack of answers, or lack of wisdom. Sometimes we cope with needs that seem to have no provision, or crises that seem to have no answer. When problems come, we must refocus on our Lord Jesus Christ. We must go to Him. Whatever He says, do it. He will meet the need.

A GREAT AGE

Anna, a prophetess... was of a great age.... And coming in that instant she gave thanks to the Lord, and spoke of Him to all those who looked for redemption in Jerusalem.

LUKE 2:36-38

In his book *Nearing Home,* Billy Graham wrote, "Scripture is filled with examples of men and women whom God used late in life, often with great impact ...men and women who refused to use old age as an excuse to ignore what God wanted them to do."[39]

Many of the godly characters in Genesis—Methuselah, Noah, and Abraham—did their best work in advanced years. Moses and Joshua were in their eighties when God called them to a new work. In the Gospels, the story of Christ begins with the aged couple, Zacharias and Elizabeth, who bore John the Baptist.

And don't forget the prophetess Anna in the temple in Luke 2. The Bible says she was "of a great age." What a wonderful phrase! Anna was at least eighty-four, perhaps older. But the Bible calls it "a great age." It's great because the years help us mature in love, gentleness, thoughtfulness, and wisdom. We have the accumulated experiences of a lifetime and a rich history in our walk with God.

According to Luke 2:36, *old* age is a *great* age in God's sight. Make the most of it!

39 Billy Graham, *Nearing Home* (Nashville, TN: Thomas Nelson, 2011), 11-13.

GOOD HANDS

. . . casting all your care upon Him, for He cares for you.

1 PETER 5:7

Supposedly, the phrase "in good hands" has been used to mean competency, safety, or care since the 1300s. Seven centuries later, we may see the original meaning of skill when a coach says of a star player, "He's got great hands"—meaning, he never drops the ball. A major insurance company today calls itself the "good hands people," suggesting safety and protection. If you are facing major surgery, it's comforting for a nurse to say, "Don't worry, you're in good hands with this doctor."

As good as the hands of highly skilled people are, can they compete with the hands of God in terms of safety, comfort, or skill? God doesn't have hands, of course (John 4:24). But the "hand of God" is mentioned some fifteen times in Scripture, usually as a reference to His power and authority. But wait—isn't that what we hope for when we are in a difficult circumstance? Don't we want someone with power and authority to step in and meet our need? Of course—and that is likely what Peter had in mind when he wrote that we should cast all our cares upon God since God cares for us (1 Peter 5:7).

This very day, you are in God's good hands. Cast your cares *upon* Him and put your faith *in* Him.

Fruits of Faith

*For we are His workmanship, created in Christ
Jesus for good works, which God prepared
beforehand that we should walk in them.*

Ephesians 2:10

The phrase "catch-22" refers to a problem that has a solution that is prohibited by the problem itself. For example, if you need glasses to see, and you lose your glasses, you can't find them because you need them to carry out the search. A typical "catch-22" is when a job seeker is denied a job because of a lack of experience which he will never get unless he can get a job.

Not exactly a "catch-22" puzzle, but a conundrum nonetheless, is this theological problem: We cannot be saved *with* good works, but neither can we be saved *without* good works. How is that possible? The Bible clearly says we are saved by grace through faith, not by works (Ephesians 2:8-9). But it also says that faith without works is dead (James 2:17). Actually, we can be saved without good works—like the thief on the cross who died immediately after placing his faith in Christ (Luke 23:43). But as a rule, good works are evidence of our faith, a sign that our faith is alive and well (Ephesians 2:10).

We should look regularly—examine ourselves—for the fruits of our faith: the good works we were saved to carry out.

SYMPATHY OR EMPATHY?

For in that He Himself has suffered, being tempted,
He is able to aid those who are tempted.

HEBREWS 2:18

Speakers of English often confuse two similar sounding words: sympathy and empathy. But their meanings are significantly different. Sympathy is a feeling of pity or sorrow because of someone else's suffering. Empathy is the ability to identify with, understand, and share another's feelings. Sympathy can only *imagine* another person's suffering, while empathy *knows* exactly how the sufferer feels because of having suffered the same way.

Regarding our temptations to sin: Does Jesus *sympathize* with our temptations or *empathize*? Does He feel sorrow when we feel tempted or does He know exactly how we feel, having been tempted Himself? Some people find it hard to believe that the Son of God could be tempted to sin. Yet that is the clear testimony of Scripture. The Holy Spirit led Jesus into the wilderness "to be tempted by the devil" for forty days (Matthew 4:1-3). And the writer of Hebrews says Jesus was "in all points tempted as we are" (Hebrews 2:18; 4:15). It's how He learned to obey God (Hebrews 5:8).

When you are tempted, know that Jesus is able to intercede and help you on the basis of empathy, not sympathy (Hebrews 7:25).

IN JESUS' NAME

*For I have come down from heaven, not to do My
own will, but the will of Him who sent Me.*

JOHN 6:38

When ambassadors or other official representatives present themselves to a foreign king or government, a long-standing tradition has been to present "papers"—that is, official documents stating that the delegate comes "in the name of" his or her government and is authorized to speak on its behalf. Delegates don't speak their own will, but the will of those they represent.

That is what it means to pray "in Jesus' name." Somewhere along the way, "in Jesus' name, amen" became the habitual way for Christians to end their prayers. It is certainly appropriate, of course, but prayers could begin the same way: "Father, I come into Your presence in Jesus' name"—that is, "I am not coming to demand my will; I am coming to ask that which I believe is pleasing to Your Son, my Lord, Jesus Christ. I ask You to honor this prayer as You would honor Your Son's prayers, as I make this request in His name." The purpose of prayer is not to bend God to our will, but to align ourselves to His will as we pray.

By abiding in Christ, and letting His Word abide in us, we will learn to pray according to His will, not our own (John 15:7).

THE NATIVITY

And they came with haste and found Mary and Joseph, and the Babe lying in a manger.

LUKE 2:16

Your family may have one—it may have even been passed down from prior generations: a Nativity set that finds its honored place on a mantel or side table every Christmas season. The English "Nativity" comes from the Latin *nativus*—"arisen by birth." Francis of Assisi gets credit for the first Nativity scene in 1223, a live scene such as many churches host for several nights preceding December 25. But by far the most popular Nativity scenes are those we use in our homes—especially the beautiful sets carved from olive wood by craftsmen in Bethlehem.

A complete Nativity set reminds us of all the elements of the first Christmas: Mary and Joseph, the humble shepherds, the wealthy Magi, even the animals whose manger (feeding trough) served as the bassinet for the baby Jesus. Each element of the Nativity is important: Joseph from the House of David, Mary an obedient servant, shepherds and Magi representing the full spectrum of humanity, and lowly animals representing all creation.

A Nativity scene is a wonderful teaching tool for children and for Christmas family devotions—bringing the first Christmas into the present.

ALWAYS BE READY

But sanctify the Lord God in your hearts, and
always be ready to give a defense to everyone who
asks you a reason for the hope that is in you.

1 PETER 3:15

When Martin Luther helped launch the German Reformation, he emphasized the wonder of the Incarnation; and from that heritage came many Old World celebrations that still yield an evocative Christmas. Many of our modern traditions hail from Germany. But when the Nazis took over in the 1930s, they tried to change that. In his book, *Hitler's Cross,* Erwin Lutzer wrote, "Since Germans had for centuries celebrated Christmas and Easter, Hitler had to reinterpret their meaning. Christmas was turned into a totally pagan festival…. Carols and Nativity plays were banned from the schools in 1938, and even the name Christmas was changed to Yuletide."[40]

Lutzer points out that the same changes are happening today. In every age the devil wants to minimize the wonder of Christ, who came into the world to be our Redeemer and Savior.

We can't control a secular society, but in our own hearts we can sanctify Jesus as Lord. We can always be ready to give a reason to everyone who asks us about our Christmas hope and heritage.

40 Erwin Lutzer, *Hitler's Cross* (Chicago: Moody Publishers, 1998).

The Never-Ending Wonder

Where is He who has been born King of the Jews?

Matthew 2:2

The *Baptist Press* reported about a missionary who saw a collection of nativity sets in an open-air market in a staunchly Buddhist area of Southeast Asia. This region had no knowledge of Christianity. The missionary tracked down the family making the nativities and learned they had started selling them after a French tourist suggested it. The family had no idea what the nativity sets meant. They just started making the figures for business based on the tourist's description. This missionary had the joy of taking up the various characters of the set, one at a time, and telling the family the story of the Lord Jesus. Now the whole village is responding.[41]

Imagine hearing about Christmas for the first time! Imagine first learning about the One born King of the Jews! The wonder of the Christmas message is that God revealed Himself and His love to us by becoming a man.

Keep Christmas fresh in your heart. Our Lord is a Savior worth worshiping, and His Gospel is a message worth sharing.

---

41 Evelyn Adamson, "Nativity Set Maker in Asia Begins Learning the Real Story," *Baptist Press*, November 1, 2013.

THE TRUE SPIRIT OF CHRISTMAS

For He has regarded the lowly state of His maidservant; for behold, henceforth all generations will call me blessed.

LUKE 1:48

The three most prominent women in the Gospels were all named Mary. The first was Mary of Nazareth. God chose her to raise Jesus because of her servant's heart. "He has regarded the lowly state of His maidservant," she said.

The second was Mary of Bethany. She was His student. Whenever she appeared in the Gospels, she was at the feet of Jesus. In Luke 10:42, the Lord said of her habit of sitting at His feet hearing His words: "One thing is needed, and Mary has chosen that good part."

The third was Mary of Magdala. Though successful in business, she had deep spiritual needs in her life. Jesus freed her from demons, saved her, and she became His zealous supporter. She supported His ministry from her own resources, according to Luke 8:1-3.

Three Marys—a servant, a student, a supporter.

That's the true spirit of Christmas. Jesus came to earth to die for us and rise again. He meets our deepest needs. Today, let's rededicate ourselves to being His faithful servants, students, and supporters. That's the way to have a *Mary* Christmas!

ADDICTED TO STRESS

For God is not the author of confusion but of peace.

1 CORINTHIANS 14:33

According to a report this year by NPR (National Public Radio) and the Harvard School of Public Health, more than 63 percent of Americans are battling stress; and a significant number describe their stress as "great." The report suggested that some of us have become addicted to stress. We've become so conditioned to stress, we don't know what to do with ourselves if we're not insanely busy. The study suggested our busyness may be a way of distracting ourselves from how unsatisfied we inwardly feel with life.

That's not how God wants us to live. Jesus said, "Peace I leave with you, My peace I give to you" (John 14:27). Paul talked about "the peace of God, which surpasses all understanding" (Philippians 4:7). Romans 8:6 says, "To be carnally minded *is* death, but to be spiritually minded *is* life and peace."

Peace with God is obtainable through faith in Jesus, and He wants to give you peace like a river (Isaiah 66:12). Don't wait until the New Year to give your life to Jesus. Do so today. Claim His peace and let Him bestow the inward satisfaction you seek. He isn't the author of confusion, but of peace.

WORRIED?

For unto us was the gospel preached, as well as unto them: but the word preached did not profit them, not being mixed with faith in them that heard it.

HEBREWS 4:2, KJV

Worry can lead to stress, which can result in all manner of negative physical manifestations. But what is the downside of worry from a spiritual point of view? Connecting a number of biblical dots results in a serious conclusion: Worry can be viewed as sin; sin is not pleasing to God; sin can keep God from working in our life.

Several times Jesus used the phrase, "O you of little faith" to describe people who were worried about the future: their physical needs (Matthew 6:30), their physical safety (Matthew 8:26), their inability to find a solution to a problem (Matthew 14:31), and their lack of resources for ministry (Matthew 16:8). In each situation, people were worried about their circumstances, and Jesus linked their worry to a lack of faith. The writer to the Hebrews says that "without faith it is impossible to please [God]" (Hebrews 11:6), and Paul wrote that "whatever is not from faith is sin" (Romans 14:23). Worry is not from faith, so a lifestyle of worry is certainly not pleasing to God.

If you are worried today, confess it to God and put your faith in Him (Philippians 4:6-7).

SECURE IN HIM

*And the Word became flesh and dwelt among us,
and we beheld His glory, the glory as of the only
begotten of the Father, full of grace and truth.*

JOHN 1:14

A man-on-the-street poll to determine the most important event in world history would reveal a variety of answers. But for Christians, the answer is clear: the coming of God to earth. To consider the importance of that event is to invite wonder and awe. And there is no shortage of ways to consider its importance for us.

For example, Christ lived in complete dependence on His Father and trusted in God's will for His life (John 4:34; 5:30; 6:38; 8:28, 42). And even though He was tempted (Matthew 4:1-11) and at times suffered (Hebrews 5:8), He never questioned His experiences; He was always confident that the Father's will for His life was perfect and His to obey. Christ proceeded from the Godhead to earth, bringing the will of God with Him. He *was* the will of God—and He never faltered. Now, the apostle Paul says, all who believe in Christ are *in Him* (Colossians 2:9-10). Therefore, as Christ fulfilled, and continues to fulfill, the will of God, so do we who live in Him by faith.

If you are a Christian, trust today that, in Christ, your life is secure in the purposes and plans of God.

DECEMBER 29

A CONTINUAL SOURCE OF PEACE

This Book of the Law shall not depart from your mouth, but you shall meditate in it day and night, that you may observe to do according to all that is written in it. For then you will make your way prosperous, and then you will have good success.

JOSHUA 1:8

Scientists tell us that the very act of stroking a pet dog or cat can reduce stress. Such intimacy releases oxytocin into the blood stream—the so-called "bonding hormone"—resulting in feelings of well-being and security.

But what if your pet is not around, or if you don't have a pet? Scripture suggests that meditating on the Word of God can have an always-on effect of peace and strength in difficult times. The psalmist wrote that the man who meditates on God's Word is like a fruitful tree planted by a river (Psalm 1). God told Joshua, just before entering the Promised Land of Canaan, that if he kept his mind focused on His Word, he would be prosperous and successful (Joshua 1:8). The writer to the Hebrews said that God's Word can help us understand our own heart (Hebrews 4:12).

Enjoy your pet if you have one. But don't neglect a more permanent source of encouragement: the great and precious promises in the living and active Word of God (2 Peter 1:4).

MOVE FORWARD

The backslider in heart will be filled with his own ways, but a good man will be satisfied from above.

PROVERBS 14:14

We seldom hear the term "backsliding" now, but it's still in the Bible. Jeremiah 3:22 says, "Return, you backsliding children, *and* I will heal your backslidings." Hosea 11:7 says, "My people are bent on backsliding from Me."

The word "backslider" is a visual term that describes someone who, having made progress in his or her Christian life, slides back into old patterns. It's like a man climbing a hill who takes a step forward but slides two steps backward. Is that you? We're all prone to backsliding. Dr. Harry Ironside said, "Any Christian who is not at the present time enjoying Christ as much as he did in a past day, or living for God as devotedly as he once did, is just to that extent a backslider."

But how great is God's mercy! He says of the backslider, "I have seen his ways, and will heal him; I will also lead him, and restore comforts to him" (Isaiah 57:18). If you're sliding backward into some bad habits, change direction. Now is the time to make *forward* progress in your Christian life!

NEVER ALONE

*For He Himself has said, "I will never
leave you nor forsake you."*

HEBREWS 13:5

We often hear or read of a person expressing comfort this way: "I know she is with me." Or, "I could sense him guiding me." They are referring, of course, to a sense of the presence of a departed loved one. While the memory of a loved one can be a comfort in life—the memory of love, wisdom, and experiences shared—we have no biblical warrant for anticipating the presence of a departed loved one as we complete our journey through life.

But we have good news! We absolutely have biblical warranty for expecting the presence of Jesus Christ with us. The Holy Spirit indwells every Christian to make the words of Galatians 2:20 a reality: "Christ lives in me." Christ promised His apostles He would be with them, and Mark noted how Christ worked with them as they spread the Gospel (Mark 16:20). The writer to the Hebrews affirms the same promise to all believers—we are never left alone in this life (Hebrews 13:5).

A mark of maturity in the Christian life is moving from believing that promise to *living as if we truly believe* Christ is with us. Consider today: What would that belief look like in your life?

DAVID JEREMIAH